Seeing Differently

The Harvard Business Review Book Series

Seeing Differently: Insights on Innovation

Edited with an Introduction by
John Seely Brown

A Harvard Business Review Book

The *Harvard Business Review* articles in this collection are available as
individual reprints. Discounts apply to quantity purchases. For information
and ordering contact Customer Service, Harvard Business School
Publishing, Boston, MA 02163. Telephone: (617) 495–6192, 9 A.M. to 5 P.M.
Eastern Time, Monday through Friday. Fax: (617) 495–6985, 24 hours a
day.

The paper used in this publication meets the requirements of the American
National Standard for Permanence of Paper for Printed Library Materials
Z39.48–1984

Library of Congress Cataloging-in-Publication Data

Seeing differently : insights on innovation / edited with an
    introduction by John Seely Brown.
      p. cm.—(Harvard business review book)
    Includes index.
    ISBN 0-87584-755-2 (alk. paper)
    1. Organizational change. 2. Technological innovations—
Management. I. Brown, John Seely. II. Series: Harvard business
review book series.
HD58.8.S44   1997
658.5'14—dc21
96-48033
CIP

The greatest thing a human soul ever does in this world is to *see* something, and tell what it *saw* in a plain way. Hundreds of people can talk for one who can think, but thousands can think for one who can see. To see clearly is poetry, prophecy, and religion—all in one.

    —John Ruskin, *Modern Painters*, 1888

Contents

Introduction
Rethinking Innovation
in a Changing World

John Seely Brown

Fundamental changes are under way in the world of business. Pick up any newspaper, magazine, or business book and there it is: Chaos reigns. Living on the cusp of the twenty-first century, we are experiencing structural shifts in our economy brought about by revolutions in computation and communication technologies. The accelerating pace of change is real. As the speeds and bandwidths of these technologies increase, a transition is in motion from a manufacturing economy based on the production and processing of materials to a digital economy based on the production and processing of knowledge. With this shift, we are finding many of our background assumptions and time-honored business models inadequate to help us understand what is going on, let alone how to compete.

Many of us—business leaders, technologists, entrepreneurs, and managers—are confused about how to interpret the Internet, the World Wide Web, and the impact of the cyber-revolution. Questions abound. What is the role of the publisher of tomorrow? The retailer? The bank? The document company? What does it mean if there are no clear-cut competitors but networks of alliances? How is trust established among members? What are the organizational structures of virtual organizations? Where is the accountability of these organizations to consumers?

The questions we ask are as infinite as the opportunities they afford. The challenge lies in our ability to make sense of the rapidly changing context in which we are doing business. We need to find new ways of doing things, whether we are working on new solutions to old problems or creating new ways of doing things that have never been done—or even thought of—before.

To do things differently, we must learn to see things differently. Seeing differently means learning to question the conceptual lenses though which we view and frame the world, our businesses, our core competencies, our competitive advantage, and our business models. It means finding new eyeglasses that will enable us to see strategies and structures taking shape, even if we feel that we are on the edge of chaos; it is a matter of survival in the new world of business. If there is anything that is actually coming *into* focus today, it is the realization that we need to question much of what we think we know about how to conduct commerce, including marketing, distribution, service, and the notion of competition itself. Hardest of all, we need to be able to think about changing the architecture of our revenue streams, that is, the way we make money.[1]

Innovation, in the largest sense, is center stage in this evolving arena. While the long-standing challenges in our existing businesses are still with us, we need to seize the expanding opportunities to innovate new markets and new businesses. Maintaining the status quo is no longer a viable option. We need to develop a multiplicity of methods to bend and break out of old frames built for old conditions. It is in this spirit that I have selected the articles in this book.

This collection of *Harvard Business Review* articles is intended to provide a starter kit of tools and frameworks to help make sense of the world that is taking shape. It is not intended as a textbook for a standard course on innovation, but as a selected set of conceptual lenses that I have found useful in my own efforts to see differently. In varying ways and degrees, each article suggests a new way of thinking about some aspect of the way we do business: strategy, financial analysis, product design, competitive analysis, organizational structure, marketing, and research. With new ways of thinking, we can begin to envision opportunities for innovation at every stage of the value chain.

The Innovation of Xerox

My perspective on innovation has been shaped by my having worked for many years in corporate research at Xerox. The history of Xerox offers a wonderful object lesson in the power of seeing differently.[2]

After the invention of xerography, for a long time it appeared as if the commercial photocopier would never see the light of day. Numerous manufacturers were offered the patent and turned it down. The market analysts could see little value in the photocopier and forecast a market of no more than a few thousand machines.

If we have trouble seeing back to the world at that time to understand this oversight, the market analysts and manufacturers had far more difficulty looking forward to our world today—a world that takes for granted the inescapable usefulness of copiers in every office and on almost every street corner. We know the value of the copier. Why couldn't they see it?

In retrospect, we can understand how the market forecasts for the copier were, you might say, filtered through the carbon paper that copiers were intended to replace. Whereas at the time, people used carbon paper to make copies at the same time as they typed, using the new machine would add an extra step. First, people would have to type. Then they would have to go to a different machine in a different place to make copies. It is not difficult to see why this didn't seem like progress.

What no one could predict was that the copy machine would not be used just for making a copy of an original. It would be used for making copies of copies, and copies of copies of copies, and so on. If people had continued making copies only of originals, market growth for the photocopying machine would have been a simple linear progression. But if people started making copies of copies, the progression would be exponential. The number of copies and the copier market would explode. And that's what happened.

An entirely new set of work practices developed around the technology. People started to realize the power of copying for supporting collaborative work, and this changed the way people work. The copier created the process of "midcasting," as opposed to narrowcasting or broadcasting, in which a document could be shared among a group. Since this couldn't be done with carbons, no one could see the demand for it coming. The Xerox copier, in effect, was invented for an office with work practices that didn't yet exist.

But people don't buy machines for practices that don't exist. So sales of the first copier had to rely on two innovations. One was the copier itself, a technological innovation. The other was the means of putting it into circulation, an equally profound marketing innovation. Instead of trying to sell into a hesitant market, Haloid, the firm that bought the patent (and later renamed itself Xerox), elected to take its return from use fees. Every time someone made a copy, Xerox made money. This marketing innovation allowed people to take a chance on the machine at minimal cost, without requiring a leap of faith, unfathomable foresight, or monumental risk taking. And it allowed the machines to make it into offices and from there into both technological and marketing history.

These stories are frequently told. But one is usually recounted in a technological arena and the other in a marketing one. Telling the two together reveals the synergy of technological and marketing foresight that made xerography—and Xerox—possible. Foresight is not just the purview of research labs; it is a coproduction of multiple perspectives.[3]

Innovation at Xerox

As I describe in the last article of this collection, the Xerox Palo Alto Research Center (PARC) was founded in 1970 to do basic research in computing and electronics and to explore how organizations use information. Broadly construed, our mission is to enhance the adaptability of Xerox. Over the years, we have launched a number of initiatives to make corporate research more effective by facilitating coproduction with other parts of the organization. One of the most successful of these initiatives was a coproduction itself between Xerox and the Harvard Business School, led by Mark Myers of Xerox, and Richard Rosenbloom, a professor at the Harvard Business School. The "Business Model Workshops" were created to train our technical staff to be conversant in notions like "sustainable competitive advantage," "value proposition," and the construction of business plans. The aim is to teach our research managers leading-edge business ideas in order to open up broader conversations between the technologists and the strategists, the marketers, and so on.

By changing the discourse and enabling research technologists to traffic in these ideas, we are facilitating the movement of inventions into the marketplace. And this is what we mean by "innovation": invention implemented. Instead of merely hurling inventions over the transom into the hands of business developers, technologists share in the responsibility for making inventions into innovations. Just as the first copier was as dependent on marketing innovation as on technological innovation, PARC researchers learn that as much, if not more, creativity goes into the implementation part of the innovation as into the invention itself.

Linking, Listening, Learning, Leading

The great challenge in innovation is linking emerging technologies with emerging markets. If it were just a matter of linking emerging technologies with existing markets (or vice versa), the coupling would be relatively easy. But when both are emerging, it is a delicate, coevolutionary process: as technologies emerge, they affect the markets, and as markets emerge, they influence the technologies. It's not a question of "technology push" or "market pull" but more along the lines of "how tight is the coevolutionary loop?"

When a product is completely new, no matter how much work has gone into it in the research lab, it usually isn't exactly right. To get it right, one needs to listen closely to the emergent market. This requires that new technologies and emerging market needs be brought together in a series of market-learning experiences, and that the learning be used to modify, improve, and fine-tune the product rapidly.

The process by which we at PARC do this developed, in part, out of a companywide quality program called "Leadership through Quality" (LTQ). Despite some initial skepticism about LTQ, the research staff came to see that we could use the concept to facilitate our ability to listen to our customers, both internally and externally. Moreover, we discovered that we could reconfigure LTQ to carry the message about customer response to a particular innovation from the research lab back into the corporation. By letting our customers do the talking for us, we found a new way of communicating with the rest of the corporation. I think of the adapted quality program as QTL[4]: Quality Through

> Linking to the world,
> Listening through those linkages,
> Learning and reflecting through those listenings, and then
> Leading.

I have found this framework useful for thinking about innovation opportunities. Many of our initiatives at PARC concern finding innovative ways to do each of these four things. Through linking and listening, for example, we have come to understand that innovation is not about technology alone but also about the work practices in which technologies are used. In fact, we have anthropologists, psychologists, and sociologists on our research staff to help us find better techniques for linking to the world, listening in different ways for latent needs and tacit knowledge, and learning from actual work practices.

I have also used this framework in selecting the articles in this book. Several of the articles, such as "Competing on Resources" and "Research That Reinvents the Corporation," touch on innovative ways to link. Others, for example, "Disruptive Technologies" and "Breaking Compromises, Breakaway Growth," discuss the difficulty and importance of listening.

Virtually all the articles have to do with learning. We learn through conceptual frameworks. While we can expand what we know incrementally with our existing frameworks, our evolving world increasingly calls upon us to challenge the assumptions that underlie these conceptual models. One reason the new digital world can seem so chaotic is that we are imposing old frameworks on a world that requires new ones. To see differently, we need new intellectual constructs. In its own way, each of these articles is proposing a new way of seeing.

Finally, there is leading. Disciplined leading requires that all the pieces be in order: the right organizational forms, the right alliances, the right competencies and resources, the right products, the right channels of distribution, and the right strategies. Moreover, leading requires the discipline and courage to carry forth, understanding that there are no definitive rules, and that what we are managing are the tensions inherent in the uncertainties and risks underlying virtually every aspect of the process of innovation.

In the next few pages, I will briefly discuss each of the articles in this collection. In some cases, I will use an article as a springboard for my own thoughts on the topic. I encourage readers to do likewise and to use their imaginations to explore how each one might apply to their own situations. To gain footholds in our fast-evolving world, we must be willing to step back, listen, learn, reflect—and act.

The Changing Business Context

I selected the first three articles in the collection to give the flavor of the new business context and to provide a framework for thinking about how the world is evolving. In the first, "Increasing Returns and the New World of Business," W. Brian Arthur describes that, at the beginning of this century, Western economies were based primarily on the bulk-processing of resources and now, at the close of the century, they are based increasingly on the processing of both resources *and* information. Western economies now comprise two overlapping, intertwined worlds that operate under fundamentally different economic principles. With the evolution from processing resources to processing information, the mechanisms that determine economic behavior have shifted from those of diminishing returns to those of increasing returns. And with this shift, many of our assumptions about how business operates are being turned on their heads.

The article is a compelling analysis of the transition and the new world of business now taking shape. For those of us in companies that came into existence in the bulk-processing economy, it is not the case that the new knowledge-based economy simply replaces the traditional one. Most companies—Xerox among them—struggle with how to do business in both worlds at the same time. As is the case with all paradigm shifts, we are experiencing, in many cases, a clash between these two world views. And yet, in most companies, they have to co-exist and move ahead simultaneously. While there is no reason why this can't be done, it is critical to realize that both these world views are present. The real challenge is to combine the strengths of the bulk-processing economy with insights from the digital economy; to use current product platforms to launch fundamentally new initiatives in the digital economy.

Many companies are now using the Internet to extend their strategic information systems, such as FedEx with its on-line tracking system and American Airlines and United Airlines with their on-line reservation systems. Other examples of businesses' expanding their existing product offerings through on-line technology are magazines and newspapers that augment the conventional form of publication with Web sites that provide additional information and chat rooms. In the near future, we will see companies using that technology to create synergistic initiatives that broaden and complement their core business. An example would be a health insurance company that uses the Web to build a virtual community focused on health and well-being, building customer loyalty while dispensing information, and potentially lowering the number of claims.

Another way to describe the transition under way is that the traditional world has to do with producing products—or making *stuff*—and the new world has more to do with making *sense*. As companies outsource more and more of what they produce, the competencies left at the core are sense-making capabilities. This emphasis on sense making represents a significant shift in thinking, especially because, in the digital world, we are all making up the rules as we go along. It is no longer just a question of optimization, standardization, or rapid improvements; it's also a question of making sense, creating the right rules, building the ecologies[4] and alliances, and moving out to market quickly. Given the pace of change and the uncertainty surrounding technology, the challenge is to make enough sense of patterns, possibilities, and opportunities to place the bets we want to place and to create the game we want to play.

In the next article, "Strategy as Revolution," Gary Hamel argues that companies are reaching the limits of what can be achieved through incremental improvement. Every industry is made up of three kinds of companies: rule makers, the incumbents that built the industry; rule takers, the companies that follow the rules of the incumbents; and rule breakers, the revolutionaries that are rewriting the rules and reinventing industries. Companies that are not naturally inclined to be revolutionaries have the choice of either surrendering the future to revolutionary challengers or revolutionizing the way they create strategy. Hamel offers a number of new ways to think about and create strategy to help companies liberate their "revolutionary spirit."

Senior managers, for example, must give up their monopoly on strategy making. Strategy has to be informed by insights that percolate from the bottom up, from the outside in. Traditional strategic planning tends to be little more than a calendar-driven ritual in which deeply held assumptions and industry conventions are reinforced rather than challenged. Managers must now learn to embrace a process that will give voice to the renegades that exist in every company.

Although the focus of this article is strategy, I see close ties to innovation. One of the challenges in innovation is putting into place the processes and organizational structure that will honor emergent notions wherever they occur and facilitate the deep listening I discussed earlier. A company that has control-oriented hierarchical organizational structures limits its ability to listen to a changing world by not honoring its periphery, from which new ideas often emerge. I'm not proposing anarchy or chaos; the organizations that will prove most effective are those that have discipline with *enabling*—rather than coercive[5]—business processes and that have the ability to hear and act on unusual signals before others do.

"Strategy as Revolution" also reminded me of the importance of being grounded in reality. Organizations ground themselves through listening. If an organization's researchers are grounded—that is, if they have a deep and intuitive understanding of why the problems they are working on are important—and the organization has enabling business processes with systems to support emergent communities of practice, it is in a position to create meaningful strategies that are informed by what has come up from the bottom, in from the outside, from where the rubber hits the road. That's when the sparks start to fly and innovation takes hold.

As Hamel points out, those sparks need to come from multiple points of view, some of which will be outside our current frame: "There can be no innovation in the creation of strategy," he tells us, "without a change in perspective." In my mind, this also brings up the critical role that diversity is coming to play. The organizations that will survive and thrive are those that can leverage the diverse capabilities and multiple perspectives embedded within them to achieve unity of purpose. Having a diverse work force is not merely a social goal; it is a competitive advantage and, increasingly, a strategic imperative. In the new economy, creativity and diversity will be the coin of the day. The management of intellectual capital—the nurturing, utilization, and leveraging of creativity and intellectual resources—requires an ability to honor the diversity of ideas all around us. Doing so intelligently and strategically constitutes a true management challenge.

I selected the next article, "How Architecture Wins Technology Wars," because it demonstrates how seeing things differently can define an entirely new competitive arena and open up new ways of thinking about strategy and innovation. Looking at the winners and losers in the information technology industry, Charles Morris and Charles Ferguson propose that a new paradigm is needed to explain success and failure. Success, it seems, is not tied to what we consider critical in the production economy (for instance, scale, manufacturing process, superior design). Instead it is tied to the ability to "establish proprietary architectural control over a broad, fast-moving, competitive space. . . . Architectural battles are fast-moving, hotly challenged, and rarely completely settled. The rewards to a winner, however, can be great."

People had previously thought of open systems and proprietary architectures almost as opposites. This article, however, provided an explanation for the evolving dynamics of the computer industry that were difficult to understand in the context of the diminishing returns business model. To create and maintain an open yet proprietary architecture requires substantial implementation skills, along with shrewd business acumen and an understanding of how to nurture an ecology comprising positive feedback loops and lock-ins of the sort that W. Brian Arthur describes. The reason these open, proprietary architecture systems are so powerful is that, once they *do* lock in, we see the winner-take-all, increasing returns dynamic at work. We see companies like Microsoft.

New Tools, New Rules

While the first three articles propose new ways of looking at the world and the need for new rules, the next few provide new tools for fostering and leveraging innovation. In "The Right Game: Use Game Theory to Shape Strategy," Adam Brandenburger and Barry Nalebuff present a new way of thinking about opportunities for launching new products, creating new markets, and so on. The Value Net is a novel, game theory–based construct that provides a schematic framework for thinking about the ecology of competition. It is a conceptual lens through which one can look at all the players in a business game and identify innovative win-win strategies. Most important, it offers guidelines for "actively shaping the game you play, not just playing the game you find." "Making the game you want" is a key component of competing in the new world of business.

Through the lens of the Value Net, one can see the multiple roles that a firm plays as, for example, a complementor, supplier, substitutor, and customer. For me, the power of this article is in its emphasis on rethinking the interrelationship of those roles, and on the importance of rapidly building alliances that create win-win situations. In the digital economy, we need to consider how to align our multiple complementors and suppliers so that everything works together in our particular ecology. Again, this evokes W. Brian Arthur's world of increasing returns, in which players compete "by building *webs*—loose alliances of companies organized around a mini-ecology—that amplify positive feedbacks." It is this web of alliances that allows firms to move out quickly and take hold of opportunities that lead to the kind of lock-ins that Arthur discusses.

In "The Options Approach to Capital Investment" we are given another analytic tool, in this case, to help manage the risk in innovation. The need for such tools is greater than ever in the new world of business, where we are developing new technologies for new markets as fast as we can. Avinash Dixit and Robert Pindyck argue that companies make capital investments—including investments in research and development—in order to produce opportunities to take some future action. "Opportunities are *options*—rights but not obligations to take some action in the future."

Thinking about investing in innovation as creating options changes the way a manager might determine whether to invest in a new project. The article points out the weakness in using the net present value method to analyze investment decisions and provides a more useful method of analysis that incorporates a range of possibilities, such as investing today or waiting and investing at a later time. The options method takes into account the irreversibility of investment expenditures and the ability to delay making a major product decision while still investing in a technology option for that product. To make intelligent investment choices, managers need to consider the value of keeping their options open. Dixit and Pindyck point out that the lost option value is an opportunity cost that must be included as part of the cost of the investment.

The article also raises an important point about the need for discipline in innovation. There is a danger that the options model lends itself to being misused in R&D because it provides a great excuse for saying, "We're not wasting money, we're creating a technology option." The discipline comes in being able to say, at some point, "That's it! This option has run out," which is, of course, one of the hardest things in the world to do. This model works as an analytic tool only if one is willing to call, or terminate, an option.

Managing innovation has much to do with managing "future time," and that has much to do with managing—and even capitalizing on—uncertainties: uncertainties with the technology or uncertainties about the market, let alone their coupling. If used correctly, the options method allows one to manage risk intelligently. It seems a particularly useful tool for risky situations like establishing de facto standards that relate to the increasing returns winner-take-all economy. In such situations, payoff distributions are exceedingly nonlinear with potentially counterintuitive results pertaining to the value of a particular set of technology options.

In "When Is Virtual Virtuous? Organizing for Innovation," Henry

Chesbrough and David Teece successfully take aim at the currently popular belief that there is nothing that can't be done in a virtual organization. The article introduces the notion of *types* of innovation, autonomous versus systemic, and shows how alliances and outsourcing can be effective for some innovations and strategically dangerous for others. The authors provide a matrix for thinking through the appropriate organizational design, given the type of innovation and the capabilities needed. We are given a sense of the tension in finding the right balance between internal development versus buying from suppliers versus forming alliances.

Another idea that I took away from this article is the necessity of maintaining deep knowledge at the hub of the organization. We can have multiple strategic alliances and partnerships, but we must be sure to preserve a deep core competence at the hub. While people understand this at some level, an extreme notion of virtual organizations seems to be taking hold: the radically virtual organization, in which relationships emerge to solve a particular problem and then dissolve again. I believe that we need to be vigilant about maintaining a set of deep core competencies and about leveraging those competencies with careful outsourcing only when appropriate.

New Lenses for Competitive Advantage

Each of the next three articles is about how seeing things just a little differently can open up entirely new opportunities for competitive advantage.

In "Disruptive Technologies: Catching the Wave," Joseph Bower and Clayton Christensen question why established companies that invest aggressively—and successfully—in the technologies needed to retain their current customers often fail to make the technological investments that customers of the future will demand. The fundamental reason, they argue, is that leading companies succumb to one of the most popular, and valuable, management dogmas: stay close to your customer. To remain at the top of their industries, managers must first be able to spot disruptive technologies and then to pursue them while protecting them from the processes and incentives geared to serving mainstream customers.

I found this article refreshing, particularly from the perspective of one who works in a big corporation. Too often, it seems that an obsessive focus on customers eliminates judgment from the game of innovation. Innovation requires judgment, informed by a wide range of analytic tools, and it requires discipline. But in many companies, it seems it doesn't matter whether something is a good idea or if it makes strategic sense. All anyone cares about is what the current customers say they want. The problem is that customers often can't articulate what they want, and what they want isn't always what they need.

Particularly when dealing with emerging technologies and emerging markets, the voice of the customer should not be heard as definitive. One has to listen carefully, to be attuned to signals about latent needs, and to respond shrewdly and judiciously. Innovation can require being willing to ignore customers. How do you decide which customers to ignore in making this judgment? How do you find ways of getting at latent needs? The article doesn't answer these questions, but it raises the important issue of *when* they should be asked.

In "Breaking Compromises, Breakaway Growth," George Stalk, David Pecaut, and Benjamin Burnett discuss how to listen for conflict in the marketplace and how to tap into the value that is trapped in the compromises that customers have been forced to make. "The most important compromises are forced on customers simply because companies have lost touch with those customers' needs. Finding and breaking those compromises can unleash new demand and create breakaway growth." The article proposes a number of ways that companies can find and exploit compromise-breaking opportunities in virtually any industry. It is a useful framework for thinking about how to identify innovative opportunities for growth. The trick, once again, is learning to trust your intuition about which customers to listen to.

The next article, "Competing on Resources: Strategy in the 1990s," takes a more holistic approach to strategy. It offers a different approach to thinking strategically about the context in which innovation takes place and in which decisions about innovation are made. As David Collis and Cynthia Montgomery point out, over the past 35 years the field of strategy has split between two divergent models of the source of competitive advantage. On the one hand, there is a view that the structure of an industry determines the state of competition within that industry and sets the context for companies' strategies and potential profitability. The alternative view shifts the focus from the outside to the inside; it is not the external industry environment but the collective skills and learning embedded in an organization—the core competence of the corporation—that determines a company's competitive position.

The resource-based approach to strategy bridges the gap between these two views; it's not "either/or" but "both/also." Instead of industrial structure *or* core competency, the resource-based view proposes that a company's ownership of a valuable resource or capability can be a powerful source of competitive advantage. It combines the internal and external perspectives and provides a framework for assessing whether a company has the best and most appropriate resources and capabilities for its business and strategy. Moreover, by refocusing on building and leveraging unique resources and capabilities, the resource-based approach opens the door to new areas for strategic innovation.

Managing Innovation

Finally, the last three articles address managing the process of innovation in the rapidly changing new business context.

"Tough-Minded Ways to Get Innovative" reinforces the imperative of managing innovation for corporate survival. Andrall Pearson sets out five steps to make a company more innovative and dynamic, most of which reinforce points made in other articles in this collection.

Pearson notes that even the best concepts tend to develop incrementally: "They rarely ever work the first time out or unfold just as they were planned. In fact, the original concept or its execution usually gets changed considerably before it's ready to be implemented broadly." As I mentioned above, when dealing with new technologies and new markets, no matter how much we think we're going to get it right in the labs, *we have to let the market shape the innovation*. And product platform architectures must be flexible to allow rapid reshaping of a product in response to customer feedback. In the best of all possible worlds, we would have a product platform that the customers themselves could shape *in situ*, the ultimate tool for listening to customers' needs. In this world, time-to-market is basically zero; there's "in the market" and there's "being created in the market itself." As Netscape has shown, companies can also link to their customers efficiently via the Internet. By employing the same medium to distribute their product and solicit customer response, companies can embed user feedback immediately in the next generation. In other words, they can link, listen, learn, and lead almost instantaneously.

A significant challenge we face as technologies become increasingly powerful is not to create more features but to create "robust fluidity," so that users have more control over shaping products. Think, for example, of computer software. As a user, I would like to be able to tailor software seamlessly to my particular needs, to deploy the power of the machine to let me easily shape it almost as if it were Silly Putty. Of course, this is very different from the way most companies create products. How many of the features available in word processing software do any of us actually use?

Successful innovation requires that the market be honored. By building flexibility into technologies as a way of learning about latent market needs and honoring their evolution, we can let customers shape a product through their tacit knowledge—without ever having to articulate what they want. There is enormous potential for innovation in tightening the coevolutionary loop between emerging technologies and emerging markets.

In "Managing Innovation in the Information Age," Rebecca Henderson uses a study that she conducted with Iain Cockburn of the pharmaceuticals industry as a benchmark for companies that are trying to become more innovative in the information age. Citing companies founded 50 years ago that still dominate the pharmaceuticals industry, Henderson points out that—despite size, age, and success—these companies have continued to learn and grow. She discusses three of their shared characteristics: they make and maintain close connections with the scientific community, they allocate resources broadly and effectively, and they manage the tension in organizational design.

Rebecca Henderson has had a profound impact on my own thinking on innovation. Although her examples come from the pharmaceuticals industry, her conclusions about innovation provide valuable lessons for managers in all industries. "The successful companies balanced the ability to reach out beyond the company for new scientific knowledge with the ability to link that knowledge to therapeutically useful goals." This kind of balancing and connecting to the world is very important in the notion of "link" that I discussed earlier.

I particularly like Henderson's point about managing the tensions in different kinds of organizational design: "Cross-functional teams, organizing by product, or organizing by function may increase cross-disciplinary communication, but they may do so at the expense of disciplinary excellence. Companies succeed by attending to this tension, devoting organizational energy to ensuring that neither end of the continuum dominates the process." Again, what is being suggested is not "either/or" but "and/also." The trick is finding creative ways to balance and leverage the tension.

Finally, she says something else that I will note primarily because it is so closely tied to the theme of this collection. Many companies are in trouble today because "they have become prisoners of the deeply ingrained assumptions, information filters, and problem-solving strategies that make up their world views, changing the solutions that once made them great into new problems to be resolved."

And then there is my article, "Research That Reinvents the Corporation." Reading it now, it is interesting to see how our thinking at PARC has evolved in the five years since it was published. In the article, I describe what we call pioneering research, a concept that has played a defining role in how we think about innovation, research, and technology at PARC. Pioneering research is radical, in the sense of going to the root, and it is grounded, in that it is closely tied to real problems. What we have come to realize is that pioneering research is built on two distinct and sometimes contradictory components—strategic capability and strategic exploration. Managing innovation requires the ability to honor both of these activities and to find ways of bringing them together, thus turning the tension between them into a creative tension.

Exhibit I illustrates the necessary coexistence of strategic capability—using science to create fundamentally new technological options, to make creative ideas more robust—and strategic exploration—uncovering and discovering new ideas, practices, products, and markets. These are the essential components of pioneering research; one without the other isn't particularly interesting. The problem is that the activities involved in each are done best by very different kinds of people who traditionally thrive in very different kinds of cultures. One is scientific, the other is inventive. It is rare to find people who are capable of making major scientific breakthroughs *and* of being playful and thinking in out-of-the-box ways about using technologies. We have come to see that the challenge in managing innovation in the research lab is, once again, about managing the tensions between two world views, bringing them together, and productively leveraging the strengths of each.

What we have done at PARC is to create a milieu that is ambidextrous,[6] in that it honors the two worlds. We have a remarkably broad group of disciplines represented on our staff, including everything from computer science and physics to psychology, linguistics, anthropology, and art. Being in this kind of culture, the researchers are more likely to have conversations and form associations that will facilitate their ability to see differently. The milieu is a powerful tool in leveraging and capitalizing on the active engagement of all these points of

Exhibit I. Pioneering Research: Grounded and Radical

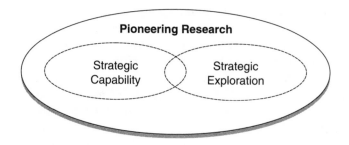

Strategic Capability	Strategic Exploration
Frames	Reframes
Makes Robust	Discovers
Extends	Undermines
Advances	Destabilizes
Defines	Creates
Is Moderately Predictable	Is Unpredictable

Mission: Enhancing the adaptability of the corporation.

view, making innovation at PARC as much a product of the environment as of the individuals who comprise it.

On the one hand, we have serious scientists who do what we call "white space research." I think of this kind of radical research as lashing one's self to a problem and taking it wherever it goes. The only guide to where to go is the problem itself; if it takes you out of your discipline, you go with it. If you have the wrong tools, you find new ones. It's easy to see how white space research is greatly facilitated by being conducted in the context of a multi-disciplinary group, where all around are people who have different sets of tools and lenses. (Although this is also true at universities, such research seldom happens because peer review and tenure mechanisms tend to favor research that stays well within established disciplines.)

On the other hand, we have "edge designers," researchers engaged in strategic exploration. The problems they work on tend to be as much about the use of technology as about technology itself. Their research is radical in the sense of being "out of the box " and pushing the boundaries. It often goes to the edge: the scientific edge, the edge between functions, between products, between work practices, and between markets. Being an edge designer means not only exploring these outer reaches, but also finding ways to actively shape what one finds there, almost like an artist creating a new genre.

Innovation requires a great deal of interplay between the serious scientists and the edge designers. A lot of tightrope walking is required on both sides. To do it well, one needs to be ambidextrous: intuitive and analytical, open and focused, capable of leading and honoring multiple points of view, creative and disciplined. People often ask how we at PARC bring together researchers with such diverse interests and backgrounds and get them to take part in grounded conversations among themselves, let alone with other parts of the corporation. The answer has to do with the people we hire. We look for people who have deep intuition and a passion to make an impact on the world. People with this passion want to learn how to motivate others; they want to play the games—and invent new ones—in order to have an impact.

Innovation means finding new markets for existing technologies, new technologies for existing markets, and new technologies for new markets. It means finding new ways of doing business: reaching customers, listening to the market, distributing products, managing people, managing uncertainty, and connecting to the ecologies surrounding our businesses. Doing any of these things requires that we see *something* differently. Moreover, we need to have the courage to follow our intuitions. Often we have no way of knowing—as we go way out on these limbs with emergent technologies and markets—if we are kidding ourselves. Who knows if our intuitions will prove correct? These leaps of faith make up the honest terror that lies beneath carrying out radical innovation. It takes resolution and it takes vision. But this is what innovation is really about.

Closing Thoughts

In this Introduction I have discussed the notion of seeing differently in the sense of challenging background assumptions, developing new intellectual constructs, and finding new lenses for looking at the world. There is another sense of seeing differently that plays an equally critical role in fostering innovation, and that is seeing from another person's point of view. When people from different worlds are able to come together and engage in a productive way, innovation is more likely to happen. Much of what we think of as innovation is the product of the creative tension between varied perspectives.

Many of the articles in this collection have to do with bringing together and balancing two worlds. We begin with W. Brian Arthur's discussion of the two worlds of business and end with my description of the two worlds that make up pioneering research at Xerox PARC. In between we read about developing product platforms that are both open and proprietary, and a way of thinking about strategy that brings together divergent schools of thought. Innovation, it seems, has to do with blurring distinctions between boundaries, transforming tension into creative energy, balancing formal work processes and social work practices, and leveraging the resources of divergent worlds. Innovation lies at the nexus of communities, of perspectives, and of paradigms.

Much of our current confusion about how to gain control in this shifting landscape has to do with the difficulty of living in two worlds at the same time. The transition from the factory-oriented, bulk processing way of doing things to the digitally based knowledge economy is fraught with peril. Yet, as we look at the companies that are making the transition successfully, we see how many of them are balancing both worlds and building on the strengths of the old to take hold in the new. The opportunities are boundless for those who are able to step back, adjust their vision, and begin to make sense.

Notes

1. The concept of "architecture of revenue" comes out of conversations with Mark Myers, senior vice president for Corporate Research and Technology at Xerox, about why it is so hard to build a capacity for radical innovation into corporations. The business models that underlie revenue streams provide the fundamental filters though which companies look at the world. It is because they represent the most deeply ingrained assumptions that these models are so difficult to change.

2. The xerography story is adapted from "Changing the Game of Corporate Research: Learning to Thrive in the Fog of Reality," to appear in the *International Journal of Technology Management* special issue on technology and learning, to be published by Inderscience Enterprise Ltd., Geneva, Switzerland.

3. This talk, given by John Seely Brown at many conferences, will be printed in a forthcoming issue of the *International Journal of Tech-*

nology Management. Reprinted by permission of Inderscience Enterprise Ltd.

4. See James F. Moore, "Predators and Prey: A New Ecology of Competition," *Harvard Business Review,* May–June 1993, 75.

5. Paul S. Adler and Bryan Borys, "Two Types of Bureaucracy: Enabling versus Coercive," *Administrative Science Quarterly* 41, no.1 (March 1996): 61–89.

6. The concept of ambidextrous organizations has been more fully developed by Michael L. Tushman and Charles A. O'Reilly, III in *Winning through Innovation* (Boston: Harvard Business School Press, 1996).

Seeing Differently

PART

I

Perspectives on the Changing Business Context

1
Increasing Returns and the New World of Business

W. Brian Arthur

Our understanding of how markets and businesses operate was passed down to us more than a century ago by a handful of European economists—Alfred Marshall in England and a few of his contemporaries on the continent. It is an understanding based squarely upon the assumption of diminishing returns: products or companies that get ahead in a market eventually run into limitations, so that a predictable equilibrium of prices and market shares is reached. The theory was roughly valid for the bulk-processing, smokestack economy of Marshall's day. And it still thrives in today's economics textbooks. But steadily and continuously in this century, Western economies have undergone a transformation from bulk-material manufacturing to design and use of technology—from processing of resources to processing of information, from application of raw energy to application of ideas. As this shift has occurred, the underlying mechanisms that determine economic behavior have shifted from ones of diminishing to ones of *increasing* returns.

Increasing returns are the tendency for that which is ahead to get further ahead, for that which loses advantage to lose further advantage. They are mechanisms of positive feedback that operate—within markets, businesses, and industries—to reinforce that which gains success or aggravate that which suffers loss. Increasing returns generate not equilibrium but instability: If a product or a company or a technology—one of many competing in a market—gets ahead by chance or clever strategy, increasing returns can magnify this advantage, and the product or company or technology can go on to lock in the market. More than causing products to become standards, increasing returns cause businesses to work differently, and they stand many of our notions of how business operates on their head.

Mechanisms of increasing returns exist alongside those of diminishing returns in all industries. But roughly speaking, diminishing returns hold sway in the traditional part of the economy—the processing industries. Increasing returns reign in the newer part—the knowledge-based industries. Modern economies have therefore bifurcated into two interrelated worlds of business corresponding to the two types of returns. The two worlds have different economics. They differ in behavior, style, and culture. They call for different management techniques, strategies, and codes of government regulation.

They call for different understandings.

Alfred Marshall's World

Let's go back to beginnings—to the diminishing-returns view of Alfred Marshall and his contemporaries. Marshall's world of the 1880s and 1890s was one of bulk production: of metal ores, aniline dyes, pig iron, coal, lumber, heavy chemicals, soybeans, coffee—commodities heavy on resources, light on know-how. In that world it was reasonable to suppose, for example, that if a coffee plantation expanded production it would ultimately be driven to use land less suitable for coffee. In other words, it would run into diminishing returns. So if coffee plantations competed, each one would expand until it ran into limitations in the form of rising costs or diminishing profits. The market would be shared by many plantations, and a market price would be established at a predictable level—depending on tastes for coffee and the availability of suitable farmland. Planters would produce coffee so long as doing so was profitable, but because the price would be squeezed down to the average cost of production, no one would be able to make a killing. Marshall said such a market was in perfect competition, and the economic world he envisaged fitted beautifully with the Victorian values of his time. It was at equilibrium and therefore orderly, predictable and therefore amenable to scientific analysis, stable and therefore safe, slow to change and therefore continuous. Not too rushed, not too profitable. In a word, mannerly. In a word, genteel.

With a few changes, Marshall's world lives on a century later within that part of the modern economy still devoted to bulk processing: of grains, livestock, heavy chemicals, metals and ores, foodstuffs, retail goods—the part where operations are largely repetitive day to day or week to week. Product differentiation and brand names now mean that a few companies rather than many compete in a given market. But typically, if these companies try to expand, they run into some limitation: in numbers of consumers who prefer their brand, in regional demand, in access to raw materials. So no company can corner the market. And because such products are normally substitutable for one another, something like a standard price emerges. Margins are thin and nobody makes a killing. This isn't exactly Marshall's perfect competition, but it approximates it.

The Increasing-Returns World

What would happen if Marshall's diminishing returns were reversed so that there were *increasing* returns? If products that got ahead thereby got further ahead, how would markets work?

Let's look at the market for operating systems for personal computers in the early 1980s when CP/M, DOS, and Apple's Macintosh systems were competing. Operating systems show increasing returns: if one system gets ahead, it attracts further software developers and hardware manufacturers to adopt it, which helps it get further ahead. CP/M was first in the market and by 1979 was well established. The Mac arrived later, but it was wonderfully easy to use. DOS was born when Microsoft locked up a deal in 1980 to supply an operating system for the IBM PC. For a year or two, it was by no means clear which system would prevail. The new IBM PC—DOS's platform—was a kludge. But the growing base of DOS/IBM users encouraged software developers such as Lotus to write for DOS. DOS's prevalence—and the IBM PC's—bred further prevalence, and eventually the DOS/IBM combination came to dominate a considerable portion of the market. That history is now well known. But notice several things: It was not predictable in advance (before the IBM deal) which system would come to dominate. Once DOS/IBM got ahead, it locked in the market because it did not pay for users to switch. The dominant system was not the best: DOS was derided by computer professionals. And once DOS locked in the market, its sponsor, Microsoft, was able to spread its costs over a large base of users. (For more on Microsoft, see "In the Case of Microsoft . . .") The company enjoyed killer margins.

In the Case of Microsoft . . .

What should be legal in this powerful and as yet unregulated world of increasing returns? What constitutes fair play? Should technology markets be regulated, and if so in what way? These questions have come to a head with the enormous amount of publicity generated by the U.S. Justice Department's current antitrust case against Microsoft.

In Marshall's world, antitrust regulation is well understood. Allowing a single player to control, say, more than 35% of the silver market is tantamount to allowing monopoly pricing, and the government rightly steps in. In the increasing-returns world, things are more complicated. There are arguments in favor of allowing a product or company in the web of technology to dominate a market, as well as arguments against. Consider these pros and cons:

Convenience. A locked-in product may provide a single standard of convenience. If a software company such as Microsoft allows us to double-click all the way from our computer screen straight to our bank account (by controlling all the technologies in between), this avoids a tedious balkanizing of standards, where we have to spend useless time getting into a succession of on-line connection products.

Fairness. If a product locks in because it is superior, this is fair, and it would be foolish to penalize such success. If it locks in merely because user base was levered over from a neighboring lock-in, this is unfair.

Technology Development. A locked-in product may obstruct technological advancement. If a clunker such as DOS locks up the PC market for ten years, there is little incentive for other companies to develop alternatives. The result is impeded technological progress.

Pricing. To lock in, a product usually has been discounted, and this established low price is often hard to raise. So monopoly pricing—of great concern in bulk-processing markets—is therefore rarely a major worry.

Added to these considerations, high tech is not a commodity industry. Dominance may consist not so much in cornering a single product as in successively taking over more and more threads of the web of technology, thereby preventing other players from getting access to new, breaking markets. It would be difficult to separate out each thread and to regulate it. And of course it may be impracticable to regulate a market before it forms—before it is even fully defined. There are no simple answers to antitrust regulation in the increasing-returns world. On balance, I would favor a high degree of regulatory restraint, with the addition of two key principles:

Do not penalize success. Short-term monopolization of an increasing-returns market is correctly perceived as a reward or prize for innovation and risk taking. There is a temptation to single out dominant players and hit them with an antitrust suit. This reduces regulation to something like a brawl in an Old West saloon—if you see a head, hit it. Not a policy that preserves an incentive to innovate in the first place.

Don't allow head starts for the privileged. This means that as a new market opens up—such as electronic consumer banking—companies that already dominate standards, operating systems, and neighboring technologies should not be allowed a ten-mile head start in the land rush that follows. All competitors should have fair and open access to the applicable technologies and standards.

In practice, these principles would mean allowing the possibility of winner-take-all jackpots in each new subindustry, in each new wave of technology. But each contender should have access to whatever degree possible to the same technologies, the same open standards, so that all are lined up behind the same starting line. If industry does not make such provisions voluntarily, government regulation will impose them.

These properties, then, have become the hallmarks of increasing returns: market instability (the market tilts to favor a product that gets ahead), multiple potential outcomes (under different events in history, different operating systems could have won), unpredictability, the ability to lock in a market, the possible predominance of an inferior product, and fat profits for the winner. They surprised me when I first perceived them in the late 1970s. They were also repulsive to economists brought up on the order, predictability, and optimality of Marshall's world. Glimpsing some of these properties in 1939, English economist John Hicks warned that admitting increasing returns would lead to "the wreckage of the greater part of economic theory." But Hicks had it wrong: the theory of increasing returns does not destroy the standard theory—it complements it. Hicks felt repugnance not just because of unsavory properties but also because in his day no mathematical apparatus existed to analyze increasing-returns markets. That situation has now changed. Using sophisticated techniques from qualitative dynamics and probability theory, I and others have developed methods to analyze increasing-returns markets. The theory of increasing returns is new, but it already is well established. And it renders such markets amenable to economic understanding.

In the early days of my work on increasing returns, I was told they were an anomaly. Like some exotic particle in physics, they might exist in theory but would be rare in practice. And if they did exist, they would last for only a few seconds before being arbitraged away. But by the mid-1980s, I realized increasing returns were neither rare nor ephemeral. In fact, a major part of the economy was subject to increasing returns—high technology.

Why should this be so? There are several reasons:

UP-FRONT COSTS. High-tech products—pharmaceuticals, computer hardware and software, aircraft and missiles, telecommunications equipment, bioengineered drugs, and suchlike—are by definition complicated to design and to deliver to the marketplace. They are heavy on know-how and light on resources. Hence they typically have R&D costs that are large relative to their unit production costs. The first disk of Windows to go out the door cost Microsoft $50 million; the second and subsequent disks cost $3. Unit costs fall as sales increase.

NETWORK EFFECTS. Many high-tech products need to be compatible with a network of users. So if much downloadable software on the Internet will soon appear as programs written in Sun Microsystems' Java language, users will need Java on their computers to run them. Java has competitors. But the more it gains prevalence, the more likely it will emerge as a standard.

CUSTOMER GROOVE-IN. High-tech products are typically difficult to use. They require training. Once users invest in this training—say, the maintenance and piloting of Airbus passenger aircraft—they merely need to update these skills for subsequent versions of the product. As more market is captured, it becomes easier to capture future markets.

In high-tech markets, such mechanisms ensure that products that gain market advantage stand to gain further advantage, making these markets unstable and subject to lock-in. Of course, lock-in is not forever. Technology comes in waves, and a lock-in such as DOS's can last only as long as a particular wave lasts.

So we can usefully think of two economic regimes or worlds: a bulk-production world yielding products that essentially are congealed resources with a little knowledge and operating according to Marshall's principles of diminishing returns, and a knowledge-based part of the economy yielding products that essentially are congealed knowledge with a little resources and operating under increasing returns. The two worlds are not neatly split. Hewlett-Packard, for example, designs knowledge-based devices in Palo Alto, California, and manufactures them in bulk in places like Corvallis, Oregon, or Greeley, Colorado. Most high-tech companies have both knowledge-based operations and bulk-processing operations. But because the rules of the game differ for each, companies often separate them—as Hewlett-Packard does. Conversely, manufacturing companies have operations such as logistics, branding, marketing, and distribution, which belong largely to the knowledge world. And some products—like the IBM PC—start in the increasing-returns world but later in their life cycle become virtual commodities that belong to Marshall's processing world.

The Halls of Production and the Casino of Technology

Because the two worlds of business—processing bulk goods and crafting knowledge into products—differ in their underlying economics, it follows that they differ in their character of competition and their culture of management. It is a mistake to think that what works in one world is appropriate for the other.

There is much talk these days about a new management style that involves flat hierarchies, mission orientation, flexibility in strategy, market positioning, reinvention, restructuring, reengineering, repositioning, reorganization, and re-everything else. Are these new insights or are they fads? Are they appropriate for all organizations? Why are we seeing this new management style?

Let us look at the two cultures of competition. In bulk processing, a set of standard prices typically emerges. Production tends to be repetitive—much the same from day to day or even from year to year. Competing therefore means keeping product flowing, trying to improve quality, getting costs down. There is an art to this sort of management, one widely discussed in the literature. It favors an environment free of surprises or glitches—an environment characterized by control and planning. Such an environment requires not just people to carry out production but also people to plan and control it. So it favors a hierarchy of bosses and workers. Because bulk processing is repetitive, it allows constant improvement, constant optimization. And so, Marshall's world tends to be one that favors hierarchy, planning, and controls. Above all, it is a world of optimization.

Competition is different in knowledge-based industries because the economics are different. If knowledge-based companies are competing in winner-take-most markets, then managing becomes redefined as a series of quests for the next technological winner—the next cash cow. The goal becomes the search for the Next Big Thing. In this milieu, management becomes not production oriented but mission oriented. Hierarchies flatten not because democracy is suddenly bestowed on the workforce or because computers can cut out much of middle management. They flatten because, to be effective, the deliverers of the next-thing-for-the-company need to be organized like commando units in small teams that report directly to the CEO or to the board. Such people need free rein. The company's future survival depends upon them. So they—and the commando teams that report to them in turn—will be treated not as employees but as equals in the business of the company's success. Hierarchy dissipates and dissolves.

Does this mean that hierarchy should disappear in meatpacking, steel production, or the navy? Contrary to recent management evangelizing, a style that is called for in Silicon Valley will not necessarily be appropriate in the processing world. An aircraft's safe arrival depends on the captain, not on the flight attendants. The cabin crew can usefully be "empowered" and treated as human beings. This approach is wise and proper. But forever there will be a distinction—a hierarchy—between cockpit and cabin crews.

In fact, the style in the diminishing-returns Halls of Production is much like that of a sophisticated modern factory: the goal is to keep high-quality product flowing at low cost. There is little need to watch the market every day, and when things are going smoothly the tempo can be leisurely. By contrast, the style of competition in the increasing-returns arena is more like gambling. Not poker, where the game is static and the players vie for a succession of pots. It is casino gambling, where part of the game is to choose which games to play, as well as playing them with skill. We can imagine the top figures in high tech—the Gateses and Gerstners and Groves of their industries—as milling in a large casino. Over at this table, a game is starting called multimedia. Over at that one, a game called Web services. In the corner is electronic banking. There are many such tables. You sit at one. How much to play? you ask. Three billion, the croupier replies. Who'll be playing? We won't know until they show up. What are the rules? Those'll emerge as the game unfolds. What are my odds of winning? We can't say. Do you still want to play?

High technology, pursued at this level, is not for the timid.

In fact, the art of playing the tables in the Casino of Technology is primarily a psychological one. What counts to some degree—but only to some degree—is technical expertise, deep pockets, will, and courage. Above all, the rewards go to the players who are first to make sense of the new games looming out of the technological fog, to see their shape, to cognize them. Bill Gates is not so much a wizard of technology as a wizard of precognition, of discerning the shape of the next game.

We can now begin to see that the new style of management is not a fad. The knowledge-based part of the economy demands flat hierarchies, mission orientation, above all a sense of direction. Not five-year plans. We can also fathom the mystery of what I've alluded to as *re-everything*. Much of this "re-everything" predilection—in the bulk-processing world—is a fancy label for streamlining, computerizing, downsizing. However, in the increasing-returns world, especially in high tech, re-everything has become necessary because every time the quest changes, the company needs to change. It needs to reinvent its purpose, its goals, its way of doing things. In short, it needs to adapt. And adaptation never stops. In fact, in the increasing-returns environment I've just sketched, standard optimization makes little sense. You cannot optimize in the casino of increasing-returns games. You can be smart. You can be cunning. You can position. You can observe. But when the games themselves are not even fully defined, you cannot optimize. What you *can* do is adapt. Adaptation, in the proactive sense, means watching for the next wave that is coming, figuring out what shape it will take, and positioning the company to take advantage of it. Adaptation is what drives increasing-returns businesses, not optimization.

Playing the High-Tech Tables

Suppose you are a player in the knowledge-industry casino, in this increasing-returns world. What can you do to capitalize on the increasing returns at your disposal? How can you use them to capture markets? What strategic issues do you need to think about? In the processing world, strategy typically hinges upon capitalizing on core competencies, pricing competitively, getting costs down, bringing quality up. These are important also in the knowledge-based world, but so, too, are other strategies that make use of the special economics of positive feedbacks.

Two maxims are widely accepted in knowledge-based markets: it pays to hit the market first, and it pays to have superb technology. These maxims are true but do not guarantee success. Prodigy was first into the on-line services market but was passive in building its sub-scriber base to take advantage of increasing returns. As a result, it has fallen from its leading position and currently lags the other services. As for technology, Steve Jobs's NeXT workstation was superb. But it was launched into a market already dominated by Sun Microsystems and Hewlett-Packard. It failed. A new product often has to be two or three times better in some dimension—price, speed, convenience—to dislodge a locked-in rival. So in knowledge-based markets, entering first with a fine product can yield advantage. But as strategy, this is still too passive. What is needed is *active* management of increasing returns.

One active strategy is to discount heavily initially to build up an installed base. Netscape handed out its Internet browser for free and won 70% of its market. Now it can profit from spin-off software and applications. Although such discounting is effective—and widely un-derstood—it is not always implemented. Companies often err by pric-ing high initially to recoup expensive R&D costs. Yet even smart dis-counting to seed the market is ineffective unless the resulting installed base is exploited later. America Online built up a lead of more than 4.5 million subscribers by giving away free services. But because of the Internet's dominance, it is not yet clear whether it can transform this huge base into later profits.

Let's get a bit more sophisticated. Technological products do not stand alone. They depend on the existence of other products and other technologies. The Internet's World Wide Web operates within a group-ing of businesses that include browsers, on-line news, E-mail, network retailing, and financial services. Pharmaceuticals exist within a net-work of physicians, testing labs, hospitals, and HMOs. Laser printers are part of a grouping of products that include computers, publishing software, scanners, and photo-input devices. Unlike products of the processing world, such as soybeans or rolled steel, technological prod-ucts exist within local groupings of products that support and enhance them. They exist in mini-ecologies.

This interdependence has deep implications for strategy. When, in the mid-1980s, Novell introduced its network-operating system, Net-

Ware, as a way of connecting personal computers in local networks, Novell made sure that NetWare was technically superior to its rivals. It also heavily discounted NetWare to build an installed base. But these tactics were not enough. Novell recognized that NetWare's success depended on attracting software applications to run on NetWare—which was a part of the ecology outside the company's control. So it set up incentives for software developers to write for NetWare rather than for its rivals. The software writers did just that. And by building NetWare's success, they ensured their own. Novell managed these cross-product positive feedbacks actively to lock in its market. It went on to profit hugely from upgrades, spin-offs, and applications of its own.

Another strategy that uses ecologies is linking and leveraging. This means transferring a user base built up upon one node of the ecology (one product) to neighboring nodes, or products. The strategy is very much like that in the game Go: you surround neighboring markets one by one, lever your user base onto them, and take them over—all the time enhancing your position in the industry. Microsoft levered its 60-million-person user base in DOS onto Windows, then onto Windows 95, and then onto Microsoft Network by offering inexpensive upgrades and by bundling applications. The strategy has been challenged legally. But it recognizes that positive feedbacks apply across markets as well as within markets.

In fact, if technological ecologies are now the basic units for strategy in the knowledge-based world, players compete not by locking in a product on their own but by building *webs*—loose alliances of companies organized around a mini-ecology—that amplify positive feedbacks to the base technology. Apple, in closing its Macintosh system to outsiders in the 1980s, opted not to create such a web. It believed that with its superior technology, it could hold its increasing-returns market to itself. Apple indeed dominates its Mac-based ecology. But this ecology is now only 8% of the personal computer business. IBM erred in the other direction. By passively allowing other companies to join its PC web as clones, IBM achieved a huge user base and locked in the market. But the company itself wound up with a small share of the spoils. The key in web building is active management of the cross-company mutual feedbacks. This means making a careful choice of partners to build upon. It also means that, rather than attempting to take over all products in the ecology, dominant players in a web should allow dependent players to lock in their dependent products by piggybacking on the web's success. By thus ceding some of the profits, the dominant players ensure that all participants remain committed to the alliance.

Important also to strategy in knowledge-based markets is psychological positioning. Under increasing returns, rivals will back off in a market not only if it is locked in but if they *believe* it will be locked in by someone else. Hence we see psychological jockeying in the form of preannouncements, feints, threatened alliances, technological preening, touted future partnerships, parades of vaporware (announced products that don't yet exist). This posturing and puffing acts much the way similar behavior does in a primate colony: it discourages competitors from taking on a potentially dominant rival. No moves need be made in this strategy of premarket facedown. It is purely a matter of psychology.

What if you hold a losing hand? Sometimes it pays to hold on for residual revenue. Sometimes a fix can be provided by updated technology, fresh alliances, or product changes. But usually under heavy lock-in, these tactics do not work. The alternatives are then slow death or graceful exit—relinquishing the field to concentrate on positioning for the next technology wave. Exit may not mean quitting the business entirely. America Online, Compuserve, Prodigy, and Microsoft Network have all ceded dominance of the on-line computer networking market to the Internet. But instead of exiting, they are steadily becoming adjuncts of the Net, supplying content services such as financial quotations or games and entertainment. They have lost the main game. But they will likely continue in a side game with its own competition for dominance within the Net's ecology.

Above all, strategy in the knowledge world requires CEOs to recognize that a different kind of economics is at work. CEOs need to understand which positive and negative feedback mechanisms are at play in the market ecologies in which they compete. Often there are several such mechanisms—interbraided, operating over different time frames, each needing to be understood, observed, and actively managed.

What About Service Industries?

So far, I've talked mainly about high tech. Where do service industries such as insurance, restaurants, and banking fit in? Which world do they belong to? The question is tricky. It would appear that such industries belong to the diminishing-returns, processing part of the economy because often there are regional limits to the demand for a given service, most services do consist of "processing" clients, and services are low-tech.

The truth is that network or user-base effects often operate in services. Certainly, retail franchises exist because of increasing returns. The more McDonald's restaurants or Motel 6 franchises are out there geographically, the better they are known. Such businesses are patronized not just for their quality but also because people want to know exactly what to expect. So the more prevalent they are, the more prevalent they can become. Similarly, the larger a bank's or insurance company's customer base, the more it can spread its fixed costs of headquarters staff, real estate, and computer operations. These industries, too, are subject to mild increasing returns.

So we can say more accurately that service industries are a hybrid. From day to day, they act like bulk-processing industries. But over the long term, increasing returns will dominate—even though their destabilizing effects are not as pronounced as in high tech. The U.S. airline business, for example, processes passengers day to day. So it seemed in 1981 that deregulation should enhance competition, as it normally does under diminishing returns. But over the long term, airlines in fact experience a positive feedback: under the hub-and-spoke system, once an airline gets into trouble, it cannot work the feeder system for its routes properly, its fleet ages, it starts a downward spiral, and it loses further routes. The result of deregulation over the long term has been a steady decline in large carriers, from 15 airlines in 1981 to approximately 6 at present. Some routes have become virtual monopolies, with resulting higher fares. None of this was intended. But it should have been predicted—given increasing returns.

In fact, the increasing-returns character of service industries is steadily strengthening. One of the marks of our time is that in services everything is going software—everything that is information based. So operations that were once handled by people—designing fancy financial instruments or automobiles or fashion goods, processing insurance claims, supplying and inventorying in retail, conducting paralegal searches for case precedents—are increasingly being handled by software. As this reengineering of services plays out, centralized software facilities come to the fore. Service providers become hitched into software networks, regional limitations weaken, and user-base network effects kick in.

This phenomenon can have two consequences. First, where the

local character of service remains important, it can preserve a large number of service companies but clustered round a dominant software provider—like the large numbers of small, independent law firms tied in to the dominant computer-search network, Lexis-Nexis. Or physicians tied in to an HMO. Second, where locality is unimportant, network effects can transform competition toward the winner-take-most character we see in high tech. For example, when Internet-based retail banking arrives, regional demand limitations will vanish. Each virtual bank will gain in advantage as its network increases. Barring regulation, consumer banking will then become a contest among a few large banking networks. It will become an increasing-returns business.

Services belong to both the processing and the increasing-returns world. But their center of gravity is crossing over to the latter.

Thoughts for Managers

Where does all this leave us? At the beginning of this century, industrial economies were based largely on the bulk processing of resources. At the close of the century, they are based on the processing of resources *and* on the processing of knowledge. Economies have bifurcated into two worlds—intertwined, overlapping, and different. These two worlds operate under different economic principles. Marshall's world is characterized by planning, control, and hierarchy. It is a world of materials, of processing, of optimization. The increasing-returns world is characterized by observation, positioning, flattened organizations, missions, teams, and cunning. It is a world of psychology, of cognition, of adaptation.

Many managers have some intuitive grasp of this new increasing-returns world. Few understand it thoroughly. Here are some questions managers need to ask themselves when they operate in knowledge-based markets:

DO I UNDERSTAND THE FEEDBACKS IN MY MARKET? In the processing world, understanding markets means understanding consumers' needs, distribution channels, and rivals' products. In the knowledge world, success requires a thorough understanding of the self-negating and self-reinforcing feedbacks in the market—the diminishing- and increasing-returns mechanisms. These feedbacks are interwoven and operate at different levels in the market and over different time frames.

WHICH ECOLOGIES AM I IN? Technologies exist not alone but in an interlinked web, or ecology. It is important to understand the ecologies a company's products belong to. Success or failure is often decided not just by the company but also by the success or failure of the web it belongs to. Active management of such a web can be an important magnifier of increasing returns.

DO I HAVE THE RESOURCES TO PLAY? Playing one of the increasing-returns games in the Casino of Technology requires several things: excellent technology, the ability to hit the market at the right time, deep pockets, strategic pricing, and a willingness to sacrifice current profits for future advantage. All this is a matter not just of resources but also of courage, resolution, will. And part of that resolution, that courage, is also the decisiveness to leave the market when increasing returns are moving against one. Hanging on to a losing position that is being further eroded by positive feedbacks requires throwing reinforcements into a battle already lost. Better to exit with financial dignity.

WHAT GAMES ARE COMING NEXT? Technology comes in successive waves. Those who have lost out on this wave can position for the next. Conversely, those who have made a killing on this cycle should not become complacent. The ability to profit under increasing returns is only as good as the ability to see what's coming in the next cycle and to position oneself for it—technologically, psychologically, and cooperatively. In high tech, it is as if we are moving slowly on a ship, with new technologies looming, taking shape, through a fog of unknowingness. Success goes to those who have the vision to foresee, to imagine, what shapes these next games will take.

These considerations appear daunting. But increasing-returns games provide large payoffs for those brave enough to play them and win. And they are exciting. Processing, in the service or manufacturing industries, has its own risks. Precisely because processing is low-margin, operations must struggle to stay afloat. Neither world of business is for the fainthearted.

In his book *Microcosm*, technology thinker George Gilder remarked, "The central event of the twentieth century is the overthrow of matter. In technology, economics, and the politics of nations, wealth in the form of physical resources is steadily declining in value and significance. The powers of mind are everywhere ascendant over the brute force of things." As the economy shifts steadily away from the brute force of things into the powers of mind, from resource-based bulk processing into knowledge-based design and reproduction, so it is shifting from a base of diminishing returns to one of increasing returns. A new economics—one very different from that in the textbooks—now applies, and nowhere is this more true than in high technology. Success will strongly favor those who understand this new way of thinking.

2
Strategy as Revolution

Gary Hamel

Let's admit it. Corporations around the world are reaching the limits of incrementalism. Squeezing another penny out of costs, getting a product to market a few weeks earlier, responding to customers' inquiries a little bit faster, ratcheting quality up one more notch, capturing another point of market share—those are the obsessions of managers today. But pursuing incremental improvements while rivals reinvent the industry is like fiddling while Rome burns.

Look at any industry and you will see three kinds of companies. First are the rule makers, the incumbents that built the industry. IBM, CBS, United Airlines, Merrill Lynch, Sears, Coca-Cola, and the like are the creators and protectors of industrial orthodoxy. They are the oligarchy. Next are the rule takers, the companies that pay homage to the industrial "lords." Fujitsu, ABC, U.S. Air, Smith Barney, J.C. Penney, and numerous others are those peasants. Their life is hard. Imagine working at Fujitsu for 30 years trying to catch IBM in the mainframe business, or being McDonnell Douglas to Boeing, or Avis to Hertz. We Try Harder may be a great advertising slogan, but it's depressingly futile as a strategy. What good will it do to work harder to follow the rules when some companies are rewriting them? IKEA, the Body Shop, Charles Schwab, Dell Computer, Swatch, Southwest Airlines, and many more are the rule breakers. Shackled neither by convention nor by respect for precedent, these companies are intent on overturning the industrial order. They are the malcontents, the radicals, the industry revolutionaries.

Never has the world been more hospitable to industry revolutionaries and more hostile to industry incumbents. The fortifications that protected the industrial oligarchy are crumbling under the weight of deregulation, technological upheaval, globalization, and social change. But it's not just the forces of change that are overturning old industrial structures—it's the actions of companies that harness those forces for the cause of revolution. (See "Nine Routes to Industry Revolution.")

Nine Routes to Industry Revolution

Unless you are an industry leader with an unassailable position—a status that, given the lessons of history, not even Microsoft would be wise to claim—you probably have a greater stake in staging a revolution than in preserving the status quo. The opportunities for revolution are many and mostly unexplored. How should a would-be revolutionary begin? By looking for ways to redefine products and services, market space, and even the entire structure of an industry.

Reconceiving a Product or Service

1. RADICALLY IMPROVING THE VALUE EQUATION. In every industry, there is a ratio that relates price to performance: X units of cash buy Y units of value. The challenge is to improve that value ratio and to do so radically— 500% or 1,000%, not 10% or 20%. Such a fundamental redefinition of the value equation forces a reconception of the product or service.

Fidelity Investments, for instance, wondered why a person couldn't invest in foreign equity markets for tens or hundreds of dollars rather than thousands. On a recent flight, I heard one flight attendant say to another, "I just moved some of my investments from the Europe Fund to the Pacific Basin Fund." Such a comment would have been inconceivable a decade or two ago, but Fidelity and other mutual-fund revolutionaries have redefined the industry's value equation. Hewlett-Packard's printer business and IKEA are other value revolutionaries.

2. SEPARATING FUNCTION AND FORM. Another way to challenge the existing concept of a product or service is to separate core benefits (function) from the ways in which those benefits are currently embodied in a product or service (form). Any organization that is able to distinguish form from function and then reconceive one or both has the opportunity to create an industry revolution.

Consider credit cards, which perform two functions. First, a credit card inspires a merchant to trust that you are who the card says you are: your name is embossed on the front, your signature appears on the back, and your photo may even appear in the corner. Nevertheless, credit card fraud is a rapidly escalating problem. In what form will "trust" be delivered in the future? Probably through biometric data: a handprint, voiceprint, or retinal scan. Any credit card maker that is not investing in those technologies today may be surprised by interlopers. Second, a credit card gives you permission to charge up to your credit limit. What new opportunities appear if you distinguish permission as a general function from the particular case of permission to charge? In many hotels, a card with a magnetic stripe gives guests "permission" to enter their rooms. Did credit card makers see the opportunity to use the cards in this way? No, the card security market is owned largely by newcomers.

3. ACHIEVING JOY OF USE.   We live in a world that takes ease of use for granted. The new goal is joy of use. We want our products and services to be whimsical, tactile, informative, and just plain fun. Any company that can wrap those attributes around a mundane product or service has the chance to be an industry revolutionary.

What's the most profitable food retailer per square foot in the United States? Probably Trader Joe's, a cross between a gourmet deli and a discount warehouse, which its CEO, John Shields, calls a "fashion food retailer." Essentially without competition, its 74 stores were averaging annual sales of $1,000 per square foot in 1995—twice the rate of conventional supermarkets and more than three times that of most specialty food shops. Customers shop Trader Joe's as much for entertainment as for sustenance. The store stocks dozens of offbeat foods—jasmine fried rice, salmon burgers, and raspberry salsa—as well as carefully selected, competitively priced staples. By turning shopping from a chore into a culinary treasure hunt, Trader Joe's has more than doubled its sales over the last five years to $605 million.

Redefining Market Space

4. PUSHING THE BOUNDS OF UNIVERSALITY.   Every company has an implicit notion of its served market: the types of individuals and institutions that are—and are not—customers. Revolutionary companies, however, focus not just on their served market but on the total imaginable market.

A few years back, who would have considered children a likely market for 35-millimeter film? Would you have given your $500 Nikon to an eight-year-old? Probably not. Parents today, however, think nothing of giving a disposable camera to a child for a day at the beach, a birthday party, or the family's vacation. The single-use camera has made access to photography virtually universal. In 1995, the single-use-camera market reached 50 million units, worth close to $1 billion at retail. From class to mass, adult to child, professional to consumer, and national to global, the traditional boundaries of market space are being redefined by revolutionary companies.

5. STRIVING FOR INDIVIDUALITY. No one wants to be part of a mass market. We'll all buy the same things—but only if we have to. Deep in our need to be ourselves, to be unique, are the seeds of industry revolution.

A woman who wants a perfect-fitting pair of jeans, for example, can now get measured at one of Levi Strauss's Personal Pair outlets, and a computer will pick out exactly the right size. The woman's specifications are sent to Levi's by computer, and her made-to-order jeans arrive a few days later. The price? Just about $10 more than an off-the-shelf pair. Levi's plans to introduce the Personal Pair system to nearly 200 stores in the United States by the end of the decade. The company is counting on its revolutionary approach to put a considerable dent in the growing market for private-label jeans.

6. INCREASING ACCESSIBILITY. Most market spaces have temporal and geographic bounds: customers must go to a specific store at a specific location between certain hours. But market space is becoming cyber-space, and every day industry revolutionaries are resetting consumers' expectations about accessibility.

Consider First Direct, a bank that can be reached only by telephone. The fastest-growing bank in Great Britain, First Direct was opening 10,000 new accounts per month in mid-1995—the equivalent of two or three branches. The professionals and workaholics who make up First Direct's half million customers carry, on average, a balance that's ten times higher than the average balance at Midland Bank, First Direct's parent, while overall costs per client are 61% less. One of the first U.S. banks to experiment with so-called direct banking estimates that it will ultimately be able to close at least half of its branches.

Redrawing Industry Boundaries

7. RESCALING INDUSTRIES. As industry revolutionaries seek out and exploit new national and global economies of scale, industries around the world—even office cleaning and haircutting—are consolidating at a fear-some pace. Any industry that was local, such as consumer banking, is becoming national. Any industry that was national, such as the airline business, is becoming global.

Every minute and a half, Service Corporation International buries or cremates someone, somewhere in the world. Performing 320,000 funerals per year, SCI has become the world's largest funeral operator in an industry that traditionally has been very fragmented. Most funeral operators have been family businesses. By buying up small operators, SCI has reaped economies of scale in purchasing, capital utilization (sharing hearses among operators, for example), marketing, and administration.

Of course, an industry can be scaled down as well as up. Bed-and-breakfast inns, microbreweries, local bakeries, and specialty retailers are the result of industries that have scaled down to serve narrow or local customer segments more effectively.

8. COMPRESSING THE SUPPLY CHAIN. The cognoscenti use the word *disintermediation* in its literal sense: the removal of intermediaries. Wal-Mart, for instance, essentially turned the warehouse into a store, thus disintermediating the traditional small-scale retailer. And Xerox hopes to reinvent the way companies distribute printed documents by disintermediating trucking companies from the printing business. Why, Xerox asks, should annual reports, user manuals, catalogs, employee handbooks, and other printed matter be hauled across the country in trucks? Why not send the information digitally and print it close to where it is needed? Xerox is working with a variety of partners to stage this revolution.

9. DRIVING CONVERGENCE. Revolutionaries not only radically change the value-added structure within industries but also blur the boundaries between industries. Deregulation, the ubiquity of information, and new customer demands give revolutionaries the chance to transcend an industry's boundaries.

For example, a consumer can now get a credit card from General Motors, a mortgage from Prudential or GE Capital, a retirement account at Fidelity Investments, and a checkbook from Charles Schwab. Innovative hospitals "capitate" lives, guaranteeing to provide an individual with a full range of health services for a fixed sum per year. Insurance companies, such as Aetna, respond by refashioning themselves into health care providers. Boston Market offers hot family-style meals for takeout, and supermarkets respond by offering an ever wider selection of prepared foods, further blurring the boundary between the grocery and fast-food industries.

Industry revolutionaries don't ask what industry they are in. They know that an industry's boundaries today are about as meaningful as borders in the Balkans.

What if your company is more ruling class than revolutionary? You can either surrender the future to revolutionary challengers or revolutionize the way your company creates strategy. What is required is not a little tweak to the traditional planning process but a new philosophical foundation: strategy *is* revolution; everything else is tactics.

The following ten principles can help a company liberate its revolutionary spirit and dramatically increase its chances of discovering truly revolutionary strategies. Companies in industries as diverse as personal care products, information services, food processing, insurance, and telecommunications have internalized and acted on these principles. Every organization, however, must interpret and apply them in its own way. These are not a set of step-by-step instructions but a way of thinking about the challenge of creating strategy—the challenge of becoming an industry revolutionary.

PRINCIPLE 1: STRATEGIC PLANNING ISN'T STRATEGIC.   Consider your company's planning process. Which describes it best—column A or column B.

A	B
Ritualistic	Inquisitive
Reductionist	Expansive
Extrapolative	Prescient
Positioning	Inventing
Elitist	Inclusive
Easy	Demanding

Unless your company is truly exceptional, you've probably admitted that the words in column A are more fitting than those in column B. In the vast majority of companies, strategic planning is a calendar-driven ritual, not an exploration of the potential for revolution. The strategy-making process tends to be reductionist, based on simple rules and heuristics. It works from today forward, not from the future back, implicitly assuming, whatever the evidence to the contrary, that the future will be more or less like the present. Only a tiny percentage of an industry's conventions are ever challenged, rendering strategy making largely extrapolative. An industry's boundaries are taken as a given; thus the question is how to position products and services within those boundaries rather than how to invent new, uncontested competitive space. Further, the planning process is generally elitist, harnessing only a small proportion of an organization's creative potential.

Perhaps most disturbing, strategy making is often assumed to be easy, especially in comparison with implementing strategy. But of course strategy making is easy when the process limits the scope of discovery, the breadth of involvement, and the amount of intellectual effort expended. Of course the process is easy when its goal is something far short of revolution. How often has strategic planning produced true strategic innovation? No wonder that in many organizations, corporate planning departments are being disbanded. No wonder that consulting firms are doing less and less "strategy" work and more and more "implementation" work.

The essential problem in organizations today is a failure to distinguish *planning* from *strategizing*.[1] Planning is about programming, not discovering. Planning is for technocrats, not dreamers. Giving planners responsibility for creating strategy is like asking a bricklayer to create Michelangelo's *Pietà*.

Most executives know a strategy when they see one. Wal-Mart has a clear strategy; so does Federal Express. But recognizing a strategy that already exists is not enough. Where do strategies come from? How are they created? Strategizing is not a rote procedure—it is a quest. Any company that believes that planning can yield strategy will find itself under the curse of incrementalism while freethinking newcomers lead successful insurrections.

PRINCIPLE 2: STRATEGY MAKING MUST BE SUBVERSIVE.   Galileo challenged the centrality of Earth and man in the cosmos. The American colonists challenged the feudal dependencies and inherited privileges of European society. Picasso and other modernists challenged representational art. Einstein challenged Newtonian physics. Revolutionaries are subversive, but their goal is not subversion. What the defenders of orthodoxy see as subversiveness, the champions of new thinking see as enlightenment.

If there is to be any hope of industry revolution, the creators of strategy must cast off industrial conventions. For instance, Anita Roddick, the founder of the Body Shop, turned Charles Revson's hope-in-a-bottle formula on its head. Instead of assuming, as the cosmetics industry always had, that women lack self-confidence and will pay inflated prices for simple formulations if they believe that they will make them more attractive, Roddick assumed that women have self-esteem and just want lighthearted, environmentally responsible products. Roddick wasn't kidding when she said, "I watch where the cosmetics industry is going and then walk in the opposite direction."

Identify the 10 or 20 most fundamental beliefs that incumbents in your industry share. What new opportunities present themselves when you relax those beliefs? Consider the hotel industry's definition of a day, which begins when you check in and ends at noon, when you must check out. But if you check in at 1 A.M. after a grueling journey, why should you have to check out at the same time or pay the same amount as the person who arrived at 5 the previous afternoon? If a rental-car company can manage a fleet of cars on a rotating 24-hour basis, why can't a hotel do exactly the same with a fleet of rooms?

Rule makers and rule takers are the industry. Rule breakers set out to redefine the industry, to invent the new by challenging the old. Ask yourself, What are the fundamental conventions we have examined and abandoned in our company? Can you think of more than one or two? Can you think of any at all? If not, why not? As a senior executive, are you willing to embrace a subversive strategy-making process?

PRINCIPLE 3: THE BOTTLENECK IS AT THE TOP OF THE BOTTLE. In most companies, strategic orthodoxy has some very powerful defenders: senior managers. Imagine an organizational pyramid with senior managers at the apex. (It has become fashionable to draw the pyramid with customers at the top and senior managers at the bottom. But as long as senior managers retain their privileges—corporate aircraft, spacious suites, and so on—I prefer to leave the pointy end at the top.) Where are you likely to find people with the least diversity of experience, the largest investment in the past, and the greatest reverence for industrial dogma? At the top. And where will you find the people responsible for creating strategy? Again, at the top.

The organizational pyramid is a pyramid of experience. But experience is valuable only to the extent that the future is like the past. In industry after industry, the terrain is changing so fast that experience is becoming irrelevant and even dangerous. Unless the strategy-making process is freed from the tyranny of experience, there is little chance of industry revolution. If you're a senior executive, ask yourself these questions: Has a decade or two of experience made me more willing or less willing to challenge my industry's conventions? Have I become more curious or less curious about what is happening beyond the traditional boundaries of my industry? Be honest. As Ralph Waldo Emerson wrote, "There are always two parties, the party of the past and the party of the future; the establishment and the movement." To which party do you belong?

PRINCIPLE 4: REVOLUTIONARIES EXIST IN EVERY COMPANY. It is often said that you cannot find a pro-change constituency in a successful company. I disagree. It is more accurate to say that in a successful company you are unlikely to find a pro-change constituency among the top dozen or so officers.

Make no mistake: there are revolutionaries in your company. If you go down and out into your organization—out into the ranks of much maligned middle managers, for instance—you will find people straining against the bit of industrial orthodoxy. All too often, however, there is no process that lets those revolutionaries be heard. Their voices are muffled by the layers of cautious bureaucrats who separate them from senior managers. They are isolated and impotent, disconnected from others who share their passions. So, like economic refugees seeking greater opportunity in new lands, industry revolutionaries often abandon their employers to find more imaginative sponsors.

No one doubts that Jack Welch of General Electric, Percy Barnevik of ABB Asea Brown Boveri, and Ray Smith of Bell Atlantic are pro-change leaders. But rather than celebrating the exceptions—the few truly transformational executives who populate every tome on leadership—isn't the greater challenge to help the pro-change constituency that exists in every company find its voice? Sure, there are some radical corporate leaders out there. But weren't they always revolutionaries at heart? Why couldn't they have had a much greater impact on their companies earlier in their careers? Perhaps they, too, found it difficult to challenge the combined forces of precedence, position, and power. It would be sad to conclude that a company can fully exploit the emotional and intellectual energy of a revolutionary only if he or she succeeds in navigating the tortuous route to the top. How many revolutionaries will wait patiently for such a chance?

As a corporate leader, do you know where the revolutionaries are in your own organization? Have you given them a say in the strategy-making process? One thing is certain: if you don't let the revolutionaries challenge you from within, they will eventually challenge you from without in the marketplace.

PRINCIPLE 5: CHANGE IS NOT THE PROBLEM; ENGAGEMENT IS. Senior executives assume two things about change that squelch revolutionary strategies. The first assumption is that "people"—that is, middle managers and all the rest—are against change. The second assumption follows from the first: only a hero-leader can force a timid and backward-looking organization into the future. All too often, change epics portray the chief executive dragging the organization kicking and screaming into the twenty-first century. Enough of top-management grandstanding. Humankind would not have accomplished what it has over the past millennium if it was ambivalent about change or if the responsibility for change was vested in the socially or politically elite.

Imagine that I coax a flatlander to the top of a snow-covered mountain. After strapping two well-waxed skis onto the flatlander's feet, I give the nervous and unprepared nonskier a mighty push. He or she goes screaming over a precipice; I'm booked for murder. One could well understand how the novice might not appreciate the "change" I sought to engineer. Now imagine that the nonskier takes lessons for a few days. The now fledgling skier may ascend the same mountain and, though full of caution, voluntarily point the skis downhill. What has changed? Even with a bit of training, skiing is not without risks. But in the second scenario, the skier has been given a modicum of control—an ability to influence speed and direction.

All too often, when senior managers talk about change, they are talking about fear-inducing change, which they plan to impose on unprepared and unsuspecting employees. All too often, *change* is simply a code word for something nasty: a wrenching restructuring or reorganization. This sort of change is not about opening up new opportunities but about paying for the past mistakes of corporate leaders.

The objective is not to get people to support change but to give them responsibility for engendering change, some control over their destiny. You must engage the revolutionaries, wherever they are in your company, in a dialogue about the future. Does your strategy-making process do this? Do you secretly believe that change is better served by a more compliant organization than by a more vociferous one? When senior managers engage their organization in a quest for revolutionary strategies, they are invariably surprised to find out just how big the pro-change constituency actually is.

PRINCIPLE 6: STRATEGY MAKING MUST BE DEMOCRATIC. Despite years of imploring people to bring their brains to work, to get involved in quality circles, process reengineering, and the like, senior managers have seldom urged them to participate in the process of strategy creation. But if senior managers can't address the challenge of operational improvements by themselves—witness their reliance on quality circles, suggestion systems, and process-improvement task forces—why would they be able to take on the challenge of industry revolution? After all, what do a company's top 40 or 50 executives have to learn from one another? They've been talking at one another for years. Their positions are well rehearsed, and they can finish one another's sentences. In fact, there is often a kind of intellectual incest among the top officers of a large company.

The capacity to think creatively about strategy is distributed widely in an enterprise. It is impossible to predict exactly where a revolutionary idea is forming; thus the net must be cast wide. In many of the companies I work with, hundreds and sometimes thousands of people get involved in crafting strategy. They are asked to look deeply into potential discontinuities, help define and elaborate the company's core competencies, ferret out corporate orthodoxies, and search for unconventional strategic options. In one company, the idea for a multimillion-dollar opportunity came from a twenty-something secretary. In another company, some of the best ideas about the organization's core competencies came from a forklift operator.

To help revolutionary strategies emerge, senior managers must supplement the hierarchy of experience with a hierarchy of imagination. This can be done by dramatically extending the strategy franchise. Three constituencies that are usually underrepresented in the strategy-making process must have a disproportionate say. The first constituency is young people—or, more accurately, people with a youthful perspective. Of course, some 30-year-olds are "young fogies," but most young people live closer to the future than people with gray hair. It is ironic that the group with the biggest stake in the future is the most disenfranchised from the process of strategy creation.

My definition of success in a strategy-creation process is exemplified by an executive committee spending half a day learning something new from a 25-year-old. Recently, a young technical employee in an accounting company explained the implications of virtual reality to the senior partners. His pitch went like this: "Think about a complex set of corporate accounts. How easily and quickly can you uncover the subtle relationships among the numbers that might point to a problem or opportunity? Virtual reality will allow you to 'fly' over a topography of corporate accounts. That big black hole over there is a revenue shortfall, and that red mountain is unsold inventory. A few small companies are already working on applying virtual reality to financial accounts. Are we going to get on board or risk getting left behind?" The partners actually learned something new that day. When was the last time a Generation-X employee in your company exchanged ideas with the executive committee?

The people at an organization's geographic periphery are the second constituency that deserves a larger say in strategy making. The capacity for strategic innovation increases proportionately with each mile you move away from headquarters. For a U.S. company, the periphery might be India, Singapore, Brazil, or even the West Coast. For a Japanese company, it might be Indonesia or the United States. At the periphery of an organization, people are forced to be more creative because they usually have fewer resources, and they are exposed to ideas and developments that do not conform to the company's orthodoxies. Remember the old Chinese defense of local exceptions to central rule: The emperor is far away and the hills are high. But again, in many companies the periphery has little say in the strategy-making process. If a company aims to generate 40% or 50% of its revenues in international markets, international voices should have a say in the strategy-making process to match.

The third constituency that deserves a disproportionate say is newcomers, people who have not yet been co-opted by an industry's dogma. Perhaps you've looked outside your company or industry for senior executives with fresh perspectives. But how systematically have you sought the advice of newcomers at all levels who have not yet succumbed to the dead hand of orthodoxy? Think about last year's strategic-planning process. How many new voices were heard? How hard did you work to create the opportunity to be surprised?

Inviting new voices into the strategy-making process, however, is not enough. Senior executives must ensure that they don't drown out people who are overly inclined to deference. In one company, the young representative of a strategy-creation team presented the group's findings to the management committee. When the anxious young employee showed up at the appointed place and hour, he was confronted by a daunting spectacle: 12 executives, most with more than 20 years of seniority, ensconced in high-backed leather chairs arranged around an enormous boardroom table. The brave young manager never stood a chance. Less than five minutes into the four-hour talk, he was being pelted with disbelief and skepticism. The management committee demonstrated its capacity for (unwitting) intimidation and learned little.

After this fiasco, the people attempting to facilitate the dialogue saw to it that the setting for the next meeting was very different. First, it was held off-site on neutral territory. Second, all 25 members of the strategy-creation team were invited; thus they outnumbered the executives. Third, the management committee sat in ordinary chairs arranged in a semicircle—they had no table behind which to hide. Finally, the management committee was asked to hold all comments during the presentation. Afterward, each member of the management committee was assigned two members of the team for a four-hour discussion that focused on how the team had arrived at its conclusions. The next morning, the executives were willing to admit that they had learned a lot, and they were able to give helpful advice to the team members about where they should deepen and expand their work.

That is strategy making as a democratic process. People should have a say in their destiny, a chance to influence the direction of the enterprise to which they devote their energy. The idea of democracy has become so enervated, and the individual's sense of responsibility to the community so feeble, that they can both be summarized in the slogan One Person, One Vote. That notion represents not the full ideal of democracy but its minimal precondition. If one exercises the rights of citizenship only once every 1,461 days, can one claim to be a citizen in any meaningful sense? In the corporate sphere, suggestion schemes and town hall meetings are but the tender shoots of a pluralistic process. Democracy is not simply about the right to be heard; it is about the opportunity to influence opinion and action. It is about being impatient and impassioned, informed and involved. The real power of democracy is that not only the elite can shape the agenda. One's voice can be bigger than one's vote. Susan B. Anthony, Martin Luther King, Jr., Ralph Nader, Rush Limbaugh, and Jesse Jackson have all had an influence on political thought and action that has gone far beyond a single vote.

What percentage of the employees in your company have ever seen a copy of the corporate strategy, much less participated in its creation? No wonder that what passes for strategy is usually sterile and uninspiring. Saul Alinsky, one of the most effective social revolutionaries in the United States this century, wrote this about the output of top-down, elitist planning: "It is not a democratic program but a monumental testament to lack of faith in the ability and intelligence of the masses of people to think their way through to the successful solution of their problems . . . the people will have little to do with it." That which is imposed is seldom embraced. An elitist approach to strategy creation engenders little more than compliance.

PRINCIPLE 7: ANYONE CAN BE A STRATEGY ACTIVIST. Perhaps senior managers are reluctant to give up their monopoly on the creation of strategy. After all, how often has the monarch led the uprising? What can so-called ordinary employees do to ensure that their company becomes or remains the author of industry revolution? Plenty. They can become strategy activists. Today frontline employees and middle managers are inclined to regard themselves more as victims than as activists. They have lost confidence in their ability to shape the future of their organizations. They have forgotten that from Gandhi to Mandela, from the American patriots to the Polish shipbuilders, the makers of revolutions have not come from the top. Notwithstanding all the somber incantations that change must start at the top, is it realistic to expect that, in any reasonable percentage of cases, senior managers will start an industry revolution? No.

In one large company, a small group of middle managers who were convinced that their company was in danger of forfeiting the future to less conventional rivals established what they called a "delta team." The managers, none of whom was a corporate officer, had no mandate to change the company and asked no one for permission to do so. Over several months, they worked quietly and persistently to convince their peers that it was time to rethink the company's basic beliefs. This conviction gradually took root among a cross section of managers, who started asking senior executives difficult questions about whether the company was actually in control of its destiny. Did the company have a unique and compelling view of its future? Was the company ahead of or behind the industry's change curve? Was it at the center or on the periphery of the coalitions that were reshaping the industry? Ultimately, senior managers conceded that they could not answer those questions. The result was a concerted effort, spanning several months and hundreds of employees, to find opportunities to create industry revolution. Out of this effort came a fundamental change in the company's concept of its mission, a score of new and unconventional business opportunities, and a doubling of revenues over the next five years.

Activists are not anarchists. Their goal is not to tear down but to reform. They know that an uninvolved citizenry deserves whatever fate befalls it, as do cautious and cringing middle managers. People who care about their country—or their organization—don't wait for permission to act. Activists don't shape their opinions to fit the prejudices of those they serve. They are patriots intent on protecting the enterprise from mediocrity, self-interest, and mindless veneration of the past. Not every activist ends up a hero. Shortly after he became president of the Supreme Soviet, Nikita Khrushchev gave a speech to a large group of Communist Party leaders in which he denounced the excesses of Stalin. During a pause, a voice rang out from the back of the hall, "You were there. Why didn't you stop him?" Taken aback by such impertinence, Khrushchev thundered, "Who said that?" The questioner slunk low in his seat and was silent. After a long, uncomfortable minute in which his eyes raked the audience, Khrushchev replied, "Now you know why." It is often safer to be silent. The corporate equivalent of Lubyanka is an office without a telephone or a window. Dissenters aren't shot for treason; they're asked to take a "lateral career move."

Listen to Thomas Paine: "Let them call me rebel and welcome, I feel no concern from it; but I should suffer the misery of devils, were I to make a whore of my soul." In a corporate context, this sounds like hyperbole. But think of the great companies that have fallen hopelessly behind the change curve because middle managers and first-level employees lacked the courage to speak up. To be an activist, one must care more for one's community than for one's position in the hierarchy. The goal is not to leave senior executives behind. The goal is not to stage a palace coup. But when senior managers are distracted, when planning has supplanted strategizing, and when more energy is being devoted to protecting the past than to creating the future, activists must step forward.

PRINCIPLE 8: PERSPECTIVE IS WORTH 50 IQ POINTS.[2] Without enlightenment, there can be no revolution. To discover opportunities for industry revolution, one must look at the world in a new way, through a new lens. It is impossible to make people smarter, but you can help them see with new eyes. Remember when you took your first economics course? I do. It didn't make me any smarter, but it gave me a new lens through which to look at the world. Much that had been invisible—the link between savings and investment, between interest rates and exchange rates, and between supply and demand—suddenly became visible.

A view of the corporation as a bundle of core competencies rather than a collection of business units is a new perspective. A view of discontinuities as levers for change rather than threats to the status quo is a new perspective. A view that imagination rather than investment determines an organization's capacity to be strategic is a new perspective.

Any company intent on creating industry revolution has four tasks. First, the company must identify the unshakable beliefs that cut across the industry—the industry's conventions. Second, the company must search for discontinuities in technology, lifestyles, working habits, or geopolitics that might create opportunities to rewrite the industry's rules. Third, the company must achieve a deep understanding of its core competencies. Fourth, the company must use all this knowledge to identify the revolutionary ideas, the unconventional strategic options, that could be put to work in its competitive domain. What one sees from the mountaintop is quite different from what one sees from the plain. There can be no innovation in the creation of strategy without a change in perspective.

PRINCIPLE 9: TOP-DOWN AND BOTTOM-UP ARE NOT THE ALTERNATIVES. The creation of strategy is usually characterized as either a top-down or bottom-up process. Strategy either emerges as a grand design at the top—think of Jack Welch's famous "three circles," which defined GE's future business focus—or bubbles up from lone entrepreneurs, such as the man who invented Post-It Notes at 3M. But all too often, top-down strategies are dirigiste rather than visionary. And in all too many companies, the entrepreneurial spark is more likely to be doused by a flood of corporate orthodoxy than fanned by resources and the support of senior executives. In my experience, new-venture divisions, skunk works, and the musings of research fellows are no more likely to engender an industry revolution than is an annual planning process.

Just as a political activist who fails to influence those with legislative authority will make little lasting difference, a strategy activist who fails to win senior managers' confidence will achieve nothing. Senior managers may not have a monopoly on imagination, but they do have a board-sanctioned monopoly on the allocation of resources. To bankroll the revolution, senior executives must believe, both intellectually and emotionally, in its aims. So although the revolution doesn't need to start at the top, it must ultimately be understood and endorsed by the top. In the traditional model of strategy creation, the thinkers are assumed to be at the top and the doers down below. In reality, the thinkers often lie deep in the organization, and senior managers simply control the means of doing.

To achieve diversity of perspective and unity of purpose, the strategy-making process must involve a deep diagonal slice of the organization. A top-down process often achieves unity of purpose: the few who are involved come to share a conviction about the appropriate course of action and can secure some degree of compliance from those below. A bottom-up process can achieve diversity of perspective: many voices are heard and many options are explored. But unity without diversity leads to dogma, and diversity without unity results in competing strategy agendas and the fragmentation of resources. Only a strategy-making process that is deep and wide can achieve both diversity and unity.

Bringing the top and bottom together in the creation of strategy will help bypass the usually painful and laborious process whereby a lowly employee champions an idea up the chain of command. Managers, many of whom may be more intent on protecting their reputations for prudence than on joining the ranks of the lunatic fringe, are likely to shoot down any revolutionary idea that reaches them. There are many ways of linking those on the bottom with those in the officer corps. Senior executives can sponsor a process of deep thinking about discontinuities, core competencies, and new rules that involves a cross section of the organization. Senior managers can participate as team members—together with secretaries, salespeople, and first-level engineers—in the search for revolutionary opportunities. An executive committee can devote one week per month to keeping up to speed with the revolutionary ideas that are gestating deep in the organization.

What senior executives must not do is ask a small, elite group or the "substitute brains" of a traditional strategy-consulting firm to go away and plot the company's future. With neither senior managers nor a substantial cross section of the organization involved, the output will likely be considered a bastard by all except those who created it.

Of course, senior managers must ultimately make hard choices about which revolutionary strategies to support and what resources to commit, but they must avoid the temptation to judge prematurely. In the quest for revolutionary strategies, a senior executive must be more student than magistrate. In one company, the CEO believed that the strategy-making team was responsible for convincing him that it had come up with the right answers. That is the wrong attitude. It is the CEO's responsibility to stay close enough to the organization's learning process that he or she can share employees' insights and understand their emerging convictions. In the traditional planning process, outcomes are likely to cluster closely around senior managers' prejudices; the gap between recommendations and preexisting predilections is likely to be low. But that is not the case in a more open-ended process of strategic discovery. If the goal is to ensure that the resource holders and the revolutionaries end up at the same place at the same time, senior executives must engage in a learning process alongside those at the vanguard of industry revolution.

PRINCIPLE 10: YOU CAN'T SEE THE END FROM THE BEGINNING. A strategy-making process that involves a broad cross section of the company, delves deeply into discontinuities and competencies, and encourages employees to escape an industry's conventions will almost inevitably reach surprising conclusions. At EDS, such a process convinced many in the organization that it was not enough to be a business-to-business company. As the dividing line between professional life and personal life was blurring, EDS realized that it had to become capable of serving individuals as well as businesses. After an open and creative strategy-making process, EDS installed automated teller machines in many 7-Eleven stores. Months earlier, few would have anticipated, much less credited, such a move.

Not everyone enjoys surprises. Senior managers cannot predict where an open-ended strategy-making process will lead, but they cannot go only part of the way to industry revolution. If nervous executives open up a dialogue and then ignore the outcome, they will poison the well. In one company, senior managers articulated their reluctance to staff a strategy-making team with a cohort of young, out-of-the-box employees. The CEO was convinced that he needed to set clear boundaries on the work of the eager revolutionaries. Defending his desire to impose prior restraint on the strategy-creation process, he asked, "What if the team comes back with dumb ideas?" The response: "If that is the case, you have a bigger problem—dumb managers." Senior managers should be less worried about getting off-the-wall suggestions and more concerned about failing to unearth the ideas that will allow their company to escape the curse of incrementalism.

Though it is impossible to see the end from the beginning, an open-ended and inclusive process of strategy creation substantially lessens the challenge of implementation. Implementation is often more difficult than it need be because only a handful of people have been involved in the creation of strategy and only a few key executives share a conviction about the way forward. Too often, the planning process ends with the challenge of getting "buy-in," of getting what is in the heads of the bosses into the heads of the worker bees. But when several hundred employees share the task of identifying and synthesizing a set of unconventional strategic options, the conclusions take on an air of inevitability. In such a process, senior managers' task is less to "sell" the strategy than to ensure that the organization acts on the convictions that emerge. How often does the planning process start with senior executives asking what the rest of the organization can teach them about the future? Not often enough.

To invite new voices into the strategy-making process, to encourage new perspectives, to start new conversations that span organizational boundaries, and then to help synthesize unconventional options into a point of view about corporate direction—those are the challenges for senior executives who believe that strategy must be revolution.

Notes

1. Thanks to James Scholes, my colleague at Strategos, for suggesting this distinction.
2. I owe this aphorism to Alan Kay, a research fellow at Apple Computer. Kay's point that new thinking depends more on perspective than on raw intelligence is as apropos to strategy innovation as it is to new-product innovation.

3

How Architecture Wins Technology Wars

Charles R. Morris and Charles H. Ferguson

The global computer industry is undergoing radical transformation. IBM, the industry's flagship, is reeling from unaccustomed losses and is reducing staff by the tens of thousands. The very survival of DEC, the industry's number two company, is open to question. A roll call of the larger computer companies—Data General, Unisys, Bull, Olivetti, Siemens, Prime—reads like a waiting list in the emergency room.

What's more, the usual explanations for the industry's turmoil are at best inadequate. It is true, for example, that centralized computing is being replaced by desktop technology. But how to explain the recent troubles at Compaq, the desktop standard setter through much of the 1980s? Or the battering suffered by IBM's PC business and most of the rest of the desktop clone makers, Asian and Western alike?

And the Japanese, for once, are unconvincing as a culprit. The fear that Japanese manufacturing prowess would sweep away the Western computer industry has not materialized. True, Japanese companies dominate many commodity markets, but they have been losing share, even in products they were expected to control, like laptop computers. Earnings at their leading electronics and computer companies have been as inglorious as those of Western companies.

Explanations that look to the continuing shift in value added from hardware to software, while containing an important truth, are still too limited. Lotus has one of the largest installed customer bases in the industry. Nevertheless, the company has been suffering through some very rough times. Meanwhile, Borland continues to pile up losses.

Nor are innovation and design skills a surefire recipe for success. LSI

Logic and Cypress Semiconductor are among the most innovative and well-managed companies in the industry, yet they still lose money. Design-based "fabless," "computerless" companies such as MIPS have fared very badly too. MIPS was saved from bankruptcy only by a friendly takeover. And Chips and Technologies is in dire straits.

Government protection and subsidies are no panacea either. The European computer industry is the most heavily subsidized in the world but still has no serious players in global computer markets.

Scale, friendly government policies, world-class manufacturing prowess, a strong position in desktop markets, excellent software, top design and innovative skills—none of these, it seems, is sufficient, either by itself or in combination with each other, to ensure competitive success in this field.

A new paradigm is required to explain patterns of competitive success and failure in information technology. Simply stated, competitive success flows to the company that manages to establish proprietary architectural control over a broad, fast-moving, competitive space.

Architectural strategies have become of paramount importance in information technology because of the astonishing rate of improvement in microprocessors and other semiconductor components. The performance/price ratio of cheap processors is roughly doubling every eighteen months or so, sweeping greater and greater expanses of the information industry within the reach of ever-smaller and less expensive machines. Since no single vendor can keep pace with the deluge of cheap, powerful, mass-produced components, customers insist on stitching together their own local system solutions. Architectures impose order on the system and make the interconnections possible.

An architectural controller is a company that controls one or more of the standards by which the entire information package is assembled. Much current conventional wisdom argues that, in an "open-systems" era, proprietary architectural control is no longer possible, or even desirable. In fact, the exact opposite is true. In an open-systems era, architectural coherence becomes even more necessary. While any single product is apt to become quickly outdated, a well-designed and open-ended architecture can evolve along with critical technologies, providing a fixed point of stability for customers and serving as the platform for a radiating and long-lived product family.

Proprietary architectures in open systems are not only possible but also indispensable to competitive success—and are also in the best interest of the consumer. They will become increasingly critical as the worlds of computers, telecommunication, and consumer electronics continue to converge.

Architectures in Open Systems

In order to understand architecture as a tool for competitive success in information technology, consider first the many components that make up a typical information system and the types of companies that supply those components.

Take the computer configuration in a typical Wall Street trading or brokerage operation. Powerful workstations with 50 MIPS (millions of instructions per second)—comparable to the power of standard mainframes—sit on every desk. The workstations are connected in a network so they can communicate with each other or with several others at a time. Teams of workstations can be harnessed together to crunch away on a truly big problem. Powerful computers called servers support the network and manage the huge databases—bond pricing histories, for instance—from which the workstations draw.

Such a modern network will be almost entirely open, or externally accessible by other vendors; critical elements, from perhaps as many as a hundred vendors, plug interchangeably into the network. The workstations themselves are from companies like Sun Microsystems, Hewlett-Packard, and IBM, or they may be powerful personal computers from Apple or any of a number of IBM-compatible PC manufacturers. IBM and Hewlett-Packard make their own workstation microprocessors; most workstation or personal computer makers buy microprocessors from companies like Intel, Motorola, Texas Instruments, LSI Logic, AMD, and Cyrix. Almost all the display screens are made in Japan by Sony, NEC, and many other companies; the disk drives come from American companies like Seagate or Conner Peripherals. The memory chips are made in Japan or Korea. The network printers will typically have laser printing engines from Japan or, if they are high-performance printers, from Xerox or IBM; the powerful processors needed to control modern printers will come from AMD, Motorola, or Intel. The rest of the standardized hardware components on the network, like modems, accelerator boards, coprocessors, network interface boards, and the like, will be made by a wide variety of Asian and American companies.

The network will have many layers of software, most of it "shrink-wrapped" from American companies. The operating system—the software that controls the basic interaction of a computer's components—may be a version of AT&T's UNIX, specially tailored by the workstation vendor, as with Sun and IBM, or it may come from a third party, like Microsoft. Many vendors, like Lotus and Borland, will supply applications software. The complex software required to manage the interaction of the servers and workstations on the network will, in most cases, be supplied by Novell. The software that converts digital data into instructions for printer engines is sold by Hewlett-Packard, Adobe, or one of their many clones. Each smaller element in the system, like a modem or video accelerator, will have its own specialized software, often supplied by a vendor other than the manufacturer.

It is possible to construct open systems of this kind because for each layer of the network there are published standards and interface protocols that allow hardware and software products from many vendors to blend seamlessly into the network. The standards define how programs and commands will work and how data will move around the system—the communication protocols and formats that hardware components must adhere to, the rules for exchanging signals between applications software and the operating system, the processor's command structure, the allowable font descriptions for a printer, and so forth. We call this complex of standards and rules an "architecture."

A small handful of the companies supplying components to the network will define and control the system's critical architectures, each for a specific layer of the system. The architectural standard setters typically include the microprocessor designer (such as Sun or Intel); operating system vendors (possibly Sun or Microsoft); the network system (usually Novell); the printer page-description system (Adobe or Hewlett-Packard); and a small number of others, depending on the nature of the network. Each of these is a proprietary architecture; although the rules for transmitting signals to an Intel processor, for example, are published openly for all vendors, the underlying design of the processor is owned by Intel, just as the design of Sun's operating system is owned by Sun, and so on for Microsoft's Windows/DOS, Novell's Netware, or Adobe's PostScript.

Companies that control proprietary architectural standards have an advantage over other vendors. Since they control the architecture, they are usually better positioned to develop products that maximize its capabilities; by modifying the architecture, they can discipline competing product vendors. In an open-systems era, the most consistently successful information technology companies will be the ones who manage to establish a proprietary architectural standard over a substantial competitive space and defend it against the assaults of both clones and rival architectural sponsors.

It has been conventional wisdom to argue that users, and the cause of technological progress, are better served by *nonproprietary* systems architectures. This is emphatically untrue. There are many examples of nonproprietary architectures, like the CCITT fax standard or the NTSC television standard, most of them established by government bodies or industry groups. Because they are set by committees, they usually settle on lowest-common-denominator, compromise solutions. And they are hard to change. The NTSC has been upgraded only once (for color) in a half-century; committees have been squabbling over an improved fax standard for years. *Proprietary* architectures, by contrast, because they are such extremely valuable franchises, are under constant competitive attack and must be vigorously defended. It is this dynamic that compels a very rapid pace of technological improvement.

Architectural Competitions

The computer industry has been competing on architecture for years. Take the example of the product that established IBM's dominance in the mainframe computer business—the IBM System/360. The 360 was arguably the first pervasive, partially open, information technology architecture. In the late 1960s, once the System/360 became the dominant mainframe solution, IBM began to unbundle component pricing and selectively open the system, in part because of government pressure. Published standards permitted competitors and component suppliers to produce a wide range of IBM-compatible products and programs that were interchangeable with, and sometimes superior to, IBM's own. By licensing its MVS operating system to Amdahl, for example, IBM made it possible for Fujitsu, Amdahl's partner, to produce clones of the IBM mainframe. Much of what was not licensed away voluntarily was acquired anyway by the Japanese through massive intellectual property theft.

Hundreds of new companies selling IBM-compatible mainframe products and software placed intense competitive pressure on IBM. But they also assured that the IBM standard would always be pervasive throughout the mainframe computing world. As a result, even today IBM controls some two-thirds of the IBM-compatible mainframe market and an even higher share of its profits, not only for central processing units but also for disk drives, systems software, and aftermarket products like expanded memory. Because they have no choice but to maintain compatibility with the IBM standard, competitors must wait to reverse-engineer IBM products after they are introduced. Typically, by the time competitive products are on the market, IBM is well down the learning curve or already moving on to the next generation. And as the owner of the dominant architecture, IBM can subtly and precisely raise the hurdles whenever a particular competitor begins to pose a threat. For over 20 years, in generation after generation, IBM has played this game brilliantly and won every time.

Ironically, IBM badly fumbled an equivalent opportunity in desktop computing, handing over the two most critical PC architectural control points—the systems software and the microprocessor—to Microsoft and Intel. Since any clone maker could acquire the operating system software from Microsoft and the microprocessor from Intel, making PCs became a brutal commodity business. As a high-cost manufacturer, IBM now holds only about 15% of the market it created.

In a related error, Compaq made the mistake of assuming that IBM would always control the PC architectural standard. On that premise, the company geared its cost structure and pricing policy to IBM's, only to find itself almost fatally vulnerable when the savage PC price wars of the early 1990s exposed the commoditized character of PC manufacturing. Tellingly, while IBM and Compaq struggle to eke out profits from their PC businesses, Microsoft and Intel are enjoying after-tax margins of about 20%, on sales of more than $4 billion and $6 billion respectively, and together they have more cash than IBM.

For a similar example, consider the case of Lotus. Lotus got its start in a market—spreadsheet software—where products are complex and feature-rich, hardly commodities. And over the years, the company acquired or developed a broad array of other products—Jazz, Manuscript, Improv, AmiPro, Notes, and Freelance—some of which are technically excellent. Lotus's competitive problem, however, is that these products lack any deep architectural commonality. Indeed, even the embedded spreadsheet software in the company's various offerings is incompatible from one to another.

Point product vendors like Lotus can be very profitable for a time. However, they are always at risk when an architectural leader changes the rules of the game. For example, while Lotus was accumulating a grab bag of point products, Microsoft was creating an architectural lock on the graphical user interface (GUI) for DOS-based computers. (See "Scenarios for Architectural Competition: Graphical User Interfaces.")

And Windows now defines the environment in which Lotus's software must compete. The great power of Windows is that it creates a relatively simple, intuitive, and reasonably uniform interface between a user and a very wide range of applications software. As users become accustomed to the greater ease of Windows, they insist on it, and point product vendors like Lotus are forced to adapt their software to run under the Windows architecture. But Microsoft also offers its own line of point products, like Excel and Word, and since they arguably better exploit the Windows architecture, they are steadily encroaching on Lotus's market share.

Scenarios for Architectural Competition: Graphical User Interfaces

Graphical User Interfaces (GUIs) are the software that permits users to maneuver around applications visually—for example, issuing commands by pointing to icons—providing a simple, consistent method of working with many different programs. The evolution of the GUI market provides a dramatic example of the dynamics of architectural competition.

The original GUI was developed at Xerox's famed Palo Alto Research Center (PARC) and unveiled with the Xerox Star in the early 1980s. The Star was a brilliant achievement for its time—a high-performance, if very expensive, easy-to-use networked workstation. But it was a completely closed system; there was no published applications-program interface, so no one but Xerox could supply software to run on the Star. Its appeal was therefore far too limited ever to become a pervasive desktop standard.

Steve Jobs adapted the Star technology to Apple, but it took several tries before Apple began to make inroads in the GUI arena. Apple's first try was the Lisa, a substantially closed system that failed to attract any market share. The company got it more nearly right with the Macintosh. At least in later incarnations, the Mac has been hospitable to third-party software developers. It is considerably less expensive than the Lisa and has a superb operating system/GUI architecture. But Apple has still sharply limited its distribution potential by insisting on bundling its architecture with only its own, second-rate hardware. The Mac is hardly a failure, but had Apple licensed its systems software broadly, Apple and its microprocessor partner, Motorola, could have exercised the same architectural control over personal computing that Microsoft and Intel do now.

The operating system/GUI architectural struggle is far from over and will be one of the most heated competitive arenas of the 1990s. IBM OS/2 2.0 is technically excellent but suffers from a very late start; Microsoft's brand new NT system, which will run Windows applications, will raise the hurdles yet again. A variety of UNIX-based standards are alternatives to systems derived from the original DOS. And IBM and Apple have joined forces on a next-generation operating system/GUI in their Taligent partnership.

As the ongoing GUI contest suggests, architectural battles are fast-moving, hotly challenged, and rarely completely settled. The rewards to a winner, however, can be great.

The irony is that for a time in the 1980s, Lotus had such a powerful market position that it almost certainly could have established a GUI standard itself. But the company neglected to do so. Such strategic errors spell the difference between an architectural winner and loser.

Principles and Phases of Architectural Competition

There are five basic imperatives that drive most architectural contests:

1. GOOD PRODUCTS ARE NOT ENOUGH. Products distribute architectures and can contribute to the success of an architectural strategy. However, as the case of Lotus suggests, good products alone are not enough. But if the sponsor invests heavily in continuous product improvement, products of only modest capabilities can become the basis for architectural leadership. For example, both Zilog and AMD at various stages in the PC microprocessor contest made Intel-compatible chips that were superior to Intel's own; but neither company matched Intel's commitment to R&D, and both were left behind as Intel rolled out one generation of improved processor after another. Once an architecture is established, it in turn becomes a distribution channel for additional products, with the architectural controller's products holding the favored position.

2. IMPLEMENTATIONS MATTER. Manufacturing decisions are playing an increasingly important role in product strategy. But since successful architectures have a high design content and usually a high software content, manufacturing skills by themselves are not sufficient to prevail in architectural competition. Japanese and other Asian companies, for example, despite their great manufacturing prowess, have only rarely established architectural franchises. Generally, they have settled for positions as clone makers or commodity implementors. Perhaps the only area where Japanese companies have established proprietary control over an important architectural space is in video games. But even the leaders in this arena, Nintendo and Sega, are at risk. (See "Scenarios for Architectural Competition: Video Games.")

Scenarios for Architectural Competition: Video Games

The home video game industry, dominated by Nintendo and Sega, is a serious industry. Some 30 million American homes, or about 70% of all homes with a child between the ages of eight and twelve, own a video game. Both Nintendo and Sega sell video game consoles (basic, 16-bit, 286-level computers) with tightly bundled operating systems. Game software is developed by independent vendors under tightly controlled licenses but distributed only through the two companies' networks at hefty markups. Profits flow from game sales, not consoles.

Bundled architectures are ripe for attack by more open systems, just as the Apple II was overwhelmed by the IBM PC. In fact, a number of American companies have targeted the game market. Electronic Arts, for one, has won a copyright suit allowing it to reverse-engineer Sega's operating system. The availability of a Sega system clone would break that company's hold over game software and open up console manufacturing to cloners. Another company, 3DO (formerly the San Mateo Software Group), has plans to release a powerful consumer-oriented operating system that will be ideally suited for games. Specifications have been provided to a number of Asian manufacturers including Matsushita, a 3DO investor, for a CD-ROM-based console. Existing best-selling games, presumably, could readily be adapted to the new system; 3DO's objective is to own a Windows-like architectural franchise in the consumer world.

An interesting and potentially formidable dark-horse competitor is Silicon Graphics, a company that has built its industry-leading three-dimensional image manipulation technology into a billion-dollar business. From its original base in the engineering CAD industry, Silicon Graphics has found a new niche supplying the technology behind the spectacular special effects in Hollywood hits like "Terminator II." These systems could produce mind-boggling game effects; Silicon Graphics is known to have a consumer/game strategy underway.

All these companies have ambitions that extend well beyond toys. Games may be just the first of a series of image-oriented consumer platforms for everything from news services, home shopping, or endless entertainment services. On the principle that the low end always wins, such platforms eventually may supplant the current generation of personal computers. Microsoft and Intel beware.

While insufficient on their own, however, manufacturing skills may well be an essential competence for success in the architectural contests of the 1990s. The reason: implementation is increasingly becoming the key to winning architectural control. In microprocessors, for example, a good implementation can improve performance by a factor of two. That's why architectural leaders like Intel typically make their own chips. By contrast, Sun Microsystems has chosen to focus solely on the design of its SPARC microprocessor, a decision that has been a source of recent difficulty for the company because subpar supplier implementations have compromised SPARC performance. High-quality implementations are equally important in the new generations of hand-held computers. Indeed, the more advanced information technology makes inroads into consumer markets, the more manufacturing skills will prove invaluable.

3. SUCCESSFUL ARCHITECTURES ARE PROPRIETARY, BUT OPEN. Closed architectures do not win broad franchises. Choosing the right degree of openness is one of the most subtle and difficult decisions in architectural contests. IBM opened its PC architecture too broadly—it should have, and could have, retained control of either or both the operating system and microprocessor standard. Apple made the opposite mistake of bundling the Mac operating system too closely to its own hardware. Sun, in contrast to Apple, opened its SPARC RISC architecture very early, both to software developers and processor cloners; it has the lead position in workstations, and its broad base of third-party software support has helped maintain customer loyalty though a series of technical stumbles. Autodesk's computer-aided design (CAD) software for builders is open to add-on third-party packages, like kitchen design tools, and its broad base of supporting software has given it control of a small but very profitable franchise.

4. GENERAL-PURPOSE ARCHITECTURES ABSORB SPECIAL-PURPOSE SOLUTIONS. Architectures that cannot evolve to occupy an ever-broader competitive space are dead ends. Wang's lucrative word processor franchise was absorbed by general-purpose PCs. Special-purpose CAD workstations from Daisy, Applicon, and others were absorbed by more general-purpose desktop machines. Special-purpose game machines will, in all likelihood, be absorbed by more general-purpose consumer systems.

5. LOW-END SYSTEMS SWALLOW HIGH-END SYSTEMS. Minicomputers poached away huge chunks of mainframe territory and were assaulted in turn by workstations and networks. Workstations are under pressure by increasingly high performance PCs. Traditional supercomputers and very high-end mainframes are vulnerable to parallel arrays of inexpensive microprocessors. High-end data-storage systems are similarly under attack from arrays of inexpensive, redundant disks. Although IBM helped create the personal computer revolution, it steadfastly refused to recognize its implications. Until relatively recently, it even called its desktop products division "Entry Systems," ignoring the fact that today's microprocessor-based machines are a replacement for traditional computers, not an entry point or way station to them.

However, managers must keep in mind that even those companies that best follow these principles are not necessarily guaranteed continued success in the marketplace. Architectural contests typically move through a number of different phases, and only those companies that successfully navigate them all, maintaining their pace and direction in the fluid environment of rapidly evolving technologies, emerge as winners over the long term. It's a delicate balancing act, and one that requires ever-increasing flexibility as the technologies mature.

There are five principal phases to architectural competition:

Commitment. Architectural challenges usually emerge from the early-stage chaos of competing point products. Before the IBM PC, personal computers were rigid, closed systems that tended to bundle their own operating systems and applications software. Compaq had the insight that by purchasing a Microsoft operating system identical to that of the PC, it could ride the wave of the PC's success. Microsoft then insisted that all subsequent clone makers buy the same operating system and so seized the critical PC software architectural standard. Microsoft's insight was to realize that it was in an architectural contest and to take the appropriate steps, including steadily expanding the generality and scope of its systems to come out the winner.

Diffusion. Large profits come from broad franchises. Open architectures are successful because they can be broadly diffused. Xerox's Interpress page-description software, which converts digital data into printer instructions, is excellent but can be purchased only with Xerox high-end printers. Adobe, by contrast, has widely licensed its Post-Script language and has become the industry standard setter. Intel widely licensed the early versions of its xx86 processors, then sharply restricted licensing of its 386 chip after the Intel standard had become firmly entrenched. IBM, on the other hand, has long resisted diffusing its mainframe and minicomputer software.

Of course, diffusion decisions are not without risk. Once again, balance and timing are essential. For example, Philips licensed its compact disc technology to Sony to increase market penetration. But Sony outperformed Philips and took half the market. Philips's standard was a static one that it never developed further.

Lock-in. A company has a "lock" on an architecture when competitors are trained to wait until the architectural leader introduces each new product generation. Intel and Microsoft, at least temporarily, seem to have achieved this position in PC markets. Sun was on the verge of a locked-in franchise in workstations but may have fallen short; the performance of its SPARC RISC processor design has been lagging behind the competition, and the company neglected to solidify its franchise by moving rapidly down to lower end platforms.

But lock-in is sustainable only when a company aggressively and continuously cannibalizes its own product line and continually and compatibly extends the architecture itself. This is a strategic choice that many companies find difficult to make. Often, managers become over-protective of the products that brought them their original success. IBM, for example, has frittered away a powerful lock on back-office transaction processing and operating systems. In a misguided effort to protect hardware sales, it has refused to release products, long since developed internally, that would adapt its best-selling AS400 mini-computer software to the RS6000 workstation. Such reflexive self-protection simply hands over a valuable franchise to the Microsofts and other vendors storming up from the low end.

Harvest. Of course, the ultimate objective of architectural competition is to win a market leader's share of the profits. Just to give one dramatic example, profit margins on Intel's xx86 family of chips are in the 40% to 50% range and account for well over 100% of the company's earnings. But no locked-in position is ever completely safe, and companies must be careful when they harvest not to rest on their previous successes. Indeed, Intel may have harvested too aggressively, drawing out spirited recent attacks by clone makers such as AMD and Cyrix.

Obsolescence and Regeneration. Just as products must be cannibalized, so must architectures themselves. The better the architecture, the longer its lifespan; but sooner or later every architecture, no matter how well designed, becomes obsolete. And before it does, the market leader must be prepared to move ahead, to do away with the old and introduce the new. Industry leaders often fail to cannibalize their old architectures, but although nothing is more painful, to do so is absolutely necessary. Otherwise, competitors quickly move to create and introduce rival franchises, and these eventually dominate the industry. IBM's failure to cannibalize its mainframe and minicomputer franchises provides a stark example of the catastrophic effects of waiting too long.

DEC provides another example. The company developed outstanding RISC products very early. But DEC declined to cannibalize its profitable VAX-VMS architecture because its VMS operating system, the source of its franchise, was tightly integrated with its aging VAX hardware. Predictably, DEC was beaten out by vendors such as Sun Microsystems and Microsoft, which didn't hesitate to move in with their newer, more powerful alternatives. (The main developer of DEC's advanced systems, Dave Cutler, is now in charge of developing NT for Microsoft.)

There are three lessons here. First, with better architecture DEC could have kept VMS alive longer. If VMS had been "portable," that is, not restricted to VAX hardware, DEC could have ported VMS to other vendors' hardware, making VMS an industry standard. Indeed, the company could have used RISC technology itself without losing its VMS franchise. Second, DEC would have been better off cannibalizing itself, rather than waiting to be cannibalized by others.

The third lesson, though, is the most important. As DEC's experiences with VMS and IBM's mistakes with the mainframe and minicomputer franchises show, the cultural and organizational structures useful for managing traditional, closed, integrated businesses will not work for companies that intend to compete with architectural strategy. In fact, we believe that architectural competition is stimulating the development of a new form of business organization.

This new structure, which we call the Silicon Valley Model, has major implications both for information technology and for many other industries. The model is still young and rapidly changing, and although Microsoft probably comes closest, no company fits it perfectly.

Managing Architectural Competition: The Silicon Valley Model

The Silicon Valley Model arose a decade ago when early architectural competitors noticed that they faced the same problems in managing organizations that they faced with technologies and architectural strategies.

In retrospect, this is not surprising. Architecture responds to the same imperatives in both systems and organizations. It reduces complexity. It permits clean separation between centralized general-purpose functions and decentralized or specialized functions. It enables management of unpredictability and change; individual technologies, components, or products can be switched without the need to redo everything. For similar reasons, good architecture facilitates experimentation and competition: once the framework is specified, multiple approaches can compete without jeopardizing compatibility. And finally, a standard architecture permits many systems and organizations to be developed independently and still work together gracefully. (See "Scenarios for Architectural Competition: Page- and Image-Description Standards.")

Scenarios for Architectural Competition: Page- and Image-Description Standards

Page- and image-description standards are rapidly evolving from their initial base in printers into a very large business that will transform the entire printing and publishing industry. Probably most published material is now captured in electronic format, and a major competition is shaping up for control of the standard for storage, transmission, and manipulation of complex text, images, and multimedia documents. The technology involved is extraordinarily sophisticated and processing-intensive. Data compression and decompression and image-manipulation algorithms tax all but the very fastest of available processors; data storage requirements are very large; and requirements for communications capacity outpace most conventional systems. All these hurdles are falling very rapidly before a wide range of technical advances.

At the moment, Adobe must be considered the front-runner in the standards contest. Its Acrobat product, due to be introduced this year, will provide the industry's most advanced storage, compression, and transmission capabilities. The first versions will permit users to annotate, but not edit, electronically stored texts. Later releases are expected to include editing options. Microsoft is mounting a major challenge, at least in the word processing of documents and fonts. The dark horse is Xerox, which traditionally has possessed a vast array of image- and text-oriented technologies that it somehow never manages to commercialize. A number of smaller companies have also planted their pennants, including, refreshingly, two from Europe, Harlequin and Hyphen. Hewlett-Packard and Microsoft have formed an alliance to stay in contention, but their solutions are, for the moment at least, quite limited.

An early inning in the contest will involve the possibility of creating a new proprietary fax standard. The combination of faxes with high-quality plain paper printers could induce a very substantial increase in fax usage, particularly if images are of sufficiently high quality to transmit pictures, working drawings, and the like. Two new products, PostScript for Fax from Adobe and Satisfaxion from Intel, provide much improved resolution and decrease the required data compression to allow existing low-capacity communication systems to handle complex images. Both interconnect with standard fax machines to send and receive low-resolution images.

As an organizational paradigm, the Silicon Valley Model therefore has several characteristic features and advantages. Following are the most important:

1. ORGANIZATIONAL ARCHITECTURE AND DECISION MAKING THAT MIRROR TECHNICAL ARCHITECTURE. Any organization should develop and use good technical architectures. But Silicon Valley Model firms take an additional step: the structure of the firm itself mirrors the technical architectures it uses.

Thus, for example, Microsoft is structured so that its existing systems software and applications software are managed separately, as are new architectural efforts such as NT. In this manner, Microsoft can diffuse its applications across multiple operating systems (both its own and others, like the Apple Macintosh), while also marketing its operating systems by courting other vendors' applications. The two businesses can work largely independently, yet only Microsoft gains the benefits of their synergism. Most decisions can be made directly within the organization responsible for the relevant architectural domain; this minimizes complex vertical and horizontal debates.

2. MERITOCRACY AND DIRECT FEEDBACK. Silicon Valley Model firms enable and force direct performance feedback, at levels ranging from individuals to business units. At Microsoft, team members rate each other periodically in peer reviews. Outstanding performers are rewarded; laggards are warned, then fired. Technical expertise is required for a large fraction of senior management, and communication occurs directly between the relevant parties, unbuffered by hierarchy.

By contrast, performance ratings in traditional bureaucracies are determined by managers at higher levels, and compensation is rarely based on long-term corporate performance. The process is often heavily politicized; dissent is suppressed, and incompetence goes unpunished.

Architectural competition also exposes Silicon Valley Model firms to another form of peer review—product competition. To succeed as industry standard setters, firms must license their architectures to competitors, while also developing critical products themselves. As a result, each layer of the firm (and of the architecture) is exposed to direct competition and market feedback. Hence although Microsoft controls Windows, application groups still compete individually: Excel against Lotus and QuattroPro, Word against WordPerfect and AmiPro, and so forth. Architectural leadership provides an advantage, but prevents a cover-up. Silicon Valley Model firms are structured so that excellence is the only defense.

3. CLEAN BOUNDARIES, BOTH INTERNAL AND EXTERNAL. In architected corporate structures, organizations can create and dissolve alliances rapidly, both internally and externally. Organizations are very flat, and development groups have simple, clean interfaces to each other determined by architectural boundaries. Architecture and point products can be kept apart. Moreover, products can invisibly incorporate architected "engines" developed by other organizations, including competitors. For example, a start-up called InfoNow has organized alliances involving itself, Microsoft, publishers, computer vendors, and other software companies. InfoNow packages software products, together with reviews and samples of them, which are preloaded for free on computers; the software products, however, are encrypted. Users can sample them, read reviews, and then purchase them by telephone, which triggers electronic decryption. Adding new software packages is trivial.

4. INTERNAL PROPRIETARY CONTROL OF ARCHITECTURE AND CRITICAL IMPLEMENTATIONS, EXTERNALIZED COMMODITIES AND NICHES. Silicon Valley Model firms seek to externalize the maximum possible fraction of their total system, while carefully controlling those areas required to establish and hold an architectural franchise. Thus core development of the general purpose architecture is always internally controlled. So usually are critical product implementations, which cover the broadest markets and are required either for early diffusion or later harvesting. Silicon Valley firms also carefully manage their dependencies, so as not to become unilaterally dependent on architectural competitors.

On balance, however, Silicon Valley Model firms are much less autarkic than traditional large firms. Niche products, commodity components, and architectures controlled by others are outsourced, and/or relegated to licensees. In fact, Silicon Valley firms actively seek to commoditize regions not under their control.

This yields several benefits. For one, companies can focus on what they do best and on the efforts critical to architectural success. For another, broad outsourcing and licensing create competition among suppliers and licensees, which broadens the market and benefits the architectural leader. PC price wars delight Intel, Microsoft, and Novell; IBM and Compaq take the heat.

Interestingly, this contradicts the 1980s conventional wisdom that firms should avoid broad, cost-sensitive markets in favor of high-price niches. In fact, the broad market is the strategic high ground, if it is covered by a proprietary architecture. Niche product vendors can make profits, but they will remain minor players.

5. MIGRATION AND EVOLUTION OVER TIME. Just as architectures evolve and eventually become obsolete, so too with organizations. Thus the firm's internal structure and external alliances evolve along with its architecture and market position. As new layers are added to an existing architectural position (Windows on top of DOS, then NT underneath Windows), new organizations are created; a similar situation occurs when an architecture must be cannibalized. Some Silicon Valley Model firms will soon face cannibalization; it will be interesting to see how they do.

Broader Implications of the Silicon Valley Model

The Silicon Valley Model is very much a product of a few companies in the computer sector, just as mass production was invented by Ford and just-in-time production by Toyota. And as in those cases, we believe that the Silicon Valley Model will diffuse throughout the broader information technology sector as the computer, telecommunications, information services, and consumer electronics industries merge.

In addition, however, as industrial competition in all industries becomes more complex and technological change accelerates, the model may have important effects upon many other fields. We think that it provides a framework that allows proprietary leaders in general to have the greatest span of control and profitability with the least complexity and smallest size. In fact, we think that the model is appropriate for small and large companies alike; it does, however, penalize unnecessary size. (Microsoft, with fewer than 15,000 employees, has a market capitalization equal to IBM's.) We will therefore close with an example of how architectural strategy and the Silicon Valley Model could have been used more than a decade ago, by Xerox.

Xerox became a large, global company through a single proprietary technology—xerography. Xerographic "marking engines" are the core of photocopiers, printers, and facsimile machines, all of which Xerox invented. But Xerox chose to exploit its control of xerography using the traditional strategy of integrated companies.

Where Xerox felt it could not develop products profitably itself, it simply left the market vacant. As a result, when the company's patent position eroded, Japanese competitors took the bulk of the blossoming low-end markets for personal copiers, laser printers, and fax machines. Xerox's market share declined from nearly 100% to about 30%.

Instead, Xerox could have developed an architecture for a broad family of machines and control systems, including interfaces for scanners, document handlers, and "finishers" for collating, stapling, and binding. It could have licensed its technology to other firms, and/or sold them xerographic engines. It could have developed products for core markets, leaving others to niche companies.

Every few years, the company could have changed or enhanced its architectures to improve its products and competitive position. The result could have been a Microsoft-like position, with Xerox holding the lion's share of the profits in a highly competitive, dynamic market—yet one under its own effective control. We think that similar strategies are available to companies in other complex industries—aerospace and machine tools, among others. If so, the information sector's strategic and organizational innovations might prove as interesting as its technology.

PART

II

New Tools, New Rules

1
The Right Game: Use Game Theory to Shape Strategy

Adam M. Brandenburger and Barry J. Nalebuff

Business is a high-stakes game. The way we approach this game is reflected in the language we use to describe it. Business language is full of expressions borrowed from the military and from sports. Some of them are dangerously misleading. Unlike war and sports, business is not about winning and losing. Nor is it about how well you play the game. Companies can succeed spectacularly without requiring others to fail. And they can fail miserably no matter how well they play if they make the mistake of playing the wrong game.

The essence of business success lies in making sure you're playing the right game. How do you know if it's the right game? What can you do about it if it's the wrong game? To help managers answer those questions, we've developed a framework that draws on the insights of game theory. After 50 years as a mathematical construct, game theory is about to change the game of business.

Game theory came of age in 1994, when three pioneers in the field were awarded the Nobel Prize. It all began in 1944, when mathematics genius John von Neumann and economist Oskar Morgenstern published their book *Theory of Games and Economic Behavior*. Immediately heralded as one of the greatest scientific achievements of the century, their work provided a systematic way to understand the behavior of players in situations where their fortunes are interdependent. Von

The authors are grateful to F. William Barnett, Putnam Coes, Amy Guggenheim, Michael Maples, Anna Minto, Troy Paredes, Harborne Stuart, Bart Troyer, Michael Tuchen, and Peter Wetenhall, along with many other colleagues and students, for their generous comments and suggestions.

Neumann and Morgenstern distinguished two types of games. In the first type, rule-based games, players interact according to specified "rules of engagement." These rules might come from contracts, loan covenants, or trade agreements, for example. In the second type, freewheeling games, players interact without any external constraints. For example, buyers and sellers may create value by transacting in an unstructured fashion. Business is a complex mix of both types of games.

For rule-based games, game theory offers the principle, To every action, there is a reaction. But, unlike Newton's third law of motion, the reaction is not programmed to be equal and opposite. To analyze how other players will react to your move, you need to play out all the reactions (including yours) to their actions as far ahead as possible. You have to look forward far into the game and then reason backward to figure out which of today's actions will lead you to where you want to end up.[1]

For freewheeling games, game theory offers the principle, You cannot take away from the game more than you bring to it. In business, what does a particular player bring to the game? To find the answer, look at the value created when everyone is in the game, and then pluck that player out and see how much value the remaining players can create. The difference is the removed player's "added value." In unstructured interactions, you cannot take away more than your added value.[2]

Underlying both principles is a shift in perspective. Many people view games egocentrically—that is, they focus on their own position. The primary insight of game theory is the importance of focusing on others—namely, allocentrism. To look forward and reason backward, you have to put yourself in the shoes—even in the heads—of other players. To assess your added value, you have to ask not what other players can bring to you but what you can bring to other players.

Managers can profit by using these insights from game theory to design a game that is right for their companies. The rewards that can come from changing a game may be far greater than those from maintaining the status quo. For example, Nintendo succeeded brilliantly in changing the video game business by taking control of software. Sega's subsequent success required changing the game again. Rupert Murdoch's *New York Post* changed the tabloid game by finding a convincing way to demonstrate the cost of a price war without actually launching one. BellSouth made money by changing the takeover game between Craig McCaw and Lin Broadcasting. Successful business strategy is about actively shaping the game you play, not just playing the game you find. We will explore how these examples and others worked in practice, starting with the story of how General Motors changed the game of selling cars.

From Lose-Lose to Win-Win

In the early 1990s, the U.S. automobile industry was locked into an all-too-familiar mode of destructive competition. End-of-year rebates and dealer discounts were ruining the industry's profitability. As soon as one company used incentives to clear excess inventory at year-end, others had to do the same. Worse still, consumers came to expect the rebates. As a result, they waited for them to be offered before buying a car, forcing manufacturers to offer incentives earlier in the year. Was there a way out? Would someone find an alternative to practices that were hurting all the companies? General Motors may have done just that.

In September 1992, General Motors and Household Bank issued a new credit card that allowed cardholders to apply 5% of their charges toward buying or leasing a new GM car, up to $500 per year, with a maximum of $3,500. The GM card has been the most successful credit-card launch in history. One month after it was introduced, there were 1.2 million accounts. Two years later, there were 8.7 million accounts—and the program is still growing. Projections suggest that eventually some 30% of GM's nonfleet sales in North America will be to cardholders.

As Hank Weed, managing director of GM's card program, explains, the card helps GM build share through the "conquest" of prospective Ford buyers and others—a traditional win-lose strategy. But the program has engineered another, more subtle change in the game of selling cars. It replaced other incentives that GM had previously offered. The net effect has been to raise the price that a noncardholder—someone who intends to buy a Ford, for example—would have to pay for a GM car. The program thus gives Ford some breathing room to raise its prices. That allows GM, in turn, to raise its prices without losing customers to Ford. The result is a win-win dynamic between GM and Ford.

If the GM card is as good as it sounds, what's stopping other companies from copying it? Not much, it seems. First, Ford introduced its version of the program with Citibank. Then Volkswagen introduced its variation with MBNA Corporation. Doesn't all this imitation put a dent in the GM program? Not necessarily.

Imitation is the sincerest form of flattery, but in business it is often thought to be a killer compliment. Textbooks on strategy warn that if others can imitate something you do, you can't make money at it. Some go even further, asserting that business strategy cannot be codified. If it could, it would be imitated and any gains would evaporate.

Yet the proponents of this belief are mistaken in assuming that imitation is always harmful. It's true that once GM's program is widely imitated, the company's ability to lure customers away from other manufacturers will be diminished. But imitation also can help GM. Ford and Volkswagen offset the cost of their credit card rebates by scaling back other incentive programs. The result was an effective price increase for GM customers, the vast majority of whom do not participate in the Ford and Volkswagen credit card programs. This gives GM the option to firm up its demand or raise its prices further. All three car companies now have a more loyal customer base, so there is less incentive to compete on price.

To understand the full impact of the GM card program, you have to use game theory. You can't see all the ramifications of the program without adopting an allocentric perspective. The key is to anticipate how Ford, Volkswagen, and other automakers will respond to GM's initiative.

When you change the game, you want to come out ahead. That's pretty clear. But what about the fact that GM's strategy helped Ford? One common mind-set—seeing business as war—says that others have to lose in order for you to win. There may indeed be times when you want to opt for a win-lose strategy. But not always. The GM example shows that there also are times when you want to create a win-win situation. Although it may sound surprising, sometimes the best way to succeed is to let others, including your competitors, do well.

Looking for win-win strategies has several advantages. First, because the approach is relatively unexplored, there is greater potential for finding new opportunities. Second, because others are not being forced to give up ground, they may offer less resistance to win-win moves, making them easier to implement. Third, because win-win moves don't force other players to retaliate, the new game is more sustainable. And finally, imitation of a win-win move is beneficial, not harmful.

To encourage thinking about both cooperative and competitive ways to change the game, we suggest the term *coopetition*.[3] It means looking for win-win as well as win-lose opportunities. Keeping both possibilities in mind is important because win-lose strategies often backfire. Consider, for example, the common—and dangerous—strategy of lowering prices to gain market share. Although it may provide a temporary benefit, the gains will evaporate if others match the cuts to regain their lost share. The result is simply to reestablish the status quo but at lower prices—a lose-lose scenario that leaves all the players worse off. That was the situation in the automobile industry before GM changed the game.

The Game of Business

Did GM intentionally plan to change the game of selling cars in the way we have described it? Or did the company just get lucky with a loyalty marketing program that turned out better than anyone had expected? Looking back, the one thing we can say with certainty is that the stakes in situations like GM's are too high to be left to chance. That's why we have developed a comprehensive map and a method to help managers find strategies for changing the game.

The game of business is all about value: creating it and capturing it. Who are the participants in this enterprise? To describe them, we introduce the Value Net—a schematic map designed to represent all the players in the game and the interdependencies among them. (See Exhibit I.)

Interactions take place along two dimensions. Along the vertical dimension are the company's customers and suppliers. Resources such as labor and raw materials flow from the suppliers to the company, and products and services flow from the company to its customers. Money flows in the reverse direction, from customers to the company and from the company to its suppliers. Along the horizontal dimension are the players with whom the company interacts but does not transact. They are its *substitutors* and *complementors.*

Substitutors are alternative players from whom customers may purchase products or to whom suppliers may sell their resources. Coca-Cola and PepsiCo are substitutors with respect to consumers because they sell rival colas. A little less obvious is that Coca-Cola and Tyson Foods are substitutors with respect to suppliers. That is because both companies use carbon dioxide. Tyson uses it for freezing chickens, and

Exhibit I.

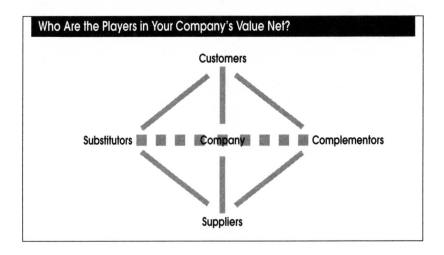

Coke uses it for carbonation. (As they say in the cola industry, "No fizziness, no bizziness.")

Complementors are players from whom customers buy complementary products or to whom suppliers sell complementary resources. For example, hardware and software companies are classic complementors. Faster hardware, such as a Pentium chip, increases users' willingness to pay for more powerful software. More powerful software, such as the latest version of Microsoft Office, increases users' willingness to pay for faster hardware. American Airlines and United Air Lines, though substitutors with respect to passengers, are complementors when they decide to update their fleets. That's because Boeing can recoup the cost of a new plane design only if enough airlines buy it. Since each airline effectively subsidizes the other's purchase of planes, the two are complementors in this instance.

We introduce the terms *substitutor* and *complementor* because we find that the traditional business vocabulary inhibits a full understanding of the interdependencies that exist in business. If you call a player a competitor, you tend to focus on competing rather than on finding opportunities for cooperation. *Substitutor* describes the market relationship without that prejudice. Complementors, often overlooked in traditional strategic analysis, are the natural counterparts of substitutors.

The Value Net describes the various roles of the players. It's possible for the same player to occupy more than one role simultaneously. Remember that American and United are both substitutors and complementors. Gary Hamel and C.K. Prahalad make this point in *Competing for the Future* (Harvard Business School Press, 1994): "On any given day . . . AT&T might find Motorola to be a supplier, a buyer, a competitor, *and* a partner."

The Value Net reveals two fundamental symmetries in the game of business: the first between customers and suppliers and the second between substitutors and complementors. Understanding those symmetries can help managers come up with new strategies for changing the game or new applications of existing strategies.

Managers understand intuitively that along the vertical dimension of the Value Net, there is a mixture of cooperation and competition. It's cooperation when suppliers, companies, and customers come together to create value in the first place. It's competition when the time comes for them to divide the pie.

Along the horizontal dimension, however, managers tend to see only half the picture. Substitutors are seen only as enemies. Complementors, if viewed at all, are seen only as friends. Such a perspective overlooks another symmetry. There can be a cooperative element to interactions with substitutors, as the GM story illustrates, and a competitive element to interactions with complementors, as we will see.

Changing the Game

The Value Net is a map that prompts you to explore all the interdependencies in the game. Drawing the Value Net for your business is therefore the first step toward changing the game. The second step is identifying all the elements of the game. According to game theory, there are five: players, added values, rules, tactics, and scope—PARTS for short. These five elements fully describe all interactions, both freewheeling and rule-based. To change the game, you have to change one or more of these elements.

Players come first. As we saw in the Value Net, the players are customers, suppliers, substitutors, and complementors. None of the players are fixed. Sometimes it's smart to change who is playing the game. That includes yourself.

Added values are what each player brings to the game. There are ways to make yourself a more valuable player—in other words, to raise your added value. And there are ways to lower the added values of other players.

Rules give structure to the game. In business, there is no universal set of rules; a rule might arise from law, custom, practicality, or contracts. In addition to using existing rules to their advantage, players may be able to revise them or come up with new ones.

Tactics are moves used to shape the way players perceive the game and hence how they play. Sometimes, tactics are designed to reduce misperceptions; at other times, they are designed to create or maintain uncertainty.

Scope describes the boundaries of the game. It's possible for players to expand or shrink those boundaries.

Successful business strategies begin by assessing and then changing one or more of these elements. PARTS does more than exhort you to think out of the box. It provides the tools to enable you to do so. Let's look at each strategic lever in turn.

Changing the Players

NutraSweet, a low-calorie sweetener used in soft drinks such as Diet Coke and Diet Pepsi, is a household name, and its swirl logo is recognized worldwide. In fact, it's Monsanto's brand name for the chemical aspartame. NutraSweet has been a very profitable business for Monsanto, with 70% gross margins. Such profits usually attract others to enter the market, but NutraSweet was protected by patents in Europe until 1987 and in the United States until 1992.

With Coke's blessing, a challenger, the Holland Sweetener Company, built an aspartame plant in Europe in 1985 in anticipation of the patent expiration. Ken Dooley, HSC's vice president of marketing and sales, explained, "Every manufacturer likes to have at least two sources of supply."

As HSC attacked the European market, Monsanto fought back aggressively. It used deep price cuts and contractual relationships with customers to deny HSC a toehold in the market. HSC managed to fend off the initial counterattack by appealing to the courts to enable it to gain access to customers. Dooley considered all this just a preview of things to come: "We are looking forward to moving the war into the United States."

But Dooley's war ended before it began. Just prior to the U.S. patent expiration, both Coke and Pepsi signed new long-term contracts with

Monsanto. When at last there was a real potential for competition between suppliers, it appeared that Coke and Pepsi didn't seize the opportunity. Or did they?

Neither Coke nor Pepsi ever had any real desire to switch over to generic aspartame. Remembering the result of the New Coke reformulation of 1985, neither company wanted to be the first to take the NutraSweet logo off the can and create a perception that it was fooling around with the flavor of its drinks. If only one switched over, the other most certainly would have made a selling point of its exclusive use of NutraSweet. After all, NutraSweet had already built a reputation for safety and good taste. Even though generic aspartame would taste the same, consumers would be unfamiliar with the unbranded product and see it as inferior. Another reason not to switch was that Monsanto had spent the previous decade marching down the learning curve for making aspartame—giving it a significant cost advantage—while HSC was still near the top.

In the end, what Coke and Pepsi really wanted was to get the same old NutraSweet at a much better price. That they accomplished. Look at Monsanto's position before and after HSC entered the game. Before, there was no good substitute for NutraSweet. Cyclamates had been banned, and saccharin caused cancer in laboratory rats. NutraSweet's added value was its ability to make a safe, good-tasting low-calorie drink possible. Stir in a patent and things looked very positive for Monsanto. When HSC came along, NutraSweet's added value was greatly reduced. What was left was its brand loyalty and its manufacturing cost advantage.

Where did all this leave HSC? Clearly, its entry into the market was worth a lot to Coke and Pepsi. It would have been quite reasonable for HSC, before entering the market, to demand compensation for its role in the form of either a fixed payment or a guaranteed contract. But, once in, with an unbranded product and higher production costs, it was much more difficult for the company to make money. Dooley was right when he said that all manufacturers want a second source. The problem is, they don't necessarily want to do much business with that source.

Monsanto did well to create a brand identity and a cost advantage: It minimized the negative effects of entry by a generic brand. Coke and Pepsi did well to change the game by encouraging the entry of a new player that would reduce their dependence on NutraSweet. According to HSC, the new contracts led to combined savings of $200 million annually for Coke and Pepsi. As for HSC, perhaps it was too quick to become a player. The question for HSC was not what it could do for Coke and Pepsi; the question was what Coke and Pepsi could do for HSC. Although it was a duopolist in a weak position when it came to selling aspartame, HSC was a monopolist in a strong position when it came to selling its "service" to make the aspartame market competitive. Perhaps Coke and Pepsi would have paid a higher price for this valuable service, but only if HSC had demanded such payment up front.

PAY ME TO PLAY.   As the NutraSweet story illustrates, sometimes the most valuable service you can offer is creating competition, so don't give it away for free. People in the takeover game have long understood the art of getting paid to play. The cellular phone business was undergoing rapid consolidation in June 1989, when 39-year-old Craig McCaw made a bid for Lin Broadcasting Corporation. With 50 million POPs (lingo for the population in a coverage area) already under his belt, McCaw saw the acquisition of Lin's 18 million POPs as the best, and possibly the only, way to acquire a national cellular footprint. He bid $120 per share for Lin, which resulted in an immediate jump in Lin's share price from $103.50 to $129.50. Clearly, the market expected more action. But Lin's CEO, Donald Pels, didn't care much for McCaw or his bid. Faced with Lin's hostile reaction, McCaw lowered his offer to $110, and Lin sought other suitors. BellSouth, with 28 million POPs, was the natural alternative, although acquiring Lin wouldn't quite give it a national footprint.

Nevertheless, BellSouth was willing to acquire Lin for the right price. But if it entered the fray, it would create a bidding war and thus make it unlikely that Lin would be sold for a reasonable price. BellSouth knew that only one bidder could win, and it wanted something in case that bidder was McCaw. Thus, as a condition for making a bid, BellSouth got Lin's promise of a $54 million consolation prize and an additional $15 million toward expenses in the event that it was outbid. BellSouth made an offer generally valued at between $105 and $112 per share. As expected, BellSouth was outbid; McCaw responded with an offer valued at $112 to $118 per share. BellSouth then raised its bid to roughly $120 per share. In return, Lin raised BellSouth's expense cap to $25 million. McCaw raised his bid to $130 and then added a few dollars more to close the deal. At the same time, he paid BellSouth $22.5 million to exit the game.[4] At this point in the bidding, Lin's CEO recognized that his stock options were worth $186 million, and the now friendly deal with McCaw was concluded.

So how did the various players make out? Lin got itself an extra billion, which made its $79 million payment to BellSouth look like a bargain. McCaw got the national network he wanted and subsequently sold out to AT&T, making himself a billionaire. And BellSouth, by getting paid first to play and then to go away, turned a weak hand into $76.5 million plus expenses.

BellSouth clearly understood that even if you can't make money in the game the old-fashioned way, you can get paid to change it. Such payments need not be made in cash; you can ask for a guaranteed sales contract, contributions to R&D, bid-preparation expenses, or a last-look provision.

The examples so far show how you can change three of the four players in the Value Net. Lin paid to bring in an extra buyer, or customer. Coke and Pepsi would, no doubt, have been prepared to pay HSC handsomely to become a second supplier. And McCaw paid to take out a rival bidder, or substitutor. That leaves complementors. The next example shows how a company can benefit from bringing players into the complements market.

CHEAP COMPLEMENTS.   Remember that hardware is the classic complement to software. One can't function without the other. Software writers won't produce programs unless a sufficient hardware base exists. Yet consumers won't purchase the hardware until a critical mass of software exists. 3DO Company, a maker of video games, is attacking this chicken-and-egg problem in the video-game business by bringing players into the complements market. To those who know 3DO's founder, Trip Hawkins, this should come as no surprise: He designed his own major at Harvard in strategy and game theory.

3DO owns a 32-bit CD-ROM hardware-and-software technology for next-generation video games. The company plans to make money by licensing software houses to make 3DO games and collecting a $3 royalty fee (hence the company name). Of course, to sell software, you first need people to buy the hardware. But those early adopters won't find much software. To start the ball rolling, 3DO needs the hardware to be cheap—the cheaper the better.

The company's strategy is to give away the license to produce the hardware technology. This move has induced hardware manufacturers such as Panasonic (Matsushita), GoldStar, Sanyo, and Toshiba to enter the game. Because all 3DO software will run on all 3DO hardware, the hardware manufacturers are left to compete on cost alone. Making the hardware a commodity is just what 3DO wants: It drives down the price of the complementary product.

But not quite enough. 3DO is discovering that to create momentum in the market, the hardware must be sold below cost, and hardware manufacturers aren't willing to go that far. As an inducement, 3DO now offers them two shares of 3DO stock for each machine sold. The company also has renegotiated its deal with software houses up to a $6 royalty, with the extra $3 earmarked to subsidize hardware sales. So Hawkins is actually paying people to play in the complements market. Is he paying enough? Time will tell.

Creating competition in the complements market is the flip side of coopetition. Just as substitutors are usually seen only as enemies, complementors are seen only as friends. Whereas the GM story shows the possibility of win-win opportunities with substitutors, the 3DO example illustrates the possibility of legitimate win-lose opportunities with complementors. Creating competition among its complementors helped 3DO at their expense.

Changing the Added Values

Just as you shouldn't accept the players of a game as fixed, you shouldn't take what they bring to the game as fixed, either. You can change the players' added values. Common sense tells us that there are two options: Raise your own added value or lower that of others.

Good basic business practices are one route to raising added values. You can tailor your product to customers' needs, build a brand, use resources more efficiently, work with your suppliers to lower their costs, and so on. These strategies should not be underestimated. But there are other, less transparent ways to raise your added value. As an example, consider Trans World Airlines' introduction of Comfort Class in 1993.

Robert Cozzi, TWA's senior vice president of marketing, proposed removing 5 to 40 seats per plane to give passengers in coach more legroom. The move raised TWA's added value; according to J.D. Power and Associates, the company soared to first place in customer satisfaction for long-haul flights. This was a win for TWA and a loss for other airlines. But elements of win-win were present as well: With fuller planes, TWA was not about to start a price war.

But what if other carriers copied the strategy? Would that negate TWA's efforts? No, because as others copied TWA's move, excess capacity would be retired from an industry plagued by overcapacity. Passengers get more legroom, and carriers stop flying empty seats around. Everyone wins. Cozzi saw a way to move the industry away from the self-defeating price competition that goes on when airlines try to fill up the coach cabin. This was business strategy at its best.[5]

The idea of raising your own added value is natural. Less intuitive is the approach of lowering the added value of others. To illustrate how the strategy works, let's begin with a simple card game.

Adam and 26 of his M.B.A. students are playing a card game. Adam has 26 black cards, and each of the students has one red card. Any red card coupled with a black card gets a $100 prize (paid by the dean). How do we expect the bargaining between Adam and his students to proceed?

First, calculate the added values. Without Adam and his black cards, there is no game. Thus Adam's added value equals the total value of the game, which is $2,600. Each student has an added value of $100 because without that student's card, one less match can be made and thus $100 is lost. The sum of the added values is therefore $5,200—made up of $2,600 from Adam and $100 from each of the 26 students. Alas, there is only $2,600 to be divided. Given the symmetry of the game, it's most likely that everyone will end up with half of his or her added value: Adam will buy the students' cards for $50 each or sell his for $50 each.

So far, nothing is surprising. Could Adam do any better? Yes, but first he'd have to change the game. In a public display, Adam burns three of his black cards. True, the pie is now smaller, at $2,300, and so is Adam's added value. But the point of this strategic move is to destroy the added values of the other players. Now no student has any added value because 3 students are going to end up without a match, and therefore no one student is essential to the game. The total value with 26 students is $2,300, and the total value with 25 students is still $2,300.

At this point, the division will not be equal. Indeed, because no student has any added value, Adam would be quite generous to offer a 90:10 split. Since 3 students will end up with nothing, anyone who ends up with $10 should consider himself or herself lucky. For Adam, 90% of $2,300 is a lot better than half of $2,600. Of course, his getting it depends on the students' not being able to get together; if they did, that would be changing the game, too. In fact, it would be changing the players, as in the previous section, and it would be an excellent strategy for the students to adopt.

Exhibit II.

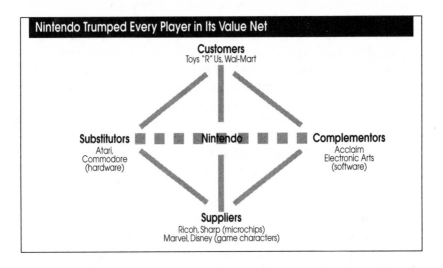

Just a card trick? No—a strategy employed by the video-game maker Nintendo (which, it so happens, used to produce playing cards). To see how the company lowered everyone else's added value, we take a tour around its Value Net. (See Exhibit II.)

NINTENDO POWER. Start with Nintendo's customers. Nintendo sold its games to a highly concentrated market—predominantly megaretailers such as Toys R Us and Wal-Mart. How could Nintendo combat such buyer power? By changing the game. Nintendo did just what Adam did when he burned the cards (although Nintendo made a lot more money): It didn't fill all the retailers' orders. In 1988, Nintendo sold 33 million cartridges, but the market could have absorbed 45 million. Poor planning? No. It's true that the pie shrank a little as some stores sold out of the game. But the important point is that retailers lost added value. Even a giant like Toys R Us was in a weaker position when not every retailer could get supplied. As Nintendomania took hold, consumers queued up outside stores and retailers clamored for more of the product. With games in short supply, Nintendo had zapped the buyers' power.

The next arena of negotiations concerned the complementors—namely, outside game developers. What was Nintendo's strategy? First, it developed software in-house. The company built a security chip into the hardware and then instituted a licensing program for outside developers. The number of licenses was restricted, and licensees were allowed to develop only a limited number of games. Because there were many Nintendo wanna-be programmers and because the company could develop games in-house, the added value of those that did get the license was lowered. Once again, Nintendo ensured that there were fewer black cards than red. It held all the bargaining chips.

Nintendo's suppliers, too, had little added value. The company used old-generation chip technology, making its chips something of a commodity. Another input was the leading characters in the games. Nintendo hit the jackpot by developing Mario. After he became a hit in his own right, the added value of comic-book heroes licensed from others, such as Spiderman (Marvel), and of cartoon icons, such as Mickey Mouse (Disney), was reduced. In fact, Nintendo turned the tables completely, licensing Mario to appear in comic books and on cartoon shows, cereal boxes, board games, and toys.

Finally, there were Nintendo's substitutors. From a kid's perspective, there were no good alternatives to a video game; the only real threat came from alternative video-game systems. Here Nintendo had the game practically all to itself. Having the largest installed base of systems allowed the company to drive down the manufacturing cost for its hardware. And with developers keen to write for the largest installed base, Nintendo got the best games. This created a positive feedback loop: More people bought Nintendo's systems, leading to a larger base, still lower costs, and even more games. Nintendo locked in its lead by requiring exclusivity from outside game developers. With few alternatives to Nintendo, that was a small price for them to pay. Potential challengers couldn't simply take successful games over to their platforms; they had to start from scratch. Although large profits might normally invite entry, no challenger could engineer any added value. The installed base, combined with Nintendo's exclusivity agreements, made competing in Nintendo's game hopeless.

What was the bottom line for Nintendo? How much could a manufacturer of a two-bit—well, eight-bit—game about a lugubrious plumber called Mario really be worth? How about more than Sony or Nissan? Between July 1990 and June 1991, Nintendo's average market value was 2.4 trillion yen, Sony's was 2.2 trillion yen, and Nissan's was 2 trillion yen.

The Nintendo example illustrates the importance of added value as opposed to value. There is no doubt that cars, televisions, and VCRs create more value in the world than do Game Boys. But it's not enough simply to create value; profits come from capturing value. By keeping its added value high and everyone else's low, Nintendo was able to capture a giant slice of a largish pie. The name of the enthusi-asts' monthly magazine, *Nintendo Power*, summed up the situation quite nicely.

Nintendo's success, however, brought it under scrutiny. In late 1989, Congressman Dennis Eckart (D-Ohio), chairman of the House Sub-committee on Antitrust, Impact of Deregulation and Privatization, requested that the U.S. Justice Department investigate allegations that Nintendo of America unfairly reduced competition. Eckart's letter ar-gued, among other things, that the Christmas shortages in 1988 were "contrived to increase consumer prices and demand and to enhance Nintendo's market leverage" and that software producers had "become almost entirely dependent on Nintendo's acceptance of their games." None of Nintendo's practices were found to be illegal.[6]

PUMPING UP PROFITS.   Protecting your added value is as important as establishing it in the first place. Back in the mid-1970s, Robert Taylor, CEO of Minnetonka, had the idea for Softsoap, a liquid soap that would be dispensed by a pump. The problem was that it would be hard to retain any added value once the likes of Procter & Gamble and Lever Brothers muscled in with their brands and distribution clout. Nothing in the product could be patented. But, to his credit, Taylor realized that the hardest part of producing the soap was manufactur-ing the little plastic pump, for which there were just two suppliers. In a bet-the-company move, he locked up both suppliers' total annual production by ordering 100 million of the pumps. Even at 12 cents apiece, this was a $12 million order—more than Minnetonka's net worth. Ultimately, the major players did enter the market, but captur-ing the supply of pumps gave Taylor a head start of 12 to 18 months. That advantage preserved Softsoap's added value during this period, allowing the company to build brand loyalty, which continues to provide added value to this day.

As the TWA, Nintendo, and Softsoap examples illustrate, added values can be changed. By reengineering them—raising your added value and lowering others'—you may be able to capture a larger slice of pie.

Game theory holds that in freewheeling interactions, no player can take away more than that player brings to the game, but that's not quite the end of the matter. First, there is no guarantee that any player will get all its added value. Typically, the sum of all the added values exceeds the total value of the game. Remember that in Adam's card game, the total prize was only $2,600 even though the added values of all the players initially totaled $5,200. Second, even if you have no added value, that doesn't prohibit you from making money. Others might be willing to pay you to enter or exit the game (as with Bell-South); similarly, you might be paid to stay out or stay in. Third, rules constrain interactions among players. We will see that in games with rules, some players may be able to capture more than their added values.

Changing the Rules

Rules determine how the game is played by limiting the possible reactions to any action. To analyze the effect of a rule, you have to look forward and reason backward.

The simplest rule is *one price to all.* According to this rule, prices are not negotiated individually with each customer. Consequently, a company can profitably enter a market even when it has no added value. If a new player enters with a price lower than the incumbent's, the incumbent has only two effective responses: match the newcomer's price across the board or stand pat and give up share. By looking forward and reasoning backward, a small newcomer can steer the incumbent toward accommodation rather than retaliation.

Imagine that a new player comes in with a limited capacity—say, 10% of the market—and a discounted price. Whether it makes any money depends on how the incumbent responds. The incumbent can recapture its lost market by coming down to match the newcomer's price, or it can give up 10% share. For the incumbent, giving up 10% share is usually better than sacrificing its profit margin. In such cases, the newcomer will do all right. But it can't get too greedy. If it tries to take away too much of the market, the incumbent will choose to give up its profit margin in order to regain share. Only when the newcomer limits its capacity does the incumbent stand pat and the newcomer make money. For this reason, the strategy is called *judo economics:* By staying small, the newcomer turns the incumbent's larger size to its own benefit.

To pull off a judo strategy, the newcomer's commitment to limit its capacity must be both clear and credible. The newcomer may be tempted to expand, but it must realize that if it does, it will give the incumbent an incentive to retaliate.

KIWI IS NO DODO. Kiwi International Air Lines understands these ideas perfectly. Named for the flightless bird, Kiwi is a 1992 start-up founded by former Eastern Air Lines pilots who were grounded after

Eastern went bankrupt. Kiwi engineered a cost advantage from its employee ownership and its use of leased planes. But it had lower name recognition and a more limited flight schedule than the major carriers—on balance, not much, if any, added value. So what did it do? It went for low prices and limited capacity. According to public statements from its then CEO, Robert Iverson, "We designed our system to stay out of the way of large carriers and to make sure they understand that we pose no threat. . . . Kiwi intends to capture, at most, only 10% share of any one market—or no more than four flights per day." Because Kiwi targets business travelers, the major airlines can't use stay-over and advance-purchase restrictions to lower price selectively against it. So Kiwi benefited from the one-price-to-all rule.

Now Kiwi, in turn, became the large player for any newcomer to the same market. That didn't leave much room to be small in relation to Kiwi, so Kiwi had to fight if someone else tried to follow suit. According to Iverson, "[The major airlines] are better off with us than without us." Even though Kiwi was Delta's rival, by staying small and keeping out other potential entrants, it managed to bring an element of coopetition into the game. From Delta's perspective, Kiwi was rather like the devil it knew.

The Kiwi story illustrates how a player can take advantage of existing rules of the marketplace—in this case, the one-price-to-all rule. In addition to practicality, rules arise from custom, law, or contracts. Common contract-based rules are most-favored-nation (most-favored-customer) clauses, take-or-pay agreements, and meet-the-competition clauses. These rules give structure to negotiations between buyers and sellers. Rules are particularly useful for players in commodity-like businesses. As an example, take the carbon dioxide industry.

SOLID PROFITS FROM GAS.   There are three major producers of carbon dioxide: Airco, Liquid Carbonic, and Air Liquide. Carbon dioxide creates enormous value (in carbonation and freezing), but it is essentially a commodity, which makes it hard for a producer to capture any of that value. One distinguishing factor, however, is that carbon dioxide is very expensive to transport, which gives some added value to the producer best located to serve a specific customer. Other sources of added value are differentiation through reliability, reputation, service, and technology. Still, a producer's added value is usually small in relation to the total value created. The question is, Can a producer capture more than its added value?

In this case the answer is yes, because of the rules of the game in the carbon dioxide industry. The producers have a meet-the-competition clause (MCC) in their contracts with customers. An MCC gives the incumbent seller the right to make the last bid.

The result of an MCC is that a producer can sustain a higher price and thereby earn more than its added value. Normally, an elevated price would invite other producers to compete on price. In this case, however, a challenger cannot come in and take away business simply by undercutting the existing price. If it tried, the incumbent could then come back with a lower price and keep the business. The back-and-forth could go on until the price fell to variable cost, but at that point stealing the business wouldn't be worth the effort. The only one to benefit would be the buyer, who would end up with a lower price.

Cutting price to go after an incumbent's business is always risky but may be justified by the gain in business. Not so when the incumbent has an MCC: The upside is lost and the downside remains. Lowering price sets a dangerous precedent and increases the likelihood of a tit-for-tat response. The incumbent may retaliate by going after the challenger's business, and even if the challenger doesn't lose customers, it certainly will lose profits. Another downside is that the challenger's customers may end up at a disadvantage. If the challenger supplies Coke and the incumbent supplies Pepsi, the challenger shouldn't help Pepsi get a lower price. Its future is tied to Coke, and it doesn't want to give Pepsi any cost advantage. It might even end up having to lower its own price to Coke without getting Pepsi's business. Finally, the challengers efforts are misplaced: It would do better to make sure that its existing customers are happy.

Putting in an MCC changes the game in a way that's clearly a win for the incumbent. Perhaps surprisingly, the challenger also ends up better off. True, it may not be able to take away market share, but the incumbent's higher prices set a good precedent: They give the challenger some room to raise prices to its own customers. There also is less danger that the incumbent will go after the challenger's share, because the incumbent, with higher profits, now has more to lose. An MCC is a classic case of coopetition.

As for the customers, why do they go along with this rule? It may be traditional in their industry. Perhaps it's the norm. Perhaps they decide to trade an initial price break in return for the subsequent lock-in. Or maybe they don't thoroughly understand the rule's implications. Whatever the reason, MCCs do offer benefits to customers. The clauses guarantee producers a long-term relationship if they so choose, even in the absence of long-term contracts. Thus producers are more willing to invest in serving their customers. Finally, even if there is no formal MCC, it's generally accepted that you don't leave your current supplier without giving it a last chance to bid.

Using an MCC is a strategy that, far from being undermined by imitation, is enhanced by it. A carbon dioxide producer benefits from unilateral adoption of an MCC, but there is an added kicker when other producers copy it. The MCCs allow them to push prices up further, so they now have even more to lose from starting a share war. As MCCs become more widespread, everyone has less prospect of gaining share. With even more at risk and even less to gain, producers refrain from going after one another's customers. A moral: Players who live in glass houses are unlikely to throw stones. So you should be pleased when others build glass houses.

Both the significance of rules and the opportunity to change the game by changing the rules are often underappreciated. If negotiations in your business take place without rules, consider how bringing in a new rule would change the game. But be careful. Just as you can rewrite rules and make new ones, so, too, can others. Unlike other games, business has no ultimate rule-making authority to settle disputes. History matters. The government can make some rules—through antitrust laws, for example. In the end, however, the power to make rules comes largely from power in the marketplace. While it's true that rules can trump added value, it is added value that confers the power to make rules in the first place. As they said in the old West, "A Smith & Wesson beats a straight flush."

Tactics: Changing Perceptions

We've changed the players, their added values, and the rules. Is there anything left to change? Yes—perceptions. There is no guarantee that everyone agrees on who the players are, what their added values are, and what the rules are. Nor are the implications of every move and countermove likely to be clear. Business is mired in uncertainty. Tactics influence the way players perceive the uncertainty and thus mold their behavior. Some tactics work by reducing misperceptions—in other words, by lifting the fog. Others work by creating or maintaining uncertainty—by thickening the fog.

Here we offer two examples. The first shows how Rupert Murdoch lifted the fog to influence how the *New York Daily News* perceived the game; the second illustrates how maintaining a fog can help negotiating parties reach an agreement.

THE NEW YORK FOG. In the beginning of July 1994, the *Daily News* raised its price from 40 cents to 50 cents. This seemed rather remarkable under the circumstances. Its major rival, Rupert Murdoch's *New York Post*, was test-marketing a price cut to 25 cents and had demonstrated its effectiveness on Staten Island. As the *New York Times* saw it (Press Notes, July 4), it was as if the *Daily News* were daring Murdoch to follow through with his price cut.

But, in fact, there was more going on than the *Times* realized. Murdoch had earlier raised the price of the Post to 50 cents, and the *Daily News* had held at 40 cents. As a result, the *Post* was losing subscribers and, with them, advertising revenue. Whereas Murdoch viewed the situation as unsustainable, the *Daily News* didn't see any problem—or at least appeared not to. A convenient fog.

Murdoch came up with a tactic to try to lift the fog. Instead of just lowering his price back down to 40 cents, he announced his intention to lower it to 25 cents. The people at the *Daily News* doubted that Murdoch could afford to pull it off. Moreover, they believed that their recent success was due to a superior product and not just to the dime price advantage. They were not particularly threatened by Murdoch's announcement.

Seeing no response, Murdoch tried a second tactic. He started the price reduction on Staten Island as a test run. As a result, sales of the *Post* doubled—and the fog lifted. The *Daily News* learned that its readers were remarkably willing to read the *Post* in order to save 15 cents. The paper's added value was not so large after all. Suddenly, it didn't seem so stupid for Murdoch to have lowered his price to a quarter. It became clear that disastrous consequences would befall the *Daily News* if Murdoch extended his price cut throughout New York City. In London, just such a meltdown scenario was taking place between Murdoch's *Times* and Conrad Black's *Daily Telegraph*. It was in the context of all these events that the *Daily News* raised its price to 50 cents.

Only the *New York Times* remained in a fog. Murdoch had never wanted to lower his price to 25 cents. He never would have expected the *Daily News* to stay at 40 cents had he initiated an across-the-board cut to 25 cents. Murdoch's announcement and the test run on Staten Island were simply tactics designed to get the *Daily News* to raise its price. With price parity, the *Post* no longer would be losing subscribers, and both papers would be more profitable than if they were priced at 25 cents or even at 40 cents. Coopetition strikes again. The *Post* took an initial hit in raising its price to 50 cents, and when the *Daily News* tried to be greedy and not follow suit, Murdoch showed it the light. When the *Daily News* raised its price, it was not daring Murdoch at all. It was saving itself—and Murdoch—from a price war.

In the case of the *Daily News* and the *Post,* the fog was convenient to the former but not to the latter. So Murdoch lifted it.

DISAGREEING TO AGREE.   Sometimes, a fog is convenient to all parties. A fee negotiation between an investment bank and its client (a composite of several confidential negotiations) offers a good example. The client is a company whose owners are forced to sell. The investment bank has identified a potential acquirer. So far, the investment bank has been working on good faith, and now it's time to sign a fee letter.

The investment bank suggests a 1% fee. The client figures that its company will fetch $500 million and argues that a $5 million fee would be excessive. It proposes a 0.625% fee. The investment bankers think that the price will be closer to $250 million and that accepting the client's proposal would cut their expected fee from $2.5 million to about $1.5 million.

One tactic would be to lift the fog. The investment bank could try to convince the client that a $500 million valuation is unrealistic and that its fear of a $5 million fee is therefore unfounded. The problem with this tactic is that the client does not want to hear a low valuation. Faced with such a prospect, it might walk away from the deal and even from the bank altogether—and then there would be no fee.

The client's optimism and the investment bankers' pessimism create an opportunity for an agreement rather than an argument. Both sides should agree to a 0.625% fee combined with a $2.5 million guarantee. That way, the client gets the percentage it wants and considers the guarantee a throwaway. With a 0.625% fee, the guarantee kicks in only for a sales price below $400 million, and the client expects the price to be $100 million higher. Because the investment bankers expected $2.5 million under their original proposal, now that this fee is guaranteed, they can agree to a lower percentage.

Negotiating over pure percentage fees is inherently win-lose. If the fee falls from 1% to 0.625%, the client wins and the investment bankers lose. Going from 1% to 0.625% plus a floor is win-win—but only when the two parties maintain different perceptions. The fog allows for coopetition.

Changing the Scope

After players, added values, rules, and tactical possibilities, there is nothing left to change within the existing boundaries of the game. But no game is an island. Games are linked across space and over time. A game in one place can affect games elsewhere, and a game today can influence games tomorrow. You can change the scope of a game. You can expand it by creating linkages to other games, or you can shrink it by severing linkages. Either approach may work to your benefit.

We left Nintendo with a stock market value exceeding both Sony's and Nissan's, and with Mario better known than Mickey Mouse. Sega and other would-be rivals had failed in the 8-bit game. But while the rest fell by the wayside, Sega didn't give up. It introduced a new 16-bit system to the U.S. market. It took two years before Nintendo responded with its own 16-bit machine. By then, with the help of its game hero, Sonic the Hedgehog, Sega had established a secure and significant market position. Today the two companies roughly split the 16-bit market.

Was Sega lucky to get such a long, uncontested period in which to establish itself? Did Nintendo simply blow it? We think not. Nintendo's 8-bit franchise was still very valuable. Sega realized that by expanding the scope, it could turn Nintendo's 8-bit strength into a 16-bit weakness. Put yourself in Nintendo's shoes: Would you jump into the 16-bit game or hold back? Had Nintendo jumped into the game, it would have meant competition and, hence, lower 16-bit prices. Lower prices for 16-bit games, substitutes for 8-bit games, would have reduced the value created by the 8-bit games—a big hit to Nintendo's bottom line. Letting Sega have the 16-bit market all to itself meant that 16-bit prices were higher than they otherwise would have been. Higher 16-bit prices cushioned the effect of the new-generation technology on the old. By staying out of Sega's way, Nintendo made a calculated trade-off: Give up a piece of the 16-bit action in order to extend the life of the 8-bit market. Nintendo's decision to hold back was reasonable, given the link between 8-bit and 16-bit games. Note that the decision not to create competition in a substitutes market is the mirror image of 3DO's strategy of creating competition in a complements market.

The Traps of Strategy

Changing the game is hard. There are many potential traps. Our mind-set, map, and method for changing the game—coopetition, the Value Net, and PARTS—are designed to help managers recognize and avoid these traps.

The first mental trap is to think you have to accept the game you find yourself in. Just realizing that you can change the game is crucial. There's more work to be done, but it's far more rewarding to be a game maker than a game taker.

The next trap is to think that changing the game must come at the expense of others. Such thinking can lead to an embattled mind-set that causes you to miss win-win opportunities. The coopetition mind-set—looking for both win-win and win-lose strategies—is far more rewarding.

Another trap is to believe that you have to find something to do that others can't. When you do come up with a way to change the game, accept that your actions might well be imitated. Being unique is not a prerequisite for success. Imitation can be healthy, as the GM card story and others illustrate.

The fourth trap is failing to see the whole game. What you don't see, you can't change. In particular, many people overlook the role of complementors. The solution is to draw the Value Net for your business; it will double your repertoire of strategies for changing the game. Any strategy toward customers has a counterpart with suppliers (and vice versa), and any strategy with substitutors has a mirror image for complementors (and vice versa).

The fifth trap is failing to think methodically about changing the game. Using PARTS as a comprehensive, theory-based set of levers helps generate strategies, but that is not enough. To understand the effect of any particular strategy, you need to go beyond your own perspective. Be allocentric, not egocentric.

For the Holland Sweetener Company, it would have helped to recognize that Coke and Pepsi would have paid a high price up front to make the aspartame market competitive. BellSouth succeeded with a weak hand only because it understood the incentives of Lin and McCaw. Nintendo's power in the 8-bit game came from lowering everyone else's added value. To craft the right choice of capacity and price, Kiwi had to put itself in the shoes of the major airlines to ensure that they would have a greater incentive to accommodate rather than fight Kiwi's entry. The effect of a meet-the-competition clause becomes clear only after you consider how a challenger thinks you would respond to an attempt it might make to steal one of your customers. To achieve his ends, Murdoch had to recognize that the *Daily News* was in a fog and find a way to lift it. By understanding how different parties perceive the game differently, a negotiator is better able to forge an agreement. Sega's success depended on the dilemma it created for Nintendo by starting a new 16-bit game linked to the existing 8-bit game.

Finally, there is no silver bullet for changing the game of business. It is an ongoing process. Others will be trying to change the game, too. Sometimes their changes will work to your benefit and sometimes not. You may need to change the game again. There is, after all, no end to the game of changing the game.

Notes

1. In-depth discussion and applications of the principle of looking forward and reasoning backward are provided in *Thinking Strategically: The Competitive Edge in Business, Politics, and Everyday Life,* by Avinash Dixit and Barry Nalebuff (W.W. Norton, 1991).

2. The argument is spelled out in Adam Brandenburger and Harborne Stuart, "Value-based Business Strategy," which will appear in a forthcoming issue of *Journal of Economics & Management Strategy.*

3. This portmanteau word can be traced to Ray Noorda, CEO of Novell, who has used it to describe relationships in the information technology business: "You have to cooperate and compete at the same time" (*Electronic Business Buyer,* December 1993).

4. McCaw paid $26.5 million to Los Angeles RCC—a joint venture between McCaw and BellSouth that was 85% owned by BellSouth. Since McCaw did not get any additional equity for his investment, it was in essence a $22.5 million payment to BellSouth and a $4 million payment to himself. Security laws override antitrust laws, so it's legal for one bidder to pay another not to be a player.

5. Unfortunately, the program provided little comfort to Cozzi, who resigned when TWA scaled it back. TWA returned to full-scale Comfort Class in the fall of 1994.

6. On a separate issue, Nintendo made a settlement with the Federal Trade Commission in which it agreed to stop requiring retailers to

adhere to a minimum price for the game console. Further, Nintendo would give previous buyers a $5-off coupon toward future purchases of Nintendo game cartridges. Reflecting on the case, Barron's suggested that "the legion of trust-busting lawyers would be far more productively occupied playing Super Mario Brothers 3 than bringing cases of this kind" (December 3, 1991).

2
The Options Approach
to Capital Investment

Avinash K. Dixit and Robert S. Pindyck

Companies make capital investments in order to create and exploit profit opportunities. Investments in research and development, for example, can lead to patents and new technologies that open up those opportunities. The commercialization of patents and technologies through construction of new plants and expenditures for marketing can allow companies to take advantage of profit opportunities. Somewhat less obviously, companies that shut down money-losing operations are also investing: The payments they make to extract themselves from contractual agreements, such as severance pay for employees, are the initial expenditure. The payoff is the reduction of future losses.

Opportunities are *options*—rights but not obligations to take some action in the future. Capital investments, then, are essentially about options. Over the past several years, economists including ourselves have explored that basic insight and found that thinking of investments as options substantially changes the theory and practice of decision making about capital investment. Traditionally, business schools have taught managers to operate on the premise that investment decisions can be reversed if conditions change or, if they cannot be reversed, that they are now-or-never propositions. But as soon as you begin thinking of investment opportunities as options, the premise changes. Irreversibility, uncertainty, and the choice of timing alter the investment decision in critical ways.

The purpose of our article is to examine the shortcomings of the conventional approaches to decision making about investment and to present a better framework for thinking about capital investment decisions. Any theory of investment needs to address the following question: How should a corporate manager facing uncertainty over future market conditions decide whether to invest in a new project? Most business schools teach future managers a simple rule to apply to such problems. First, calculate the present value of the expected stream of cash that the investment will generate. Then, calculate the present value of the stream of expenditures required to undertake the project. And, finally, determine the difference between the two—the net present value (NPV) of the investment. If it's greater than zero, the rule tells the manager to go ahead and invest.

Of course, putting NPV into practice requires managers to resolve some key issues early on. How should you estimate the expected stream of operating profits from the investment? How do you factor in taxes and inflation? And, perhaps most critical, what discount rate or rates should you use? In working out those issues, managers sometimes run into complications. But the basic approach is fairly straightforward: calculating the net present value of an investment project and determining whether it is positive or negative.

Unfortunately, this basic principle is often wrong. Although the NPV rule is relatively easy to apply, it is built on faulty assumptions. It assumes one of two things: either that the investment is reversible (in other words, that it can somehow be undone and the expenditures recovered should market conditions turn out to be worse than anticipated); or that, if the investment is *ir*reversible, it is a now-or-never proposition (if the company does not make the investment now, it will lose the opportunity forever).

Although it is true that some investment decisions fall into those categories, most don't. In most cases, investments are irreversible and, in reality, capable of being delayed. A growing body of research shows that the ability to delay an irreversible investment expenditure can profoundly affect the decision to invest. Ability to delay also undermines the validity of the net present value rule. Thus, for analyzing investment decisions, we need to establish a richer framework, one that enables managers to address the issues of irreversibility, uncertainty, and timing more directly.

Instead of assuming that investments are either reversible or that they cannot be delayed, the recent research on investment stresses the fact that companies have *opportunities* to invest and that they must decide how to exploit those opportunities most effectively. The research is based on an important analogy with financial options. A company with an opportunity to invest is holding something much like a financial call option: It has the right but not the obligation to buy an asset (namely, the entitlement to the stream of profits from the project) at a future time of its choosing. When a company makes an irreversible investment expenditure, it "exercises," in effect, its call option. So the problem of how to exploit an investment opportunity boils down to this: How does the company exercise that option optimally? Academics and financial professionals have been studying the valuation and optimal exercising of financial options for the past two decades.[1] Thus we can draw from a large body of knowledge about financial options.

The recent research on investment offers a number of valuable insights into how managers can evaluate opportunities, and it highlights a basic weakness of the NPV rule. When a company exercises its option by making an irreversible investment, it effectively "kills" the option. In other words, by deciding to go ahead with an expenditure, the company gives up the possibility of waiting for new information that might affect the desirability or timing of the investment; it cannot disinvest should market conditions change adversely. The lost option value is an opportunity cost that must be included as part of the cost of the investment. Thus the simple NPV rule needs to be modified: Instead of just being positive, the present value of the expected stream of cash from a project must exceed the cost of the project by an amount equal to the value of keeping the investment option alive.[2]

Numerous studies have shown that the cost of investing in an opportunity can be large and that investment rules that ignore the expense can lead the investor astray. The opportunity cost is highly sensitive to uncertainty over the future value of the project; as a result, new economic conditions that may affect the perceived riskiness of future cash flows can have a large impact on investment spending—much larger than, say, a change in interest rates. Viewing investment as an option puts greater emphasis on the role of risk and less emphasis on interest rates and other financial variables. (See "Irreversibility and Uncertainty in Everyday Life.")

Irreversibility and Uncertainty in Everyday Life

The decisions that individuals face in their personal lives do not typically involve billions of dollars. In many cases, the highest costs and the biggest benefits are emotional. However, we have found that the option view of investment can be applied fruitfully to all sorts of personal choices and that presenting examples that are "closer to home" can help individuals get a firmer grasp of the central ideas.

For example, one's career choice is a major and largely irreversible decision, which is made in the face of considerable uncertainty about the future prospects of one's chosen sector, one's skill in it, one's future enjoyment of it, and so on. Examples of large-scale mistakes are legendary. In the 1950s, many bright students chose physics as an exciting and rewarding career, only to find that a surplus of physicists developed in the 1970s. There are signs that the same may happen to today's medical students during the next two decades.

The option view suggests appropriate caution. First, it suggests proceeding in steps. For example, instead of committing oneself in the freshman year of college to a specialized program that leads only to medical school, one should follow a more general program to acquire a more flexible set of skills and find out more about one's own tastes. As one acquires that information and gathers more data about the likely career prospects in medicine versus, say, chemical engineering, one can gradually fine-tune decisions about the appropriate direction. Second, one should not take the final and irreversible plunge into a very specialized line unless the rate of return to the investment is sufficiently greater than the cost, with high enough rewards to justify killing the option of flexibility.

Marriage is another decision that can be analyzed in the same manner. It is costly to reverse, and there is significant uncertainty about future happiness or misery. Therefore, one should enter into it with due caution and only when the expected return is sufficiently high. The criteria should become stiffer as the social costs of separation increase: for example, in some religions or cultures. Courtship is the equivalent of exploratory or R&D investment. Even if the expected return is not very high, one should be willing to undertake courtship because it creates a valuable option— namely the opportunity but not the obligation to follow up or not to, according to the information revealed by the initial steps.

Another problem with the conventional NPV rule is that it ignores the value of creating options. Sometimes an investment that appears uneconomical when viewed in isolation may, in fact, create options that enable the company to undertake other investments in the future should market conditions turn favorable. An example is research and development. By not accounting properly for the options that R&D investments may yield, naïve NPV analyses lead companies to invest too little.

Option value has important implications for managers as they think about their investment decisions. For example, it is often highly desirable to delay an investment decision and wait for more information about market conditions, even though a standard analysis indicates that the investment is economical right now. On the other hand, there may be situations in which uncertainty over future market conditions should prompt a company to speed up certain investments. Such is the case when the investments create additional options that give a company the ability (although not the obligation) to do additional future investing. R&D could lead to patents, for example; land purchases could lead to development of mineral reserves. A company might also choose to speed up investments that would yield information and thereby reduce uncertainty.

As a practical matter, many managers seem to understand already that there is something wrong with the simple NPV rule as it is taught—that there is a value to waiting for more information and that this value is not reflected in the standard calculation. In fact, managers often require that an NPV be more than merely positive. In many cases, they insist that it be positive even when it is calculated using a discount rate that is much higher than their company's cost of capital. Some people have argued that when managers insist on extremely high rates of return they are being myopic. But we think there is another explanation. It may be that managers understand a company's options are valuable and that it is often desirable to keep those options open.

In order to understand the thought processes such managers may be using, it is useful to step back and examine the NPV rule and how it is used. For anyone analyzing an investment decision using NPV, two basic issues need to be addressed: first, how to determine the expected stream of profits that the proposed project will generate and the expected stream of costs required to implement the project; and, second, how to choose the discount rate for the purpose of calculating net present value. Textbooks don't have a lot to say about the best way to calculate the profit and cost streams. In practice, managers often seek a *consensus* projection or use an average of high, medium, and low estimates. But however they determine the expected streams of profits and costs, managers are often unaware of making an implicit faulty assumption. The assumption is that the construction or development will begin at a fixed point in time, usually the present. In effect, the NPV rule assumes a fixed scenario in which a company starts and completes a project, which then generates a cash flow during some expected lifetime—without *any* contingencies. Most important, the rule anticipates no contingency for delaying the project or abandoning it if market conditions turn sour. Instead, the NPV rule compares investing today with *never* investing. A more useful comparison, however, would examine a range of possibilities: investing today, or waiting and perhaps investing next year, or waiting longer and perhaps investing in two years, and so on.

As for selecting the discount rate, a low discount rate gives more weight to cash flows that a project is expected to earn in the distant future. On the other hand, a high discount rate gives distant cash flows much less weight and hence makes the company appear more myopic in its evaluation of potential investment projects.

Introductory corporate-finance courses give the subject of selecting discount rates considerable attention. Students are generally taught that the correct discount rate is simply the opportunity cost of capital for the particular project—that is, the expected rate of return that could be earned from an investment of similar risk. In principle, the opportunity cost would reflect the nondiversifiable, or *systematic,* risk that is associated with the particular project. That risk might have characteristics that differ from those of the company's other individual projects or from its average investment activity. In practice, however, the opportunity cost of a specific project may be hard to measure. As a result, students learn that a company's weighted average cost of capital (WACC) is a reasonable substitute. The WACC offers a good approximation as long as the company's projects do not differ greatly from one another in their nondiversifiable risk.[3]

Most students leave business school with what appears to be a simple and powerful tool for making investment decisions: Estimate the expected cash flows for a project; use the company's weighted average cost of capital (perhaps adjusted up or down to reflect the risk characteristics of the particular project) to calculate the project's NPV; and then, if the result is positive, proceed with the investment.

But both academic research and anecdotal evidence bear out time and again the hesitancy of managers to apply NPV in the manner they have been taught. For example, in a 1987 study, Harvard economist Lawrence Summers found that companies were using hurdle rates ranging from 8% to 30%, with a median of 15% and a mean of 17%. Allowing for the deductibility of interest expenses, the nominal interest rate during the period in question was only 4%, and the real rate was close to zero. Although the hurdle rate appropriate for investment with a nondiversifiable risk usually exceeds the riskless rate, it is not enough to justify the large discrepancies found. More recent studies have confirmed that managers regularly and consciously set hurdle rates that are often three or four times their weighted average cost of capital.[4]

Evidence from corporate *dis*investment decisions is also consistent with that analysis. In many industries, companies stay in business and absorb large operating losses for long periods, even though a conventional NPV analysis would indicate that it makes sense to close down a factory or go out of business. Prices can fall far below average variable cost without inducing significant disinvestment or exit from the business. In the mid-1980s, for example, many U.S. farmers saw prices drop drastically, as did producers of copper, aluminum, and other metals. Most did not disinvest, and their behavior can be explained easily once irreversibility and option value are taken into account. Closing a plant or going out of business would have meant an irreversible loss of tangible and intangible capital: The specialized skills that workers had developed would have disappeared as they dispersed to different industries and localities, brand name recognition would have faded, and so on. If market conditions had improved soon after and operations could have resumed profitably, the cost of reassembling the capital would have been high. Continuing to operate keeps the capital intact and preserves the option to resume profitable production later. The option is valuable, and, therefore, companies may quite rationally choose to retain it, even at the cost of losing money in the meantime.

The slow response of U.S. imports to changes in the exchange rate during the early 1980s is another example of how managers deviate from the NPV rule. From mid-1980 to the end of 1984, the real value of the U.S. dollar increased by about 50%. As a result, the ability of foreign companies to compete in the U.S. market soared. But the volume of imports did not begin to rise substantially until the beginning of 1983, when the stronger dollar was already well established. In the first quarter of 1985, the dollar began to weaken; by the end of 1987, it had almost declined to its 1978 level. However, import volume did not decline for another two years; in fact, it rose a little. Once established in the U.S. market, foreign companies were slow to scale back or close their export operations when the exchange rate moved unfavorably. That behavior might seem inconsistent with traditional investment theory, but it is easy to understand in the light of irreversibility and option value: The companies were willing to suffer temporary losses to retain their foothold in the U.S. market and keep alive their option to operate profitably in the future if the value of the dollar rose.

So far, we have focused on managers who seem shortsighted when they make investment decisions, and we have offered a.1 explanation based on the value of the option for waiting and investing later. But some managers appear to override the NPV rule in the opposite direction. For example, entrepreneurs sometimes invest in seemingly risky projects that would be difficult to justify by a conventional NPV calculation using an appropriately risk-adjusted cost of capital. Such projects generally involve R&D or some other type of exploratory investment. Again, we suggest that option theory provides a helpful explanation because the goal of the investments is to reveal information about technological possibilities, production costs, or market potential. Armed with this new information, entrepreneurs can decide whether to proceed with production. In other words, the exploratory investment creates a valuable option. Once the value of the option is reflected in the returns from the initial investment, it may turn out to have been justified, even though a conventional NPV calculation would not have found it attractive.

Before proceeding, we should elaborate on what we mean by the notions of irreversibility, ability to delay an investment, and option to invest. What makes an investment expenditure irreversible? And how do companies obtain their options to invest?

Investment expenditures are irreversible when they are specific to a company or to an industry. For example, most investments in marketing and advertising are company specific and cannot be recovered. They are sunk costs. A steel plant, on the other hand, is industry specific in that it cannot be used to produce anything but steel. One might think that, because in principle the plant could be sold to another steel producer, investment in a plant is recoverable and is not a sunk cost. But that is not necessarily true. If the industry is reasonably competitive, then the value of the plant will be approximately the same for all steel companies, so there is little to be gained from selling it. The potential purchaser of the steel plant will realize that the seller has been unable to make money at current prices and considers the plant a bad investment. If the potential buyer agrees that it's a bad investment, the owner's ability to sell the plant will not be worth much. Therefore, an investment in a steel plant (or any other industry-specific capital project) should be viewed largely as a sunk cost: that is, irreversible.

Even investments that are not company or industry specific are often partly irreversible because buyers of used equipment, unable to evaluate the quality of an item, will generally offer to pay a price that corresponds to the average quality in the market. Sellers who know the quality of the item they are selling will resist unloading above-average merchandise at a reduced price. The average quality of used equipment available in the market will go down and, therefore, so will the market price. Thus cars, trucks, office equipment, and computers (items that are not industry specific and can be sold to buyers in other industries) are apt to have resale values that are well below their original purchase costs, even if they are almost new.

Irreversibility can also arise because of government regulations, institutional arrangements, or differences in corporate culture. For example, capital controls may make it impossible for foreign (or domestic) investors to sell their assets and reallocate their funds. By the same token, investments in new workers may be partly irreversible because of the high costs of hiring, training, and firing. Hence most major investments are to a large extent irreversible.

The recognition that capital investment decisions can be irreversible gives the ability to delay investments added significance. In reality, companies do not always have the opportunity to delay their investments. For example, strategic considerations can make it imperative for a business to invest quickly in order to preempt investment by existing or potential competitors. In most cases, though, it is at least feasible to delay. There may be a cost—the risk of entry by other companies or the loss of cash flows—but the cost can be weighed against the benefits of waiting for new information. And those benefits are often substantial.

We have argued that an irreversible investment opportunity is like a financial call option. The holder of the call option has the right, for a specified period, to pay an exercise price and to receive in return an asset—for example, a share of stock—that has some value. Exercising the option is irreversible; although the asset can be sold to another investor, one cannot retrieve the option or the money that was paid to exercise it. Similarly, a company with an investment opportunity has the option to spend money now or in the future (the exercise price) in return for an asset of some value (the project). Again, the asset can be sold to another company, but the investment itself is irreversible. As with the financial call option, the option to make a capital investment is valuable in part because it is impossible to know the future value of the asset obtained by investing. If the asset rises in value, the net payoff from investing increases. If the value declines, the company can decide not to invest and will lose only what it has spent to obtain the investment opportunity. As long as there are *some* contingencies under which the company would prefer not to invest, that is, when there is some probability that the investment would result in a loss, the opportunity to delay the decision—and thus to keep the option alive—has value. The question, then, is when to exercise the option. The choice of the most appropriate time is the essence of the optimal investment decision.

Recognizing that an investment opportunity is like a financial call option can help managers understand the crucial role uncertainty plays in the timing of capital investment decisions. With a financial call option, the more volatile the price of the stock on which the option is written, the more valuable the option and the greater the incentive to wait and keep the option alive rather than exercise it. This is true because of the asymmetry in the option's net payoffs: The higher the stock price rises, the greater the net payoff from exercising the option; however, if the stock price falls, one can lose only what one paid for the option.

The same goes for capital investment opportunities. The greater the uncertainty over the potential profitability of the investment, the greater the value of the opportunity and the greater the incentive to wait and to keep the opportunity alive rather than exercise it by investing at once. Of course, uncertainty also plays a role in the conventional NPV rule—the fact that a risk is nondiversifiable creates an uncertainty that is added on to the discount rate used to compute present values. But in the option view of investment, uncertainty is far more important and fundamental. A small increase in uncertainty (nondiversifiable or otherwise) can lead managers to delay some investments (those that involve the exercising of options, such as the construction of a factory). At the same time, uncertainty can prompt managers to accelerate other investments (those that generate options or reveal information, such as R&D programs).

In addition to understanding the role of irreversibility and uncertainty, it is also important to understand how companies obtain their investment opportunities (their options to invest) in the first place. Sometimes investment opportunities result from patents or from ownership of land or natural resources. In such cases, the opportunities are probably the result of earlier investments. Generally, however, investment opportunities flow from a company's managerial resources, technological knowledge, reputation, market position, and possible scale, each of which may have been built up gradually. Such resources enable the company to undertake in a productive way investments that individuals or other companies cannot undertake.

Regardless of where a company gets its options to invest, the options are valuable. Indeed, a substantial part of the market value of most companies can be attributed to their options to invest and grow in the future, as opposed to the capital they already have in place. That is particularly true for companies in very volatile and unpredictable industries, such as electronics, telecommunications, and biotechnology. Most of the economic and financial theory of investment has focused on how companies should (and do) exercise their options to invest. But managers also need to understand how their companies can obtain investment opportunities in the first place. The knowledge will help them devise better long-term competitive strategies to determine how to focus and direct their R&D, how much to bid for mineral rights, how early to stake out competitive positions, and so on.

To illustrate the implications of the option theory of investment and the problems inherent in the traditional net present value rule, let us work through the process of making a capital investment decision at a hypothetical pharmaceutical company.

Suppose that you are the CEO of a company considering the development and production of a new drug. Both the costs and the revenues from the venture are highly uncertain. The costs will depend on, among other things, the purity of the output of the chemical process and the compound's overall effectiveness. The revenues will depend on the company's ability to find a principal market for the compound (and for whatever secondary uses might be discovered) and the time frame within which rival companies are able to introduce similar products.

Suppose that you must decide whether to make an initial investment of $15 million in R&D. You realize that later, if you decide to continue the project, additional money will have to be invested in a production facility. There are three possible scenarios for the cost of production: low ($40 million), middle ($80 million), and high ($120 million). To keep matters simple, we will assume that each of the scenarios is equally likely (in other words, that each has a $1/3$ probability of occurring). Let us also assume that there are two equally likely cases for the revenue (probability $1/2$ each): low ($50 million) and high ($130 million). To focus on the question of how uncertainty and option values modify the usual NPV analysis and to keep the example simple, we will also assume that the time frame is short enough that the usual discounting to reflect the time value of money can be ignored.

Should you make the $15 million investment in R&D? First, let us analyze the problem by using a simple NPV approach. The expected value (i.e., the probability-weighted average) of the cost of the production facility is ($\frac{1}{3}$ × $40 million) + ($\frac{1}{3}$ × $80 million) + ($\frac{1}{3}$ × $120 million) = $80 million. Likewise, the expected value of the revenue is ($\frac{1}{2}$ × $50 million) + ($\frac{1}{2}$ × $130 million) = $90 million. Therefore, the expected value of the operating profit is $10 million, which does not justify the expenditure of $15 million on R&D. So the conventional thinking would kill the project at the outset.

However, suppose that by doing the R&D, you are able to narrow the uncertainty by finding out which of the three possibilities for the cost of the production facility is closest to reality. After learning about the cost, you would be able to make a decision to go ahead and continue the project or to drop it. Thus the $15 million you invest in R&D creates an option—a right with no obligation to proceed with the actual production and marketing.

For a moment, we will put aside the market uncertainty and suppose that the revenue will always be $90 million. If the high-cost ($120 million) scenario is the one that materializes, you will decide not to proceed with the production, and your operating profit will be zero. In the other two cases, however, you will proceed. The operating profit is $90 million − $80 million = $10 million in the middle-cost case and $90 million − $40 million = $50 million in the low-cost case. The probability-weighted average of your operating profit across all three possible outcomes is ($\frac{1}{3}$ × 0) + ($\frac{1}{3}$ × $10 million) + ($\frac{1}{3}$ × $50 million) = $20 million. That exceeds your research and development cost of $15 million, and, therefore, the investment in R&D would be justified.

The logic shows that an action to *create* an option should be valued more highly than a naïve NPV approach would suggest. The gap between the naïve calculation and the correct one arises because the option itself is valuable. You can exercise it selectively when doing so is to your advantage, and you can let it lapse when exercising it would be unprofitable. The amount that an option should be valued over and above the $10 million expected profit (calculated on the assumption of immediate go-ahead) depends on the sizes and the probabilities of the losses that you are able to avoid.

Now let us reintroduce the notion of uncertainty with regard to the expected revenue. Suppose that you have found out that the middle-cost scenario ($80 million) is the reality. If you need to make a go-or-no-go decision about production at this point, you will choose to proceed because the expected revenue of ($\frac{1}{2}$ × $130 million) + ($\frac{1}{2}$ × $50 million) = $90 million exceeds the production cost of $80 million, resulting in an operating profit of $10 million. But suppose you can postpone the production decision until you have found out the true market potential. By waiting, you can choose to go ahead only if the revenue is high, and you can avoid the loss-making case where the revenue turns out to be low. If revenue is high (which occurs with probability $\frac{1}{2}$), you will earn an operating profit of $130 million − $80 million = $50 million, and if revenue is low (also probability $\frac{1}{2}$), you will earn zero, for an average or expected value of $25 million, which is more than the $10 million you would get if you went ahead at once.

Here the opportunity to proceed with production is like a call option. Making a go-or-no-go decision amounts to exercising that option. If you can identify some eventualities that would cause you to rethink a go-ahead decision (such as a drop in market demand for your product), then the ability to wait and avoid those eventualities is valuable: The option has a time value or a holding premium. The fact that the option is "in the money" (going ahead would yield a positive NPV) does not necessarily mean that you should exercise the option (in this case, proceeding with production). Instead, you should wait until the option is deeper in the money—that is, until the net present value of going ahead is large enough to offset the loss of the value of the option.

In this example, we have intentionally left out any explicit cost of waiting. But you can easily include potential waiting costs in the calculation. Suppose that while you wait to gauge the market potential, a rival will grab $20 million worth of your anticipated revenues. The revenues under your most favorable scenario will be only $110 million and under the unfavorable one only $30 million. Now, if you wait, you can expect an outcome of $110 million − $80 million = $30 million with probability $\frac{1}{2}$ and an outcome of zero with probability $\frac{1}{2}$, for an expected value of $15 million. That is still better than the $10 million you get if you go ahead at once.

There's an important lesson here: Just as an action that creates an option needs to be valued more than the NPV analysis would indicate, an action that *exercises* or *uses up* an option should be valued *less* than a simple NPV approach would suggest. The reason is that the option itself is valuable. You can exercise an option selectively when the action is to your advantage, or you can let it lapse when such a course would be unprofitable. Again, the extra value gain depends on the sizes and the probabilities of the losses you are able to avoid.

It is even possible to put the revenue uncertainty and the cost uncertainty together. Thus if the R&D investment reveals that costs will be at the high end, you should again wait for the resolution of the revenue uncertainty before you proceed, earning $\frac{1}{2} \times$ ($130 million − $120 million) = $5 million. If the costs fall in the middle, it is best to wait, as we saw above; the expected operating profit will be $25 million. If the cost is at the low end ($40 million), however, the operating profit is positive at both revenue levels. In that case, it is best to proceed with production at once because the expected profit is ($\frac{1}{2} \times$ $130 million) + ($\frac{1}{2} \times$ $50 million) − $40 million = $50 million. The proper calculation for NPV that results from the $15 million R&D investment is ($\frac{1}{3} \times$ $5 million) + ($\frac{1}{3} \times$ $25 million) + ($\frac{1}{3} \times$ $50 million) = $26.7 million, which is even bigger than the $20 million we calculated when we left out the revenue uncertainty. We are now valuing the production options correctly, whereas earlier we assumed, in effect, that those options would be exercised immediately; in the high-cost and middle-cost scenarios, exercising the options wouldn't have been optimal.

All of the numbers in this pharmaceutical example were chosen to facilitate simple calculations. But the basic ideas represented in the case can be applied in a variety of real-life situations. As long as there are contingencies under which the company would not wish to proceed to production, the R&D that conveys information about which contingency will materialize creates an option. And insofar as there is a positive probability that production would be unprofitable, building the plant (rather than waiting) exercises an option.

The option theory of investing also has clear implications for companies attempting to raise capital. If financial market participants understand the nature of the options correctly, they will place greater value on the investments that *create* options, and they will be more hesitant to finance those that *exercise* options. Therefore, as the pharmaceutical company proceeds from exploratory R&D (which creates options) to production and marketing (which exercises them), it will find the hurdle rate rising and sources of eager venture capital drying up. It is interesting to note that this is exactly what has been going on recently in the biotechnology industry as it has progressed from searching for several new products to trying to exploit the few it has found.[5] The increased difficulty of finding venture capital for biotechnology can be explained in other ways—disappointments over earlier biotechnology products, problems securing and enforcing patents, the risk of a health care cost crunch, to name a few. But we believe that, to a large extent, the market is making an astute differentiation between the creation of options and the exercising of options.

As companies in a broad range of industries are learning, opportunities to apply option theory to investments are numerous. Below are a few examples to illustrate the kinds of insight that the options theory of investment can provide.

INVESTMENTS IN OIL RESERVES. Nowhere is the idea of investments as options better illustrated than in the context of decisions to acquire and exploit deposits of natural resources. A company that buys deposits is buying an asset that it can develop immediately or later, depending on market conditions. The asset, then, is an option—an opportunity to choose the future development timetable of the deposit. A company can speed up production when the price is high, and it can slow it down or suspend it altogether when the price is low. Ignoring the option and valuing the entire reserve at today's price (or at future prices following a preset rate of output) can lead to a significant underestimation of the value of the asset.

The U.S. government regularly auctions off leases for offshore tracts of land, and oil companies perform valuations as part of their bidding process. The sums involved are huge—an individual oil company can easily bid hundreds of millions of dollars. It should not be surprising, then, that unless a company understands how to value an undeveloped oil reserve as an option, it may overpay, or it may lose some very valuable tracts to rival bidders.[6]

Consider what would happen if an oil company manager tried to value an undeveloped oil reserve using the standard NPV approach. Depending on the current price of oil, the expected rate of change of the price, and the cost of developing the reserve, he might construct a scenario for the timing of development and hence the timing (and size) of the future cash flows from production. He would then value the reserve by discounting these numbers and adding them together. Because oil price uncertainty is not completely diversifiable, the greater the perceived volatility of oil prices, the higher the discount rate that he would use; the higher the discount rate, the lower the estimated value of the undeveloped reserve.

But that would grossly underestimate the value of the reserve. It completely ignores the flexibility that the company has regarding when to develop the reserve—that is, when to exercise the reserve's option value. And note that, just as options are more valuable when there is more uncertainty about future contingencies, the oil reserve is more valuable when the price of oil is more volatile. The result would be just the opposite of what a standard NPV calculation would tell us: In contrast to the standard calculation, which says that greater uncertainty over oil prices should lead to less investment in undeveloped oil reserves, option theory tells us it should lead to *more*.

By treating an undeveloped oil reserve as an option, we can value it correctly, and we can also determine when is the best time to invest in the development of the reserve. Developing the reserve is like exercising a call option, and the exercise price is the cost of development. The greater the uncertainty over oil prices, the longer an oil company should hold undeveloped reserves and keep alive its option to develop them.

SCALE VERSUS FLEXIBILITY IN UTILITY PLANNING. The option view of investment can also help companies value flexibility in their capacity expansion plans. Should a company commit itself to a large amount of production capacity, or should it retain flexibility by investing slowly and keeping its options for growth open? Although many businesses confront the problem, it is particularly important for electric utilities, whose expansion plans must balance the advantages of building large-scale plants with the advantages of investing slowly and maintaining flexibility.

Economies of scale can be an important source of cost savings for companies. By building one large plant instead of two or three smaller ones, companies might be able to reduce their average unit cost while increasing profitability. Perhaps companies should respond to growth opportunities by bunching their investments—that is, investing in new capacity only infrequently but adding large and efficient plants each time. But what should managers do when demand growth is uncertain, as it often is? If the company makes an irreversible investment in a large addition to capacity and then demand grows slowly or even shrinks, it will find itself burdened with capital it doesn't need. When the growth of demand is uncertain, there is a trade-off between scale economies and the flexibility that is gained by investing more frequently in small additions to capacity as they are needed.

Electric utilities typically find that it is much cheaper per unit of capacity to build large coal-fired power plants than it is to add capacity in small amounts. But at the same time, utilities face considerable uncertainty about how fast demand will grow and what the fuel to generate the electricity will cost. Adding capacity in small amounts gives the utility flexibility, but it is also more costly. As a result, knowing how to value the flexibility becomes very important. The options approach is well suited to the purpose.

For example, suppose a utility is choosing between a large coal-fired plant that will provide enough capacity for demand growth over the next 10 to 15 years or adding small oil-fired generators, each of which will provide for about a year's worth of demand growth as needed. The utility faces uncertainty over demand growth and over the relative prices of coal and oil in the future. Even if a straightforward NPV calculation favors the large coal-fired plant, that does not mean that it is the more economical alternative. The reason is that if it were to invest in the coal-fired plant, the utility would commit itself to a large amount of capacity and to a particular fuel. In so doing, it would give up its options to grow more slowly (should demand grow more slowly than expected) or to grow with at least some of the added capacity fueled by oil (should oil prices, at some future date, fall relative to coal prices). By valuing the options using option-pricing techniques, the utility can assess the importance of the flexibility that small oil-fired generators would provide.

Utilities are finding that the value of flexibility can be large and that standard NPV methods that ignore flexibility can be extremely misleading. A number of utilities have begun to use option-pricing techniques for long-term capacity planning. The New England Electric System (NEES), for example, has been especially innovative in applying the approach to investment planning. Among other things, the company has used option-pricing techniques to show that an investment in the repowering of a hydroelectric plant should be delayed, even though the conventional NPV calculation for the project is positive. It has also used the approach to value contract provisions for the purchase of electric capacity and to determine when to retire a generating unit.[7]

PRICE VOLATILITY IN COMMODITIES. Commodity prices are notorious for their volatility. Copper prices, for example, have been known to double or drop by half in the space of several months. Why are copper prices so volatile, and how should producers decide whether to open new mines and refineries or to close old ones in response to price changes? The options approach to investment helps provide answers to such questions.

Investment and disinvestment in the copper industry involve large sunk costs. Building a new copper mine, smelter, or refinery involves a large-scale commitment of financial resources. Given the volatility of copper prices, managers understand that there is value to waiting for more information before committing resources, even if the current price of copper is relatively high. As we showed in the earlier pharmaceutical example, a positive NPV is not sufficient to justify investment. The price of copper and, correspondingly, the NPV of a new copper mine must be high enough to cover the opportunity cost of giving up the option to wait. The same is true with disinvestment. Once a mine, smelter, or refinery is closed, it cannot be reopened easily. As a result, managers will keep these facilities open even if they are losing money at current prices. They recognize that by closing a facility, they incur an opportunity cost of giving up the option to wait for higher future prices. Thus many copper mines built during the 1970s, when copper prices were high, were kept open during the mid-1980s, when copper prices fell to their lowest levels in real terms since the Great Depression.

Given the large sunk costs involved in building or closing copper-producing facilities and given the volatility of copper prices, it is essential to account for option value when making investment decisions. In reality, copper prices must rise far above the point of positive NPV to justify building new facilities and fall far below average variable cost to justify closing down existing facilities. Outside observers might see that approach as a form of myopia. We believe, however, that it reflects a rational response to option value.

Understanding option value and its implications for irreversible investment in the copper industry can also help us understand why copper prices are so volatile in the first place. Corporate inertia in building and closing down facilities feeds back into prices. Suppose that the demand for copper rises in response to higher-than-average GNP growth, causing the price of copper to rise. Knowing that the price might fall later, producers typically wait rather than respond immediately with new additions to capacity. Since greater supply is not readily forthcoming, the pressure of demand translates into rapid increases in price. Similarly, during downturns in demand, as mines remain open to preserve their options, the price collapses. Recent history has illustrated this phenomenon: The reluctance of producers to close mines during the mid-1980s, when demand was weak, allowed the price to fall even more than it would have otherwise. Thus the reaction of producers to price volatility in turn sustains the magnitude of price volatility, and any underlying fluctuations of demands or costs will appear in an exaggerated way as price fluctuations.

The economic environment in which most companies must now operate is far more volatile and unpredictable than it was 20 years ago—in part because of growing globalization of markets coupled with increases in exchange-rate fluctuations, in part because of more rapid technology-induced changes in the marketplace. Whatever its cause, however, uncertainty requires that managers become much more sophisticated in the ways they assess and account for risk. It's important for managers to get a better understanding of the options that their companies have or that they are able to create. Ultimately, options create flexibility, and, in an uncertain world, the ability to value and use flexibility is critical.

Decisions that enhance a company's flexibility by creating and preserving options (decisions, for example, about R&D and test marketing) have value that transcends a naïve calculation of NPV. More readily than conventional calculations suggest, managers should make decisions that increase flexibility. Choices that reduce flexibility by exercising options and committing resources to irreversible uses (construction of specific plants and equipment, advertising of particular products) will be valued less than their conventional NPV. Such choices should be made more hesitantly—and subjected to stiffer hurdle rates than the cost of capital—or delayed until circumstances are exceptionally favorable.

The bottom line for managers is that learning how to apply the net present value rule is not sufficient. To make intelligent investment choices, managers need to consider the value of keeping their options open. In this case, we don't think there is any option.

Notes

1. For an overview of financial options and their valuation, see John C. Cox and Mark Rubinstein, *Options Markets* (Englewood Cliffs, N.J.: Prentice-Hall, 1985); John C. Hull, *Options, Futures, and Other Derivative Securities* (Englewood, Cliffs, N.J.: Prentice-Hall, 1989); or Hans R. Stoll and Robert E. Whaley, *Futures and Options: Theory and Applications* (Cincinnati, Ohio: South-Western Publishing Co., 1993).

2. Of course, one can always redefine NPV by subtracting from the conventional calculation the opportunity cost of exercising the option

to invest and then saying that the rule "invest if NPV is positive" holds. But to do so is to accept our criticism. To highlight the importance of valuing the option, we prefer to keep it separate from the conventional NPV. But if others prefer to continue to use positive NPV terminology, they should be careful to include all relevant option values in their definition of NPV.

3. For a more comprehensive discussion of the standard techniques of capital budgeting, see a corporate finance textbook such as Richard A. Brealey and Stewart C. Myers, *Principles of Corporate Finance* (New York: McGraw-Hill, 1991).

4. See Lawrence H. Summers, "Investment Incentives and the Discounting of Depreciation Allowances," in *The Effects of Taxation on Capital Accumulation,* ed. Martin Feldstein (University of Chicago Press, 1987), 300; James M. Poterba and Lawrence H. Summers, "Time Horizons of American Firms: New Evidence from a Survey of CEOs" (MIT Working Paper, October 1991); Michael L. Dertouzos, Richard K. Lester, Robert M. Solow, and the MIT Commission on Industrial Productivity, *Made in America* (Harper Paperback, 1990), 61; and Robert H. Hayes and David A. Garvin, "Managing As If Tomorrow Mattered," *Harvard Business Review* May–June 1982, 70–9.

5. See "Panic in the Petri Dish," *The Economist,* July 23, 1994, pp. 61–2.

6. The application of option theory to offshore petroleum reserves was pioneered by James L. Paddock, Daniel R. Siegel, and James L. Smith, "Option Valuation of Claims on Real Assets: The Case of Offshore Petroleum Leases," *Quarterly Journal of Economics* 103, August 1988, 479–508.

7. For a more detailed discussion of utility industry applications and NEES's experience in this area, see Thomas Kaslow and Robert S. Pindyck, "Valuing Flexibility in Utility Planning," *The Electricity Journal* 7, March 1994, 60–5.

3

When Is Virtual Virtuous? Organizing for Innovation

Henry W. Chesbrough and David J. Teece

Champions of virtual corporations are urging managers to subcontract anything and everything. All over the world, companies are jumping on the bandwagon, decentralizing, downsizing, and forging alliances to pursue innovation. Why is the idea of the virtual organization so tantalizing? Because we have come to believe that bureaucracy is bad and flexibility is good. And so it follows that a company that invests in as little as possible will be more responsive to a changing marketplace and more likely to attain global competitive advantage.

There is no question that many large and cumbersome organizations have been outperformed by smaller "networked" competitors. Consider the eclipse of IBM in PCs and of DEC in workstations by Packard Bell and Sun Microsystems. But while there are many successful virtual companies, there are even more failures that don't make the headlines. After many years of studying the relationship between organization and innovation, we believe that the virtues of being virtual have been oversold. The new conventional wisdom ignores the distinctive role that large integrated companies can play in the innovation process. Those rushing to form alliances instead of nurturing and guarding their own capabilities may be risking their future.

What's Special About Virtual?

What gives the virtual company its advantage? In essence, incentives and responsiveness. Virtual companies coordinate much of their business through the marketplace, where free agents come together to buy and sell one another's goods and services; thus virtual companies can harness the power of market forces to develop, manufacture, market, distribute, and support their offerings in ways that fully integrated companies can't duplicate. As William Joy, vice president of research and development at Sun Microsystems, puts it, "Not all the smart people [in the workstation industry] work for Sun." Because an outside developer of workstation software can obtain greater rewards by selling software to Sun customers than by developing the same software as a Sun employee, he or she will move faster, work harder, and take more risks. Using high-powered, market-based incentives such as stock options and attractive bonuses, a virtual company can quickly access the technical resources it needs, if those resources are available. In situations where technology is changing rapidly, large companies that attempt to do everything inside will flounder when competing against small companies with highly trained and motivated employees.

But the incentives that make a virtual company powerful also leave it vulnerable. As incentives become greater and risk taking increases, coordination among parties through the marketplace becomes more and more difficult, precisely because so much personal reward is at stake. Each party to joint development activity necessarily acts in its own self-interest. Over time, innovation can generate unforeseen surprises that work to the advantage of some parties and to the disadvantage of others. The result: Once-friendly partners may be unwilling or unable to align strategically, and coordinated development activity falters. In contrast, integrated, centralized companies do not generally reward people for taking risks, but they do have established processes for settling conflicts and coordinating all the activities necessary for innovation.

This trade-off between incentives and control lies at the heart of the decision that managers must make about how to organize for innovation. (See Exhibit I.) If virtual organizations and integrated companies are at opposite ends of the spectrum, alliances occupy a kind of organizational middle ground. An alliance can achieve some of the coordination of an integrated company, but, like players in a virtual network, the members of an alliance will be driven to enhance their own positions, and over time their interests may diverge. The challenge for managers is to choose the organizational form that best matches the type of innovation they are pursuing.

Exhibit I.

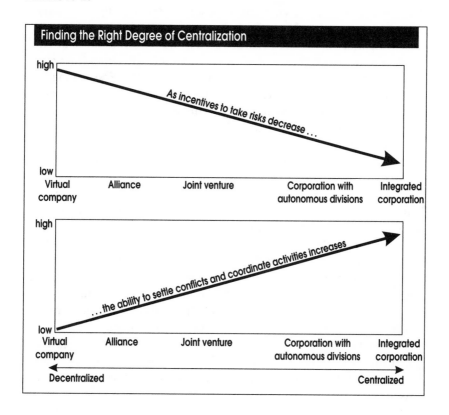

Finding the Right Degree of Centralization

As incentives to take risks decrease . . .

high / low

Virtual company — Alliance — Joint venture — Corporation with autonomous divisions — Integrated corporation

. . . the ability to settle conflicts and coordinate activities increases

high / low

Virtual company — Alliance — Joint venture — Corporation with autonomous divisions — Integrated corporation

Decentralized — Centralized

Types of Innovation

When should companies organize for innovation by using decentralized (or virtual) approaches, and when should they rely on internal organization? The answer depends on the innovation in question.

Some innovations are *autonomous*—that is, they can be pursued independently from other innovations. A new turbocharger to increase horsepower in an automobile engine, for example, can be developed without a complete redesign of the engine or the rest of the car. In contrast, some innovations are fundamentally *systemic*—that is, their benefits can be realized only in conjunction with related, complementary innovations. To profit from instant photography, Polaroid needed to develop both new film technology and new camera technology. Similarly, lean manufacturing is a systemic innovation because it requires interrelated changes in product design, supplier management, information technology, and so on.

The distinction between autonomous and systemic innovation is fundamental to the choice of organizational design. When innovation is autonomous, the decentralized virtual organization can manage the development and commercialization tasks quite well. When innovation is systemic, members of a virtual organization are dependent on the other members, over whom they have no control. In either case, the wrong organizational choice can be costly.

Consider what happened to General Motors when the automobile industry shifted from drum brakes to disc brakes, an autonomous innovation. General Motors was slow to adopt disc brakes because it had integrated vertically in the production of the old technology. GM's more decentralized competitors relied instead on market relationships with their suppliers—and the high-powered incentives inherent in those relationships. As a result, they were able to beat GM to market with the new disc brakes, which car buyers wanted. When companies inappropriately use centralized approaches to manage autonomous innovations, as GM did in this case, small companies and more decentralized large companies will usually outperform them.

To understand why the two types of innovation call for different organizational strategies, consider the information flow essential to innovation. Information about new products and technologies often develops over time as managers absorb new research findings, the results of early product experiments, and initial customer feedback. To commercialize an innovation profitably, a tremendous amount of knowledge from industry players, from customers, and sometimes from scientists must be gathered and understood. This task is easier if the information is codified.

Codified information—for example, specifications that are captured in industry standards and design rules—can often be transferred almost as effectively from one company to another as it can within a single company. Because such information is easily duplicated, it has little natural protection. Sometimes bits and pieces can be protected by intellectual property rights, but those pieces, especially trade secrets and patents, are small islands in a broad ocean of knowledge.

Other information does not travel as easily between companies. Tacit knowledge is knowledge that is implicitly grasped or used but has not been fully articulated, such as the know-how of a master craftsman or the ingrained perspectives of a specific company or work unit.

Because such knowledge is deeply embedded in individuals or companies, it tends to diffuse slowly and only with effort and the transfer of people. Established companies can protect the tacit knowledge they hold, sharing only codified information. They can be quite strategic about what they disclose and when they disclose it.

The information needed to integrate an autonomous innovation with existing technologies is usually well understood and may even be codified in industry standards. Systemic innovations, on the other hand, pose a unique set of management challenges regarding information exchange. By their very nature, systemic innovations require information sharing and coordinated adjustment *throughout an entire product system*. Here is where a market-based, virtual approach to innovation poses serious strategic hazards. Unaffiliated companies linked through arm's-length contracts often cannot achieve sufficient coordination. Each company wants the other to do more, while each is also looking for ways to realize the most gain from the innovation. Information sharing can be reduced or biased, as each seeks to get the most at the other's expense. In most cases, the open exchange of information that fuels systemic innovation will be easier and safer within a company than across company boundaries. The inevitable conflicts and choices that arise as a systemic innovation develops can best be resolved by an integrated company's internal management processes.

The Case of Industry Standards

Coordinating a systemic innovation is particularly difficult when industry standards do not exist and must be pioneered. In such instances, virtual organizations are likely to run into strategic problems. Consider how technical standards emerge. Market participants weigh many competing technologies and eventually rally around one of them. There are winners and losers among the contestants, and potential losers can try to undermine the front-runner or to fragment the standard by promoting a rival. Until a clear winner emerges, customers may choose to sit on the sidelines rather than risk making the wrong choice.

By virtue of its size and scope, an integrated company may be able to advance a new standard simply by choosing to adopt a particular technology. If a large company commits itself to one of a host of competing technologies, consumers as well as companies promoting rival technologies will probably be persuaded to follow suit. Virtual companies, however, which may be struggling to resolve conflicts within their networks, won't be able to break a deadlock in a complicated standards battle. Players in a network won't be able to coordinate themselves to act like a large company.

Once a new standard has been established, virtual organizations can manage further innovation quite well. But when an industry begins to advance technology to a new level, the cycle can begin anew. Again, technically feasible choices present new strategic trade-offs. Suppliers, competitors, and customers may fail to agree on a common path. Unless a big player emerges to break the logjam among rival technologies, the existing standard will prevail long past its usefulness.

Today computer floppy disks are frozen in an old standard because no single company has been able to establish a new one. IBM pioneered the 3.5-inch hard-case diskette in 1987 when it introduced its new line of PS/2 personal computers. Within two years, the memory capacity of 3.5-inch diskettes doubled from 720 kilobytes to 1.44 megabytes, where it has remained ever since.

Why? The technical capability to expand diskette capacity is available, but no company has the reputation and strength to set a new standard. Through the 1980s, IBM was large enough to coordinate standards among the key participants in the industry: personal computer manufacturers, diskette makers, and software publishers. If IBM told the industry it would use a particular capacity on its next generation of machines, others did the same. But in the 1990s, IBM's leadership of the PC market came to an end, perhaps permanently. Today IBM is not strong enough to move the industry by itself, and it won't move ahead of the other industry players and risk being stranded if they don't follow.

A simple rule of thumb applies: When innovation depends on a series of interdependent innovations—that is, when innovation is systemic—independent companies will not usually be able to coordinate themselves to knit those innovations together. Scale, integration, and market leadership may be required to establish and then to advance standards in an industry.

The IBM PC: Virtual Success or Failure?

IBM's development of the personal computer is a fascinating example of both the advantages and disadvantages of using virtual approaches to pursue innovation. When IBM launched its first PC in

1981, the company elected to outsource all the major components from the marketplace. By tapping the capabilities of other companies, IBM was able to get its first product to market in only 15 months. The microprocessor (the 8088) was purchased from Intel, and the operating system (which became PC-DOS) was licensed from a then fledgling software company, Microsoft. In effect, the IBM PC had an "open" architecture: It was based on standards and components that were widely available. The high-powered incentives of the market-place could coordinate the roles of component manufacturers and software vendors. IBM successfully promoted its open architecture to hundreds of third-party developers of software applications and hard-ware accessory products, knowing that those products would add to the appeal of the PC.

IBM also relied on the market to distribute the product. Although IBM launched its own IBM Product Centers as retail storefronts and had its own direct sales force for large corporate customers, the ma-jority of the company's systems were distributed through independent retailers, initially ComputerLand and Sears. Eventually, there were more than 2,000 retail outlets.

By using outside parties for hardware, software, and distribution, IBM greatly reduced its investment in bringing the PC to market. More important, those relationships allowed IBM to launch an attack against Apple, which had pioneered the market and was growing quickly. The IBM PC was an early success, and it spawned what became the dominant architecture of the entire microcomputer industry. By 1984, three years after the introduction of the PC, IBM replaced Apple as the number one supplier of microcomputers, with 26% of the PC business. By 1985, IBM's share had grown to 41%. Many observers attributed the PC's success to IBM's creative use of outside relation-ships. More than a few business analysts hailed the IBM PC develop-ment as a model for doing business in the future.

Indeed, IBM's approach in its PC business is exactly the kind of decentralized strategy that commentators are urging large, slow-mov-ing companies to adopt. The early years of the IBM PC show many of the benefits of using markets and outside companies to coordinate innovation: fast development of technology and tremendous techno-logical improvements from a wide variety of sources.

With the passage of time, though, the downside of IBM's decentral-ized approach has become apparent. IBM failed to anticipate that its virtual and open approach would prevent the company from directing the PC architecture it had created. The open architecture and the autonomy of its vendors invited design mutinies and the entry of IBM-compatible PC manufacturers. At first, competitors struggled to achieve compatibility with IBM's architecture, but after several years compatibility was widespread in the industry. And once that happened, manufacturers could purchase the same CPU from Intel and the same operating system from Microsoft, run the same application software (from Lotus, Microsoft, WordPerfect, and others), and sell through the same distribution channels (such as ComputerLand, BusinessLand, and MicroAge). IBM had little left on which to establish a competitive advantage.

To maintain technological leadership, IBM decided to advance the PC architecture. To do that, IBM needed to coordinate the many interrelated pieces of the architecture—a systemic technology coordination task. However, the third-party hardware and software suppliers that had helped establish the original architecture did not follow IBM's lead. When IBM introduced its OS/2 operating system, the company could not stop Microsoft from introducing Windows, an application that works with the old DOS operating system, thereby greatly reducing the advantages of switching to OS/2. And third-party hardware and software companies made investments that extended the usefulness of the original PC architecture. Similarly, Intel helped Compaq steal a march on IBM in 1986, when Compaq introduced the first PC based on Intel's 80386 microprocessor, an enhancement over the earlier generations of microprocessors used in IBM and compatible machines. Even though IBM owned 12% of Intel at the time, it couldn't prevent Intel from working with Compaq to beat IBM to market. This was the beginning of the end of IBM's ability to direct the evolution of PC architecture.

By the third quarter of 1995, IBM's share of the PC market had fallen to just 7.3%, trailing Compaq's 10.5% share. Today its PC business is rumored to be modestly profitable at best. Most of the profits from the PC architecture have migrated upstream to the supplier of the microprocessor (Intel) and the operating system (Microsoft), and to outside makers of application software. The combined market value of those suppliers and third parties today greatly exceeds IBM's.

IBM's experience in the PC market illustrates the strategic importance of organization in the pursuit of innovation. Virtual approaches encounter serious problems when companies seek to exploit systemic innovation. Key development activities that depend on one another must be conducted in-house to capture the rewards from long-term R & D investments. Without directed coordination, the necessary complementary innovations required to leverage a new technology may not be forthcoming.

The Virtuous Virtuals

How have the most successful virtual companies accomplished the difficult task of coordination? The virtual companies that have demonstrated staying power are all at the center of a network that they use to leverage their own capabilities. Few virtual companies that have survived and prospered have outsourced everything. Rather, the virtuous virtuals have carefully nurtured and guarded the internal capabilities that provide the essential underpinnings of competitive advantage. And they invest considerable resources to maintain and extend their core competencies internally. Indeed, without these companies' unique competencies and capabilities, their strategic position in the network would be short-lived.

Consider the well-known battle between MIPS Technologies and Sun Microsystems for control of workstation processors. (See Benjamin Gomes-Casseres, "Group Versus Group: How Alliance Networks Compete," in *Harvard Business Review,* July–August 1994.) MIPS was trying to promote its Advanced Computing Environment (ACE) against Sun's Scalable Processor Architecture (SPARC). Sun had strong internal capabilities, whereas MIPS tried to compete as a more virtual player, leveraging off of the competencies of partners such as Compaq, DEC, and Silicon Graphics. MIPS had a good technical design, but that was literally all it had, and this hollowness left the company at the mercy of its partners. As soon as DEC and Compaq reduced their commitment to the ACE initiative, the network fell apart and pulled MIPS down with it. The very reliance of virtual companies on partners, suppliers, and other outside companies exposes them to strategic hazards. Put another way, there are plenty of small, dynamic companies that have not been able to outperform larger competitors. In particular, a hollow company like MIPS is ill equipped to coordinate a network of companies. Although Sun also worked with alliance partners, it had strong internal capabilities in systems design, manufacturing, marketing, sales, service, and support. As a result, Sun can direct and advance the SPARC architecture, a dominant technology in the industry.

Many companies with superior capabilities have prospered as the dominant player in a network. Japanese keiretsu are structured that way. Consider Toyota, whose successful introduction of the lean production system—a truly systemic innovation—required tremendous coordination with its network of suppliers. Because Toyota was much larger than its suppliers, and because, until recently, it was the largest customer of virtually all of them, it could compel those suppliers to make radical changes in their business practices. In a more egalitarian network, suppliers can demand a large share of the economic benefits of innovations, using what economists call hold-up strategies. Strong central players like Toyota are rarely vulnerable to such tactics and are thus in a better position to drive and coordinate systemic innovation.

The most successful virtual companies sit at the center of networks that are far from egalitarian. Nike may rely on Asian partners for manufacturing, but its capabilities in design and marketing allow it to call all the shots. In the computer industry, Intel has effective control of the 80X86 microprocessor standard, Microsoft dominates PC operating systems, and Sun is driving the SPARC architecture. Those companies control and coordinate the advance of technologies in their areas, and in this regard they function more like integrated companies than like market-based virtuals.

Choosing the Right Organizational Design

Today few companies can afford to develop internally all the technologies that might provide an advantage in the future. In every company we studied, we found a mix of approaches: Some technologies were "purchased" from other companies; others were acquired through licenses, partnerships, and alliances; and still other critical technologies were developed internally. Getting the right balance is crucial, as IBM's disastrous experience in PCs illustrates. But what constitutes the right balance? (See "Ameritech's Strategy for Emerging Technologies.")

Ameritech's Strategy for Emerging Technologies

Ameritech, a Regional Bell Operating Company with wire and fiber assets in the Midwest, has the potential to be a major player in the development of on-demand video and interactive information services for home use. In emerging technologies such as multimedia, no one has all the information to determine what capabilities a company must develop internally or access through the market. The only certainty is that the promise of this market will depend on the codevelopment of many technologies, including data formats, throughput rates, wiring topologies, billing systems, and user interfaces.

Because the eventual configuration of the multimedia industry is unknown (and arguably unknowable ex ante), organizations such as Ameritech must become insiders to the discussions among a range of potential industry players. In emerging markets that are dependent on evolving technologies, considerable information sharing among a wide variety of companies will ultimately result in a road map for the industry. Virtual organizations can serve as catalysts to the development of industry directions and standards in ways that fully integrated organizations cannot.

Consider the role of alliances in Ameritech's multimedia strategy. By allying its own capabilities with those of companies with relevant and complementary skills, Ameritech can participate directly in defining and developing an architecture that will ultimately manage the emerging technologies. One such alliance is with Random House, a leading print publisher of books and magazines, with properties such as the *New Yorker,* Condé Nast, Fodor's, and Arthur Frommer Travel Guides. Random House is capable of supplying significant "content" over Ameritech's wires into the home. This alliance allows both companies to begin to explore the business and technical requirements of providing content into the home.

Ameritech and Random House have formed a joint venture to acquire a start-up virtual company called Worldview Systems, which publishes an electronic monthly current-events database of travel information about more than 170 destinations around the world. While Worldview Systems' products are now sold primarily through travel agents and an 800 telephone number, Ameritech and Random House believe that this type of product may turn out to be ideal for delivery to the home. As Thomas Touton, Ameritech Development's vice president for venture capital, notes, such exploratory investments "require support from senior management willing to move fast in investing but be patient in waiting for returns, and an investment focus that is strongly synergistic with the company's operations."

When and if the promise of the multimedia market becomes real, Ameritech will doubtless be competing against other powerful players. But Ameritech may already have an inside track in the race to deliver information and video on demand into the home. Through alliances such as the one with Random House and exploratory investments in virtual companies such as Worldview Systems, Ameritech has been able to share information and know-how with other potential industry participants and become an insider with the potential to influence the direction of this nascent industry. Until a technological direction becomes clear, companies must invest in capabilities and become active participants in the information dissemination process. Virtual organizations can be an extremely valuable tool at this early stage of market evolution.

Consider how a successful innovator such as Motorola evaluates the trade-offs. Motorola, a leader in wireless communications technology, has declared its long-term goal to be the delivery of "untethered communication"—namely, communication anytime, anywhere, without the need for wires, power cords, or other constraints. In order to achieve that goal, Motorola must make important decisions about where and how to advance the required technologies. Those decisions turn on a handful of questions: Is the technology systemic or likely to become systemic in the future? What capabilities exist in-house and in the current supplier base? When will needed technologies become available?

For Motorola, battery technology is critical because it determines the functionality that can be built into a handheld communications device and the length of time that the device can be used before recharging. Batteries have been a pacing technology in this area for many years.

As Motorola scans the horizon for improved battery technology, it encounters a familiar trade-off between the degree of technological advancement and the number of reliable volume suppliers. Conventional battery technologies such as nickel cadmium (Ni-Cd) have become commodities, and there are many suppliers. But few if any suppliers can offer the more advanced technologies Motorola needs. And the most exotic technologies, such as fuel cells and solid-state energy sources, are not yet commercially viable from any supplier. How should Motorola organize to obtain each of the technologies it might need? Under what circumstances should the company buy the technology from a supplier and when should it form alliances or joint ventures? When should Motorola commit to internal development of the technology? (See Exhibit II.)

For Ni-Cd technology, the clear choice for Motorola is to buy the technology, or to use the market to coordinate access to this technology, because Motorola can rely on competition among many qualified suppliers to deliver what it wants, when needed, for a competitive

Exhibit II.

Matching Organization to Innovation		

The capabilities you need . . .

Type of Innovation

	Autonomous	Systemic
. . . exist outside	go virtual	ally with caution
. . . must be created	ally or bring in-house	bring in-house

price. Motorola faces a more complex decision for fuel cells and solid-state battery technologies. Should Motorola wait until those technologies are more widely available, or should the company opt for a joint venture or internal development?

Before deciding to wait for cutting-edge battery technologies to be developed, Motorola must consider three issues. One is that Motorola could lose the ability to influence the direction of the technology; the early commercial forms may be designed for applications that do not benefit Motorola, such as electric automobiles. The second problem is that Motorola might lose the ability to pace the technology, to bring it to market at a competitively desirable time. The third issue is that if such technologies are—or become—systemic and Motorola has no control over them, the company may not be able to advance related technologies and design features to achieve its goal of untethered communication.

Those issues suggest that Motorola cannot simply wait for the technologies to be provided by the market. Rather, Motorola needs to build strong ties to suppliers with the best capabilities, thus increasing its ability to direct the path of future systemic innovation. Where Motorola itself has strong capabilities, the company should pursue the technologies on its own.

To retain its leadership over the long term, Motorola must continue to develop the critical parts of its value chain internally and acquire less critical technologies from the market or from alliances. Although networks with their high-powered incentives may be effective over the short term for an unchanging technology, they will not adapt well over the long term as technology develops and companies must depend on certain internal capabilities to keep up. The popularity of networked companies and decentralization arises, in part, from observations over a time horizon that is far too short. Remember the enthusiasm that greeted IBM's early success in PCs.

Scale and Scope

Business history presents us with a lesson of striking relevance to the organizational decisions managers face today. In the classic *Scale and Scope,* Alfred Chandler details how the modern corporation evolved in the United States, Germany, and Great Britain at the end of the nineteenth century. Managers who invested the capital to build large-scale enterprises blazed the trail for the leading industries of the second industrial revolution. Markets in railroads, steel, chemicals, and petroleum were developed and shaped by major companies, not the other way around. The most successful of those companies were the first in their industries to make the massive investments in manufacturing, management, and distribution that were needed to realize the gains from innovation.

Companies that failed to make such coordinated, internal commitments during this period were soon thrust aside. The experience of British companies provides a cautionary tale for the champions of the virtual company. Many enjoyed early technological leads in their industries, but the reluctance of those family-run companies to relinquish control to outside investors prevented them from investing to build the capabilities they needed to commercialize their technologies. When German or U.S. competitors made the requisite investments, British companies lost their leadership position. In chemicals, for example, the British lead in the 1870s was completely lost by 1890. History even provided British chemical companies with a second chance when Germany's defeat in World War I temporarily cost German chemical manufacturers their plants and distribution networks. But by 1930, German chemical companies regained the lead because the British again failed to invest adequately. The lesson is that companies that develop their own capabilities can outperform those that rely too heavily on coordination through markets and alliances to build their businesses.

The leading industries of the late nineteenth and early twentieth centuries—chemicals, steel, and railroads—all experienced rapid systemic innovation. The winners were the companies that made major internal investments to shape the markets, rather than those that relied on others to lead the way. While business conditions have certainly changed, many of the principles that worked a century ago still pertain.

Today leading companies like Intel and Microsoft make extensive investments to enhance their current capabilities and spur the creation of new ones. Because so many important innovations are systemic, decentralization without strategic leverage and coordination is exactly the wrong organizational strategy. In most cases, only a large company will have the scale and scope to coordinate complementary innovations. For both the chemicals industry 100 years ago and the microcomputer industry today, long-term success requires considerable and sustained internal investment within a company. The lessons of the second industrial revolution apply to the third: Adept, well-managed companies that commit the right internal resources to innovation will shape the markets and build the new industries of the twenty-first century.

PART

III

New Lenses for Competitive Advantage

1
Disruptive Technologies: Catching the Wave

Joseph L. Bower and Clayton M. Christensen

One of the most consistent patterns in business is the failure of leading companies to stay at the top of their industries when technologies or markets change. Goodyear and Firestone entered the radial-tire market quite late. Xerox let Canon create the small-copier market. Bucyrus-Erie allowed Caterpillar and Deere to take over the mechanical excavator market. Sears gave way to Wal-Mart.

The pattern of failure has been especially striking in the computer industry. IBM dominated the mainframe market but missed by years the emergence of minicomputers, which were technologically much simpler than mainframes. Digital Equipment dominated the minicomputer market with innovations like its VAX architecture but missed the personal-computer market almost completely. Apple Computer led the world of personal computing and established the standard for user-friendly computing but lagged five years behind the leaders in bringing its portable computer to market.

Why is it that companies like these invest aggressively—and successfully—in the technologies necessary to retain their current customers but then fail to make certain other technological investments that customers of the future will demand? Undoubtedly, bureaucracy, arrogance, tired executive blood, poor planning, and short-term investment horizons have all played a role. But a more fundamental reason lies at the heart of the paradox: leading companies succumb to one of the most popular, and valuable, management dogmas. They stay close to their customers.

Although most managers like to think they are in control, customers wield extraordinary power in directing a company's investments. Before managers decide to launch a technology, develop a product, build a plant, or establish new channels of distribution, they must look to their customers first: Do their customers want it? How big will the market be? Will the investment be profitable? The more astutely managers ask and answer these questions, the more complete.y their investments will be aligned with the needs of their customers.

This is the way a well-managed company should operate. Right? But what happens when customers reject a new technology, product concept, or way of doing business because it does *not* address their needs as effectively as a company's current approach? The large photocopying centers that represented the core of Xerox's customer base at first had no use for small, slow tabletop copiers. The excavation contractors that had relied on Bucyrus-Erie's big-bucket steam- and diesel-powered cable shovels didn't want hydraulic excavators because initially they were small and weak. IBM's large commercial, government, and industrial customers saw no immediate use for minicomputers. In each instance, companies listened to their customers, gave them the product performance they were looking for, and, in the end, were hurt by the very technologies their customers led them to ignore.

We have seen this pattern repeatedly in an ongoing study of leading companies in a variety of industries that have confronted technological change. The research shows that most well-managed, established companies are consistently ahead of their industries in developing and commercializing new technologies—from incremental improvements to radically new approaches—as long as those technologies address the next-generation performance needs of their customers. However, these same companies are rarely in the forefront of commercializing new technologies that don't initially meet the needs of mainstream customers and appeal only to small or emerging markets.

Using the rational, analytical investment processes that most well-managed companies have developed, it is nearly impossible to build a cogent case for diverting resources from known customer needs in established markets to markets and customers that seem insignificant or do not yet exist. After all, meeting the needs of established customers and fending off competitors takes all the resources a company has, and then some. In well-managed companies, the processes used to identify customers' needs, forecast technological trends, assess profitability, allocate resources across competing proposals for investment, and take new products to market are focused—for all the right reasons—on current customers and markets. These processes are designed to weed out proposed products and technologies that do *not* address customers' needs.

In fact, the processes and incentives that companies use to keep focused on their main customers work so well that they blind those companies to important new technologies in emerging markets. Many companies have learned the hard way the perils of ignoring new technologies that do not initially meet the needs of mainstream customers. For example, although personal computers did not meet the requirements of mainstream minicomputer users in the early 1980s, the computing power of the desktop machines improved at a much faster rate than minicomputer users' *demands* for computing power did. As a result, personal computers caught up with the computing needs of many of the customers of Wang, Prime, Nixdorf, Data General, and Digital Equipment. Today they are performance-competitive with minicomputers in many applications. For the minicomputer makers, keeping close to mainstream customers and ignoring what were initially low-performance desktop technologies used by seemingly insignificant customers in emerging markets was a rational decision—but one that proved disastrous.

The technological changes that damage established companies are usually not radically new or difficult from a *technological* point of view. They do, however, have two important characteristics. First, they typically present a different package of performance attributes—ones that, at least at the outset, are not valued by existing customers. Second, the performance attributes that existing customers do value improve at such a rapid rate that the new technology can later invade those established markets. Only at this point will mainstream customers want the technology. Unfortunately for the established suppliers, by then it is often too late: the pioneers of the new technology dominate the market.

It follows, then, that senior executives must first be able to spot the technologies that seem to fall into this category. Next, to commercialize and develop the new technologies, managers must protect them from the processes and incentives that are geared to serving established customers. And the only way to protect them is to create organizations that are completely independent from the mainstream business.

No industry demonstrates the danger of staying too close to customers more dramatically than the hard-disk-drive industry. Between

1976 and 1992, disk-drive performance improved at a stunning rate: the physical size of a 100-megabyte (MB) system shrank from 5,400 to 8 cubic inches, and the cost per MB fell from $560 to $5. Technological change, of course, drove these breathtaking achievements. About half of the improvement came from a host of radical advances that were critical to continued improvements in disk-drive performance; the other half came from incremental advances.

The pattern in the disk-drive industry has been repeated in many other industries: the leading, established companies have consistently led the industry in developing and adopting new technologies that their customers demanded—even when those technologies required completely different technological competencies and manufacturing capabilities from the ones the companies had. In spite of this aggressive technological posture, no single disk-drive manufacturer has been able to dominate the industry for more than a few years. A series of companies have entered the business and risen to prominence, only to be toppled by newcomers who pursued technologies that at first did not meet the needs of mainstream customers. As a result, not one of the independent disk-drive companies that existed in 1976 survives today.

To explain the differences in the impact of certain kinds of technological innovations on a given industry, the concept of *performance trajectories*—the rate at which the performance of a product has improved, and is expected to improve, over time—can be helpful. Almost every industry has a critical performance trajectory. In mechanical excavators, the critical trajectory is the annual improvement in cubic yards of earth moved per minute. In photocopiers, an important performance trajectory is improvement in number of copies per minute. In disk drives, one crucial measure of performance is storage capacity, which has advanced 50% each year on average for a given size of drive.

Different types of technological innovations affect performance trajectories in different ways. On the one hand, *sustaining* technologies tend to maintain a rate of improvement; that is, they give customers something more or better in the attributes they already value. For example, thin-film components in disk drives, which replaced conventional ferrite heads and oxide disks between 1982 and 1990, enabled information to be recorded more densely on disks. Engineers had been pushing the limits of the performance they could wring from ferrite heads and oxide disks, but the drives employing these technologies seemed to have reached the natural limits of an *S* curve. At that point, new thin-film technologies emerged that restored—or sustained—the historical trajectory of performance improvement.

On the other hand, *disruptive* technologies introduce a very different package of attributes from the one mainstream customers historically value, and they often perform far worse along one or two dimensions that are particularly important to those customers. As a rule, mainstream customers are unwilling to use a disruptive product in applications they know and understand. At first, then, disruptive technologies tend to be used and valued only in new markets or new applications; in fact, they generally make possible the emergence of new markets. For example, Sony's early transistor radios sacrificed sound fidelity but created a market for portable radios by offering a new and different package of attributes—small size, light weight, and portability.

In the history of the hard-disk-drive industry, the leaders stumbled at each point of disruptive technological change: when the diameter of disk drives shrank from the original 14 inches to 8 inches, then to 5.25 inches, and finally to 3.5 inches. Each of these new architectures initially offered the market substantially less storage capacity than the typical user in the established market required. For example, the 8-inch drive offered 20 MB when it was introduced, while the primary market for disk drives at that time—mainframes—required 200 MB on average. Not surprisingly, the leading computer manufacturers rejected the 8-inch architecture at first. As a result, their suppliers, whose mainstream products consisted of 14-inch drives with more than 200 MB of capacity, did not pursue the disruptive products aggressively. The pattern was repeated when the 5.25-inch and 3.5-inch drives emerged: established computer makers rejected the drives as inadequate, and, in turn, their disk-drive suppliers ignored them as well.

But while they offered less storage capacity, the disruptive architectures created other important attributes—internal power supplies and smaller size (8-inch drives); still smaller size and low-cost stepper motors (5.25-inch drives); and ruggedness, light weight, and low-power consumption (3.5-inch drives). From the late 1970s to the mid-1980s, the availability of the three drives made possible the development of new markets for minicomputers, desktop PCs, and portable computers, respectively.

Although the smaller drives represented disruptive technological change, each was technologically straightforward. In fact, there were engineers at many leading companies who championed the new technologies and built working prototypes with bootlegged resources before management gave a formal go-ahead. Still, the leading companies could not move the products through their organizations and into the market in a timely way. Each time a disruptive technology emerged, between one-half and two-thirds of the established manufacturers failed to introduce models employing the new architecture—in stark contrast to their timely launches of critical sustaining technologies. Those companies that finally did launch new models typically lagged behind entrant companies by two years—eons in an industry whose products' life cycles are often two years. Three waves of entrant companies led these revolutions; they first captured the new markets and then dethroned the leading companies in the mainstream markets.

How could technologies that were initially inferior and useful only to new markets eventually threaten leading companies in established markets? Once the disruptive architectures became established in their new markets, sustaining innovations raised each architecture's performance along steep trajectories—so steep that the performance available from each architecture soon satisfied the needs of customers in the established markets. For example, the 5.25-inch drive, whose initial 5 MB of capacity in 1980 was only a fraction of the capacity that the minicomputer market needed, became fully performance-competitive in the minicomputer market by 1986 and in the mainframe market by 1991. (See Exhibit I.)

A company's revenue and cost structures play a critical role in the way it evaluates proposed technological innovations. Generally, disruptive technologies look financially unattractive to established companies. The potential revenues from the discernible markets are small, and it is often difficult to project how big the markets for the technology will be over the long term. As a result, managers typically conclude that the technology cannot make a meaningful contribution to corporate growth and, therefore, that it is not worth the management effort required to develop it. In addition, established companies have often installed higher cost structures to serve sustaining technologies than those required by disruptive technologies. As a result, managers typically see themselves as having two choices when deciding whether to pursue disruptive technologies. One is to go *downmarket* and accept the lower profit margins of the emerging markets that the disruptive technologies will initially serve. The other is to go *upmarket* with sustaining technologies and enter market segments whose profit margins are alluringly high. (For example, the margins of IBM's mainframes are still higher than those of PCs.) Any rational resource-allo-

Exhibit I.

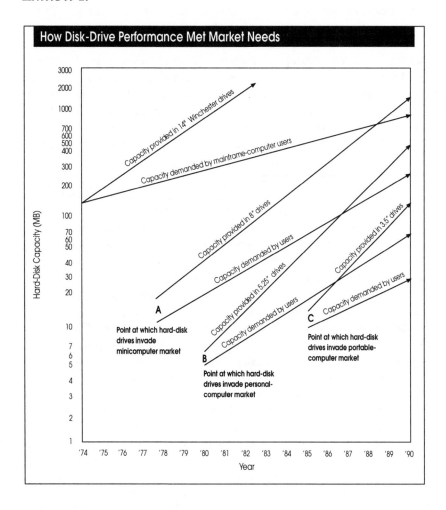

cation process in companies serving established markets will choose going upmarket rather than going down.

Managers of companies that have championed disruptive technologies in emerging markets look at the world quite differently. Without the high cost structures of their established counterparts, these companies find the emerging markets appealing. Once the companies have secured a foothold in the markets and improved the performance of their technologies, the established markets above them, served by high-cost suppliers, look appetizing. When they do attack, the entrant companies find the established players to be easy and unprepared opponents because the opponents have been looking upmarket themselves, discounting the threat from below.

It is tempting to stop at this point and conclude that a valuable lesson has been learned: managers can avoid missing the next wave by paying careful attention to potentially disruptive technologies that do *not* meet current customers' needs. But recognizing the pattern and figuring out how to break it are two different things. Although entrants invaded established markets with new technologies three times in succession, none of the established leaders in the disk-drive industry seemed to learn from the experiences of those that fell before them. Management myopia or lack of foresight cannot explain these failures. The problem is that managers keep doing what has worked in the past: serving the rapidly growing needs of their current customers. The processes that successful, well-managed companies have developed to allocate resources among proposed investments are *incapable* of funneling resources into programs that current customers explicitly don't want and whose profit margins seem unattractive.

Managing the development of new technology is tightly linked to a company's investment processes. Most strategic proposals—to add capacity or to develop new products or processes—take shape at the lower levels of organizations in engineering groups or project teams. Companies then use analytical planning and budgeting systems to select from among the candidates competing for funds. Proposals to create new businesses in emerging markets are particularly challenging to assess because they depend on notoriously unreliable estimates of market size. Because managers are evaluated on their ability to place the right bets, it is not surprising that in well-managed companies, mid- and top-level managers back projects in which the market seems assured. By staying close to lead customers, as they have been trained to do, managers focus resources on fulfilling the requirements of those reliable customers that can be served profitably. Risk is reduced—and careers are safeguarded—by giving known customers what they want.

Seagate Technology's experience illustrates the consequences of relying on such resource-allocation processes to evaluate disruptive technologies. By almost any measure, Seagate, based in Scotts Valley, California, was one of the most successful and aggressively managed companies in the history of the microelectronics industry: from its inception in 1980, Seagate's revenues had grown to more than $700 million by 1986. It had pioneered 5.25-inch hard-disk drives and was the main supplier of them to IBM and IBM-compatible personal-computer manufacturers. The company was the leading manufacturer of 5.25-inch drives at the time the disruptive 3.5-inch drives emerged in the mid-1980s.

Engineers at Seagate were the second in the industry to develop working prototypes of 3.5-inch drives. By early 1985, they had made more than 80 such models with a low level of company funding. The engineers forwarded the new models to key marketing executives, and the trade press reported that Seagate was actively developing 3.5-inch drives. But Seagate's principal customers—IBM and other manufacturers of AT-class personal computers—showed no interest in the new drives. They wanted to incorporate 40-MB and 60-MB drives in their next-generation models, and Seagate's early 3.5-inch prototypes packed only 10 MB. In response, Seagate's marketing executives lowered their sales forecasts for the new disk drives.

Manufacturing and financial executives at the company pointed out another drawback to the 3.5-inch drives. According to their analysis, the new drives would never be competitive with the 5.25-inch architecture on a cost-per-megabyte basis—an important metric that Seagate's customers used to evaluate disk drives. Given Seagate's cost structure, margins on the higher-capacity 5.25-inch models therefore promised to be much higher than those on the smaller products.

Senior managers quite rationally decided that the 3.5-inch drive would not provide the sales volume and profit margins that Seagate needed from a new product. A former Seagate marketing executive recalled, "We needed a new model that could become the next ST412 [a 5.25-inch drive generating more than $300 million in annual sales, which was nearing the end of its life cycle]. At the time, the entire market for 3.5-inch drives was less than $50 million. The 3.5-inch drive just didn't fit the bill—for sales or profits."

The shelving of the 3.5-inch drive was *not* a signal that Seagate was complacent about innovation. Seagate subsequently introduced new models of 5.25-inch drives at an accelerated rate and, in so doing, introduced an impressive array of sustaining technological improvements, even though introducing them rendered a significant portion of its manufacturing capacity obsolete.

While Seagate's attention was glued to the personal-computer market, former employees of Seagate and other 5.25-inch drive makers, who had become frustrated by their employers' delays in launching 3.5-inch drives, founded a new company, Conner Peripherals. Conner focused on selling its 3.5-inch drives to companies in emerging markets for portable computers and small-footprint desktop products (PCs that take up a smaller amount of space on a desk). Conner's primary customer was Compaq Computer, a customer that Seagate had never served. Seagate's own prosperity, coupled with Conner's focus on customers who valued different disk-drive attributes (ruggedness, physical volume, and weight), minimized the threat Seagate saw in Conner and its 3.5-inch drives.

From its beachhead in the emerging market for portable computers, however, Conner improved the storage capacity of its drives by 50% per year. By the end of 1987, 3.5-inch drives packed the capacity demanded in the mainstream personal-computer market. At this point, Seagate executives took their company's 3.5-inch drive off the shelf, introducing it to the market as a *defensive* response to the attack of entrant companies like Conner and Quantum Corporation, the other pioneer of 3.5-inch drives. But it was too late.

By then, Seagate faced strong competition. For a while, the company was able to defend its existing market by selling 3.5-inch drives to its established customer base—manufacturers and resellers of full-size personal computers. In fact, a large proportion of its 3.5-inch products continued to be shipped in frames that enabled its customers to mount the drives in computers designed to accommodate 5.25-inch drives. But, in the end, Seagate could only struggle to become a second-tier supplier in the new portable-computer market.

In contrast, Conner and Quantum built a dominant position in the new portable-computer market and then used their scale and experience base in designing and manufacturing 3.5-inch products to drive Seagate from the personal-computer market. In their 1994 fiscal years, the combined revenues of Conner and Quantum exceeded $5 billion.

Seagate's poor timing typifies the responses of many established companies to the emergence of disruptive technologies. Seagate was willing to enter the market for 3.5-inch drives only when it had become large enough to satisfy the company's financial requirements—that is, only when existing customers wanted the new technology. Seagate has survived through its savvy acquisition of Control Data Corporation's disk-drive business in 1990. With CDC's technology base and Seagate's volume-manufacturing expertise, the company has become a powerful player in the business of supplying large-capacity drives for high-end computers. Nonetheless, Seagate has been reduced to a shadow of its former self in the personal-computer market.

It should come as no surprise that few companies, when confronted with disruptive technologies, have been able to overcome the handicaps of size or success. But it can be done. There is a method to spotting and cultivating disruptive technologies.

DETERMINE WHETHER THE TECHNOLOGY IS DISRUPTIVE OR SUSTAINING. The first step is to decide which of the myriad technologies on the horizon are disruptive and, of those, which are real threats. Most companies have well-conceived processes for identifying and tracking the progress of potentially sustaining technologies, because they are important to serving and protecting current customers. But few have systematic processes in place to identify and track potentially disruptive technologies.

One approach to identifying disruptive technologies is to examine internal disagreements over the development of new products or technologies. Who supports the project and who doesn't? Marketing and financial managers, because of their managerial and financial incentives, will rarely support a disruptive technology. On the other hand, technical personnel with outstanding track records will often persist in arguing that a new market for the technology will emerge—even in the face of opposition from key customers and marketing and financial staff. Disagreement between the two groups often signals a disruptive technology that top-level managers should explore.

DEFINE THE STRATEGIC SIGNIFICANCE OF THE DISRUPTIVE TECHNOLOGY. The next step is to ask the right people the right questions about the strategic importance of the disruptive technology. Disruptive technologies tend to stall early in strategic reviews because managers either ask the wrong questions or ask the wrong people the right questions. For example, established companies have regular procedures for asking mainstream customers—especially the important accounts where new ideas are actually tested—to assess the value of innovative products. Generally, these customers are selected because they are the ones striving the hardest to stay ahead of *their* competitors in pushing the performance of *their* products. Hence these customers are most likely to demand the highest performance from their suppli-

Exhibit II.

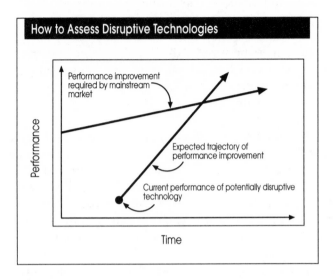

How to Assess Disruptive Technologies

Performance improvement required by mainstream market

Expected trajectory of performance improvement

Current performance of potentially disruptive technology

Performance

Time

ers. For this reason, lead customers are reliably accurate when it comes to assessing the potential of sustaining technologies, but they are reliably *in*accurate when it comes to assessing the potential of disruptive technologies. They are the wrong people to ask.

A simple graph plotting product performance as it is defined in mainstream markets on the vertical axis and time on the horizontal axis can help managers identify both the right questions and the right people to ask. First, draw a line depicting the level of performance and the trajectory of performance improvement that customers have historically enjoyed and are likely to expect in the future. Then locate the estimated initial performance level of the new technology. If the technology is disruptive, the point will lie far below the performance demanded by current customers. (See Exhibit II.)

What is the likely slope of performance improvement of the disruptive technology compared with the slope of performance improvement demanded by existing markets? If knowledgeable technologists believe the new technology might progress faster than the market's demand for performance improvement, then that technology, which does not meet customers' needs today, may very well address them tomorrow. The new technology, therefore, is strategically critical.

Instead of taking this approach, most managers ask the wrong questions. They compare the anticipated rate of performance improvement of the new technology with that of the established technology. If the new technology has the potential to surpass the established one, the reasoning goes, they should get busy developing it.

Pretty simple. But this sort of comparison, while valid for sustaining technologies, misses the central strategic issue in assessing potentially disruptive technologies. Many of the disruptive technologies we studied *never* surpassed the capability of the old technology. It is the trajectory of the disruptive technology compared with that of the *market* that is significant. For example, the reason the mainframe-computer market is shrinking is not that personal computers outperform mainframes but because personal computers networked with a file server meet the computing and data-storage needs of many organizations effectively. Mainframe-computer makers are reeling not because the performance of personal-computing technology surpassed the performance of mainframe *technology* but because it intersected with the performance demanded by the established *market.*

Consider the graph again. If technologists believe that the new technology will progress at the same rate as the market's demand for performance improvement, the disruptive technology may be slower to invade established markets. Recall that Seagate had targeted personal computing, where demand for hard-disk capacity per computer was growing at 30% per year. Because the capacity of 3.5-inch drives improved at a much faster rate, leading 3.5-inch-drive makers were able to force Seagate out of the market. However, two other 5.25-inch-drive makers, Maxtor and Micropolis, had targeted the engineering-workstation market, in which demand for hard-disk capacity was insatiable. In that market, the trajectory of capacity demanded was essentially parallel to the trajectory of capacity improvement that technologists could supply in the 3.5-inch architecture. As a result, entering the 3.5-inch-drive business was strategically less critical for those companies than it was for Seagate.

LOCATE THE INITIAL MARKET FOR THE DISRUPTIVE TECHNOLOGY. Once managers have determined that a new technology is disruptive and strategically critical, the next step is to locate the initial markets for that technology. Market research, the tool that managers have traditionally relied on, is seldom helpful: at the point a company needs to make a strategic commitment to a disruptive technology, no concrete market exists. When Edwin Land asked Polaroid's market researchers to assess the potential sales of his new camera, they concluded that Polaroid would sell a mere 100,000 cameras over the product's lifetime; few people they interviewed could imagine the uses of instant photography.

Because disruptive technologies frequently signal the emergence of new markets or market segments, managers must *create* information about such markets—who the customers will be, which dimensions of product performance will matter most to which customers, what the right price points will be. Managers can create this kind of information only by experimenting rapidly, iteratively, and inexpensively with both the product and the market.

For established companies to undertake such experiments is very difficult. The resource-allocation processes that are critical to profitability and competitiveness will not—and should not—direct resources to markets in which sales will be relatively small. How, then, can an established company probe a market for a disruptive technology? Let start-ups—either ones the company funds or others with no connection to the company—conduct the experiments. Small, hungry organizations are good at placing economical bets, rolling with the punches, and agilely changing product and market strategies in response to feedback from initial forays into the market.

Consider Apple Computer in its start-up days. The company's original product, the Apple I, was a flop when it was launched in 1977. But Apple had not placed a huge bet on the product and had gotten at least *something* into the hands of early users quickly. The company learned a lot from the Apple I about the new technology and about what customers wanted and did not want. Just as important, a group of *customers* learned about what they did and did not want from personal computers. Armed with this information, Apple launched the Apple II quite successfully.

Many companies could have learned the same valuable lessons by watching Apple closely. In fact, some companies pursue an explicit strategy of being *second to invent*—allowing small pioneers to lead the way into uncharted market territory. For instance, IBM let Apple, Commodore, and Tandy define the personal computer. It then aggressively entered the market and built a considerable personal-computer business.

But IBM's relative success in entering a new market late is the exception, not the rule. All too often, successful companies hold the performance of small-market pioneers to the financial standards they apply to their own performance. In an attempt to ensure that they are using their resources well, companies explicitly or implicitly set relatively high thresholds for the size of the markets they should consider entering. This approach sentences them to making late entries into markets already filled with powerful players.

For example, when the 3.5-inch drive emerged, Seagate needed a $300-million-a-year product to replace its mature flagship 5.25-inch model, the ST412, and the 3.5-inch market wasn't large enough. Over the next two years, when the trade press asked when Seagate would introduce its 3.5-inch drive, company executives consistently responded that there was no market yet. There actually was a market, and it was growing rapidly. The signals that Seagate was picking up about the market, influenced as they were by customers who didn't want 3.5-inch drives, were misleading. When Seagate finally introduced its 3.5-inch drive in 1987, more than $750 million in 3.5-inch drives had already been sold. Information about the market's size had been widely available throughout the industry. But it wasn't compelling enough to shift the focus of Seagate's managers. They continued to look at the new market through the eyes of their current customers and in the context of their current financial structure.

The posture of today's leading disk-drive makers toward the newest disruptive technology, 1.8-inch drives, is eerily familiar. Each of the industry leaders has designed one or more models of the tiny drives, and the models are sitting on shelves. Their capacity is too low to be used in notebook computers, and no one yet knows where the initial market for 1.8-inch drives will be. Fax machines, printers, and automobile dashboard mapping systems are all candidates. "There just isn't a market," complained one industry executive. "We've got the product, and the sales force can take orders for it. But there are no orders because nobody needs it. It just sits there." This executive has not considered the fact that his sales force has no incentive to sell the 1.8-inch drives instead of the higher-margin products it sells to higher-volume customers. And while the 1.8-inch drive is sitting on the shelf at his company and others, last year more than $50 million worth of 1.8-inch drives were sold, almost all by start-ups. This year, the market will be an estimated $150 million.

To avoid allowing small, pioneering companies to dominate new markets, executives must personally monitor the available intelligence on the progress of pioneering companies through monthly meetings with technologists, academics, venture capitalists, and other nontraditional sources of information. They *cannot* rely on the company's traditional channels for gauging markets because those channels were not designed for that purpose.

PLACE RESPONSIBILITY FOR BUILDING A DISRUPTIVE-TECHNOLOGY BUSINESS IN AN INDEPENDENT ORGANIZATION. The strategy of forming small teams into skunk-works projects to isolate them from the stifling demands of mainstream organizations is widely known but poorly understood. For example, isolating a team of engineers so that it can develop a radically new sustaining technology just because that technology is radically different is a fundamental misapplication of the skunk-works approach. Managing out of context is also unnecessary in the unusual event that a disruptive technology is more financially attractive than existing products. Consider Intel's transition from dynamic random access memory (DRAM) chips to microprocessors. Intel's early microprocessor business had a higher gross margin than that of its DRAM business; in other words, Intel's normal resource-allocation process naturally provided the new business with the resources it needed.[1]

Creating a separate organization is necessary only when the disruptive technology has a lower profit margin than the mainstream business and must serve the unique needs of a new set of customers. CDC, for example, successfully created a remote organization to commercialize its 5.25-inch drive. Through 1980, CDC was the dominant independent disk-drive supplier due to its expertise in making 14-inch drives for mainframe-computer makers. When the 8-inch drive emerged, CDC launched a late development effort, but its engineers were repeatedly pulled off the project to solve problems for the more profitable, higher-priority 14-inch projects targeted at the company's most important customers. As a result, CDC was three years late in launching its first 8-inch product and never captured more than 5% of that market.

When the 5.25-inch generation arrived, CDC decided that it would face the new challenge more strategically. The company assigned a small group of engineers and marketers in Oklahoma City, Oklahoma, far from the mainstream organization's customers, the task of developing and commercializing a competitive 5.25-inch product. "We needed to launch it in an environment in which everybody got excited about a $50,000 order," one executive recalled. "In Minneapolis, you needed a $1 million order to turn anyone's head." CDC never regained the 70% share it had once enjoyed in the market for mainframe disk drives, but its Oklahoma City operation secured a profitable 20% of the high-performance 5.25-inch market.

Had Apple created a similar organization to develop its Newton personal digital assistant (PDA), those who have pronounced it a flop might have deemed it a success. In launching the product, Apple made the mistake of acting as if it were dealing with an established market. Apple managers went into the PDA project assuming that it had to make a significant contribution to corporate growth. Accordingly, they researched customer desires exhaustively and then bet huge sums launching the Newton. Had Apple made a more modest technological and financial bet and entrusted the Newton to an organization the size that Apple itself was when it launched the Apple I, the outcome might have been different. The Newton might have been seen more broadly as a solid step forward in the quest to discover what customers really want. In fact, many more Newtons than Apple I models were sold within a year of their introduction.

KEEP THE DISRUPTIVE ORGANIZATION INDEPENDENT. Established companies can only dominate emerging markets by creating small organizations of the sort CDC created in Oklahoma City. But what should they do when the emerging market becomes large and established?

Most managers assume that once a spin-off has become commercially viable in a new market, it should be integrated into the mainstream organization. They reason that the fixed costs associated with engineering, manufacturing, sales, and distribution activities can be shared across a broader group of customers and products.

This approach might work with sustaining technologies; however, with disruptive technologies, folding the spin-off into the mainstream organization can be disastrous. When the independent and mainstream organizations are folded together in order to share resources, debilitating arguments inevitably arise over which groups get what resources and whether or when to cannibalize established products. In the history of the disk-drive industry, *every* company that has tried to manage mainstream and disruptive businesses within a single organization failed.

No matter the industry, a corporation consists of business units with finite life spans: the technological and market bases of any business will eventually disappear. Disruptive technologies are part of that cycle. Companies that understand this process can create new businesses to replace the ones that must inevitably die. To do so, companies must give managers of disruptive innovation free rein to realize the technology's full potential—even if it means ultimately killing the mainstream business. For the corporation to live, it must be willing to see business units die. If the corporation doesn't kill them off itself, competitors will.

The key to prospering at points of disruptive change is not simply to take more risks, invest for the long term, or fight bureaucracy. The key is to manage strategically important disruptive technologies in an organizational context where small orders create energy, where fast low-cost forays into ill-defined markets are possible, and where overhead is low enough to permit profit even in emerging markets.

Managers of established companies can master disruptive technologies with extraordinary success. But when they seek to develop and launch a disruptive technology that is rejected by important customers within the context of the mainstream business's financial demands, they fail—not because they make the wrong decisions, but because they make the right decisions for circumstances that are about to become history.

Note

1. Robert A. Burgelman, "Fading Memories: A Process Theory of Strategic Business Exit in Dynamic Environments," *Administrative Science Quarterly* 39 (1994), 24–56.

2
Breaking Compromises, Breakaway Growth

**George Stalk, Jr., David K. Pecaut, and
Benjamin Burnett**

When is a mature, slow-growth business not a mature business? How do rapidly growing companies emerge from stagnant, dead-in-the-water industries? The station-wagon segment of the North American auto market was dying when, in 1984, Chrysler Corporation introduced the minivan. Over the next ten years, minivan sales grew eight times faster than did the industry overall. For the last 15 years, the do-it-yourself home-improvement business as a whole has grown barely 5% per year while Home Depot has racked up 20% growth. Overcapacity and flat demand plague the airline industry, but that hasn't kept Southwest Airlines Company from growing seven times faster than the industry average over the past decade. (See Exhibit I.)

What senior managers at Chrysler, Home Depot, and Southwest have in common is the wisdom, curiosity, and perseverance to explore the compromises their industries were forcing customers to endure. And each acted on the insight that breaking those compromises would release enormous trapped value—enough to stimulate major sales and profit growth. In fact, the concept of breaking compromises is one of the most powerful organizing principles we have seen for companies that wish to achieve breakaway growth.

Compromises are not trade-offs. Trade-offs are the legitimate choices customers make among different product or service offerings. Trade-offs typically come from fundamental differences in cost structures that are usually reflected in prices. With products, the trade-offs often arise from differences in design or in the cost of materials. With

Exhibit I.

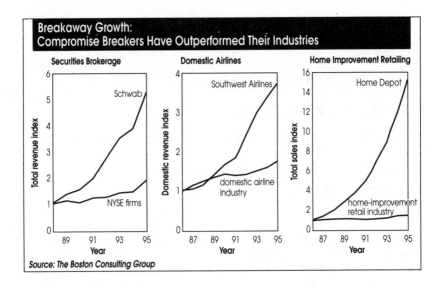

Breakaway Growth:
Compromise Breakers Have Outperformed Their Industries

Source: The Boston Consulting Group

textiles, for example, there is a trade-off between price and quality because better fabrics tend to have higher thread counts. In service, trade-offs are common because delivering greater convenience or customization often entails higher cost. Thus taxi service costs more than bus service, and a meal delivered by room service costs more than the same meal ordered in the hotel restaurant.

A compromise, in contrast, is a concession demanded of consumers by all or most service or product providers. Whereas trade-offs let customers choose their preference among alternatives, compromises offer no choice. Trade-offs allow different offerings to appeal to different segments; compromises benefit no particular segment. Trade-offs are very visible; most compromises are hidden.

In picking a hotel room, for instance, a customer can *trade off* luxury for economy by choosing between a Ritz-Carlton and a Best Western. But the hotel industry forces customers to *compromise* by not permitting check-in before 4 P.M. Similarly, until recently, most auto dealers forced a compromise on customers by not offering weekend repair and maintenance services. There is no law of nature that says that cars can't get fixed on weekends or that hotel rooms can't be ready before late afternoon. Compromises occur when an industry imposes its own operating practices or constraints on customers, leaving them no choice. It's the industry's way or no way. And often customers accept compromises as the way the business works.

Henry Ford's famous car in any color—as long as it's black—is one type of compromise. Such a compromise denies customers the selection they want. Or customers are forced to wait. Today's car buyer can custom-order virtually any car if the selection on the dealer's lot is inadequate, but the industry will make customers wait six to eight weeks for delivery. In other situations, customers may be forced to use a high-cost service or to pay a premium to get the quality they want. Because the family washing machine can't safely handle all fabrics, customers have to spend extra time and money on dry cleaning. The compromise often becomes visible when customers have to modify their behavior to use a company's product or service. Until recently, dishwashers did a satisfactory job of washing the dishes, but they made enough noise to wake the dead. Their owners had to arrange a time when they were out of hearing range to wash the dishes.

Compromises creep into businesses in various ways. Some, like hotel check-in times, are imposed by standard operating practices that no one questions. Others stem from conscious decisions that may make marginal economic sense—as long as customers adjust their behavior. For example, it may make sense for a supplier to deliver only once a week, but doing so forces customers to hold inventory between deliveries. The most important compromises, however, are forced on customers simply because companies have lost touch with those customers' needs. Finding and breaking those compromises can unleash new demand and create breakaway growth.

The Great Pasta Compromise

Contadina, an operating unit of Nestlé, has created a high-growth business by breaking the compromises imposed on consumers of pasta. Contadina's fresh pasta product is sold in supermarkets, cooks in minutes in boiling water, and comes in many varieties, including ravioli and tortellini.

Before Contadina's innovation, consumers faced one trade-off and a multitude of compromises in their quest to eat pasta. The trade-off was between eating pasta at home—where someone has to make it—and eating out at a restaurant. Pasta at home is less expensive. The restaurant has more variety and means less work, but it costs more.

The great pasta compromise begins after the decision to stay home and make it yourself. Homemade pasta is inexpensive and fresh. But making pasta from scratch is time-consuming and difficult. The first product to try to break the compromise was dry pasta. Dry pasta costs more than homemade pasta and it is not as fresh, but it is much easier and faster to make.

The next run at the great pasta compromise was frozen pasta. Frozen pasta, which often comes in a microwavable container, is even quicker and easier to cook than dry pasta and requires little cleanup. But frozen pasta costs more than either homemade or dry pasta, and it is often less tasty.

In the mid-1980s, Contadina made its run at the great pasta compromise with the introduction of a fresh pasta product. Contadina's fresh pasta is twice the price of dry pasta and comes in a smaller package that doesn't serve as many people. It is five times more expensive per serving than dry pasta. Why, then, do people buy Contadina? Consumer research provides some interesting insights. Naturally, consumers like its freshness and its ease of cooking. More surprising is the fact that consumers are choosing Contadina over a meal at a restaurant. Before Contadina's fresh pasta became available, many people said they would never eat tortellini or ravioli at home, because preparing them from scratch was just too much trouble.

Breaking the great pasta compromise not only has made it easier to prepare good-tasting pasta at home, it also has upset the old trade-off between eating at home and going to a restaurant. In this context, Contadina makes a lot of sense. Consumers get the taste, variety, and freshness that can be found at restaurants, but in a product they can cook and eat at home for less money.

Often, when segmentwide compromises imposed on consumers are broken, traditional trade-offs are sidestepped and fundamental changes in the definition of the business occur. This usually means a dramatic shift in the set of relevant competitors. Because compromise breakers often find themselves competing against companies that are higher cost and higher priced, they are often able to grow rapidly and profitably by gaining share from their new set of rivals. Contadina grew at high double-digit rates to become a leader in fresh pastas and sauces by the 1990s, with hundreds of millions of dollars in sales.

A Breakthrough for Car Buyers

Breaking compromises between an entire industry and its customers can release tremendous value. Circuit City, best known in the United States as a big-box consumer-electronics and appliance retailer, is a successful company, with sales growing at 26% per year and earnings at 30%. Its one major problem is that it is about to run out of real estate. After opening stores in virtually all major markets in the United States, Circuit City needs to go somewhere else for fast-growth opportunities.

The retailer has found what it believes to be a promising opportunity in an unlikely place—the used-car business. In October 1993, Circuit City launched CarMax, a company whose strategy is to revolutionize the way used cars are sold in the United States.

Selling used cars is a business with a stigma. In the past, most people who bought used cars couldn't afford new ones. The automakers, who naturally wanted to sell new cars, reinforced the stigma. When Chrysler introduced its successful K-car in the early 1980s, Roger Smith, then chairman of the board of General Motors Corporation, was asked how GM would respond to the threat. Smith belittled the K-car by saying that "General Motors' answer to the Chrysler K-car is a two-year-old Oldsmobile."

This attitude toward used cars has not changed much. In the summer of 1995, a *Business Week* journalist grilled the program manager for the new Ford Taurus about the car's price. In frustration, the program manager responded that the 1996 Taurus was priced to sell 400,000 units a year. "If Joe Blow can't afford to buy a new car . . . let him buy a used car" (*Business Week*, July 24, 1995).

The used-car business may get no respect, but it should. Annual used-car sales in North America top $200 billion, making used cars the third-largest consumer category after food and clothing. In fact, there are more sales of used cars and light trucks than of new ones, and demand for used cars is growing faster. Moreover, the quality of used cars has risen with the rise in the quality of new cars.

Despite improvements in product quality, the business of selling used cars is virtually unchanged. A customer who opts for a used car faces many compromises. First, the buyer has to locate a car, usually by reviewing the classified advertisements in the local paper. Product variety is limited. In Toronto, for example, 20 to 30 used Tauruses are advertised for sale in the newspaper at any one time—from individuals, from dealers specializing in used cars, and from new-car dealers who also sell used cars. In the case of private sales, the buyer must call, make an appointment, and hope the seller will actually be there at the appointed time. The buyer must drive to see the car—which is unlikely to turn out to be the one the buyer wants or in good condition or priced reasonably or even still there: it could already have been sold.

When the buyer finds an attractive car, he or she can't expect to see any maintenance records. Some dealers certify their cars, but in Ontario, for example, certification means only that the glass is not cracked, that the lights and brakes work, that the exhaust does not leak, and that the tires have sufficient tread. In other words, certification guarantees only the bare necessities for roadworthiness.

Buyers of used cars, then, risk ending up owning a car with mechanical problems. Beyond this, they must endure a time-consuming and truly horrific buying process—more accurately, up to four processes: finding and buying the car, financing it, insuring it, and selling the old car. Buyers are at a disadvantage because knowledge about the product is asymmetrical: the seller knows more than the buyer. Often the buyer is subjected to high-pressure sales tactics and forced to haggle over the price with salespeople whom he or she suspects are dishonest. And should problems arise, there is no clear recourse for the buyer.

The managers of Circuit City observed the size and growth of used-car sales and saw that many of the distinguishing capabilities of their own consumer-electronics business could break the compromises imposed on buyers of used cars.

Circuit City is known for its high variety of merchandise. CarMax takes the same approach. A typical large used-car dealer has only about 30 vehicles in stock. A large new-car dealer who sells used cars might have 130 vehicles. The first CarMax, in Richmond, Virginia, had 500 cars. The two stores that opened in Atlanta in August 1995 have 1,500 each. (See Exhibit II.)

CarMax further enhances customer choice by harnessing Circuit City's considerable systems capabilities. At CarMax, customers have access to computerized information through a kiosk that enables them to sort through the inventory of cars available not only at that site but at all the stores in the region. When CarMax advertises in any of the Richmond or Atlanta papers, it advertises inventory from both locations.

Unlike Circuit City, CarMax does not keep its inventory indoors. There is only one vehicle on display in the showroom, and it is fitted

Exhibit II.

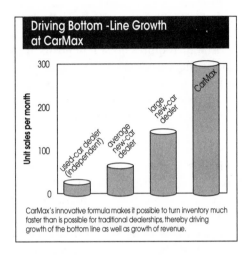

Driving Bottom-Line Growth at CarMax

CarMax's innovative formula makes it possible to turn inventory much faster than is possible for traditional dealerships, thereby driving growth of the bottom line as well as growth of revenue.

with arrows pointing to the 110 spots that have undergone performance and safety checks. The showroom's computerized kiosks provide information on the vehicles in stock, including their location on the lot. Should a customer be shopping with the family and want to see and drive a particular vehicle, CarMax provides a supervised day-care center for the children.

CarMax uses professional uniformed sales representatives, whose first job is to explain how to use the kiosk and then to help customers find the car they want. CarMax prefers *not* to hire people with experience in selling new or used cars. Instead, it wants to hire presentable people whom it can train for two weeks (compare that with the minimal or nonexistent training that employees receive at new- and used-car dealers) and pay a set dollar amount per vehicle regardless of its selling price. This is an interesting departure from Circuit City's practice of paying a percentage-of-sales commission that encourages aggressive "selling up." CarMax did not want that pressure on its customers, so it designed an incentive system that eliminates the pressure on its sales representatives.

CarMax sets prices at below the average Blue Book value and offers no-haggle pricing and no-hassle guarantees. Every CarMax vehicle comes with the 110-point safety check and a 30-day warranty. For some cars, warranties of up to four years are available. In addition, CarMax customers have a five-day return guarantee: the car may be brought back with no questions asked as long as it has not been driven more than 250 miles.

Financing is available from NationsBank Corporation or from Circuit City's financing arm. Circuit City's financing tends to be for a longer term and usually requires lower deposits. Progressive Insurance will insure both the vehicle and the driver on the spot. People buying cars from CarMax can sell their old cars as well. The sale of the used car is a separate transaction from the purchase of a car. CarMax will buy any used car—although not at a price everyone will accept.

The jury is still out on the success of CarMax. A host of imitators have emerged. Circuit City does not divulge the performance of its CarMax unit, but 4 stores were opened in 1995 and 90 more are planned by the year 2000. The race is on. Both used- and new-car dealers are likely to be bloodied. Historically, new-car dealers have sold about 80% of used cars that are less than four years old—CarMax's core offering. And those sales have accounted for anywhere from 35% to 65% of the dealers' profitability overall.

In addition, the sales of new cars are at risk. A popular saying in the automotive industry is that when you buy a new car and drive it off the lot, what you own is a very expensive used car. On average, the value of a new car plummets 28% in the first week after its sale. At CarMax, it is not uncommon to find current model-year vehicles with low mileage at substantially lower prices than those of new vehicles. In breaking so many of the compromises imposed on used-car buyers, CarMax may end the old trade-off between buying a used car and buying a new one.

CarMax is not the first to try to break the compromises imposed on used-car buyers. In northern New Jersey, there is a used-car dealership that has tackled the variety compromise by putting 600 cars on its lot and giving customers more choice. But this dealership has left everything else the same. Customers still have to haggle, obtain their financing and insurance from somewhere else, and dispose of their old car. Other dealers are touting no-haggle pricing. What sets CarMax apart is that it has put it all together: CarMax sells variety, it sells value, it sells convenience, it promises that you can be in and out in 90 minutes with a car, and it delivers a comfortable experience. Many of the car dealers near CarMax locations are matching CarMax on price, and they think, mistakenly, that the job is done. It's not. People want a different buying experience and they're getting it from CarMax.

Finding Opportunities in Any Business

Growth strategies built around the idea of breaking compromises are neither new nor limited to a few particular industries. But to visualize such a strategy requires a company's managers to clear their heads of the conventional thinking that pervades their industry. The Charles Schwab Corporation has grown steadily over two decades by breaking one industry compromise after another.

Schwab began as a discount stockbrokerage in 1975, when U.S. equity markets were deregulated and price competition on stock-trading commissions was introduced. Discount brokers ended a major compromise for individual investors, who had hitherto been forced to put up with high prices if they wanted to buy and sell securities.

Schwab, however, saw that the discount brokerage segment was itself imposing new compromises. Customers who opted for a low price worried about service reliability. Schwab tackled the problem head-on, first by investing heavily in computer technology that allowed almost immediate confirmation of orders over the telephone. At the time, even Merrill Lynch & Company could not do that. Schwab also invested in the firm's brand name and in retail offices, both of which instilled confidence in consumers. In the process, the firm broke the compromise between price and reliable service and grew dramatically through the early 1980s.

Schwab saw that other compromises remained to be broken. In exchange for low prices, customers had been compromised on convenience, flexibility, and ease of transferring funds. In the early 1980s, Schwab pioneered 24-hour-a-day, seven-day-a-week service. It introduced the Schwab One cash-management account with Visa card and checking privileges, copying a Merrill Lynch product but eliminating the need to deal with a full-commission broker. Schwab also pioneered automated phone trading and eventually electronic trading directly from the customer's personal computer.

Over time, Schwab's management realized that the company was no longer a simple discount broker but in fact a broad, value-priced provider of cash, stocks, bonds, and mutual funds. The compromises Schwab had broken had generated a 20% to 25% per year growth rate and made Schwab the largest non-full-commission broker in the United States. But Schwab was ready to break yet another compromise to fuel its next stage of growth.

Until 1992, most consumers wanting to buy mutual funds had been forced to choose among different fund companies, each of which serviced its own accounts. Because diversification and high performance were not easily accomplished within a single family of funds, many consumers placed money with a number of different fund-management companies. Most investors were frustrated by the complexity of dealing with different statements, different rules, and different sales representatives.

In 1992, Schwab changed the scenario by introducing OneSource, a single point of purchase for more than 350 no-load mutual funds in 50 different fund families. OneSource gives customers a single account with one monthly statement that tracks the performance of all their funds. There are no transaction fees on OneSource accounts, so customers can shift their money among different fund families without any charge. Schwab can do this because it is paid directly by the funds as their sales representative and subaccount processor.

OneSource has grown to include 500 mutual funds, driving Schwab's mutual-fund assets from $6 billion in 1991 to more than $60 billion in 1996 and making it the third-largest mutual-fund distributor in the United States. No longer forced to compromise on assortment, price, and convenience, consumers have been flocking to OneSource to manage their investments.

Schwab's experience illustrates that relentless breaking of compromises can be a source for continuing growth. In fact, there are at least seven ways in which companies can find and exploit compromise-breaking opportunities in any industry.

SHOP THE WAY THE CUSTOMER SHOPS. At Schwab, the most important source of ongoing insight is employees who use the company's products and services just as Schwab's customers do. For example, the belief that customers would value the convenience of 24-hour-a-day, seven-day-a-week systems was heavily supported by Schwab's own employees, who wanted that kind of flexibility in managing their own investments. Unfortunately, in many industries, executives never know how customers shop. In the auto industry, executives of the Big Three do not buy cars. Their secretaries do it for them, over the telephone. The cars are delivered to the executives clean, full of gas, and ready to go. For most Big Three executives, buying a car the way ordinary customers do would be an out-of-body experience.

PAY CAREFUL ATTENTION TO HOW THE CUSTOMER REALLY USES THE PRODUCT OR SERVICE. In all industries, people exhibit *compensatory behaviors*. They devise their own ways of using the product or service to compensate for the fact that if they did only what the company intended them to do, they wouldn't really get what they wanted. In every product category, consumers can undertake dozens of compensatory behaviors, and each of those can have significant compromise-breaking potential.

In the brokerage business, it was common knowledge that customers often called back a second or even a third time to confirm that their trade had gone through at the price they had requested. Schwab paid careful attention to customers' actual behavior and realized that the ability to provide immediate confirmation at the time an order was taken would eliminate those second and third calls—saving customers a lot of trouble and giving Schwab a significant advantage over other brokers.

EXPLORE CUSTOMERS' LATENT DISSATISFACTIONS. Most companies ask their customers to describe their dissatisfactions with existing products and services. Such surveys usually lead to helpful improvements, but truly significant breakthroughs are generally the result of tapping into much deeper dissatisfactions. Those can be called *latent dissatisfactions* because consumers are unable to articulate their unhappiness with the product or service category. Chrysler's development of the minivan, for example, tapped into latent dissatisfaction with both station wagons and full-size vans. Station wagons couldn't carry enough and were hard to load and unload. Full-size vans were more useful, but they were not fun to drive. Minivans broke the compromise by "cubing out" the box design of the station wagon. Ford Motor Company and GM had both researched customers' feelings about station wagons and had found that they could meet obvious needs with features such as two-way doors, electric rear windows, and third seats. But they did not explore the "white space" between station wagons (based on car platforms) and vans (based on truck platforms). The minivan—a van based on a car platform—was hidden in this white space defined by customers' latent dissatisfactions.

LOOK FOR UNCOMMON DENOMINATORS. Over time, companies tend to drift toward providing products or services that, on average, meet the needs of large numbers of customers. But compromises often lurk in this common-denominator approach. Schwab, for example, has now separated the service channel for the high-volume equity trader from that for the ordinary investor, whose needs are simpler. Each receives different services and pays different fees.

Some companies are reluctant to abandon the approach of averaging costs across all customers, because they believe abandoning it will reduce the profitability of their high-volume accounts. But recent history suggests that if managers don't separate out what should be discrete businesses, a new or existing rival will do it for them. Recognition of that fact begets a relentless search for new compromises to break.

PAY CAREFUL ATTENTION TO ANOMALIES. Anomalies often are a rich source for compromise breaking. The one regional sales office that significantly outperforms all others and for which there is no obvious explanation; the factory that appears to have a scale disadvantage but still has a lower production cost; the supplier who has lower cost and higher quality despite having an older product design: those anomalies are all worth exploring as potential compromise-breaking opportunities.

In Schwab's case, the idea of creating local offices grew out of an anomaly. Charles Schwab's uncle was looking for a business to run and Schwab decided to open an office in Sacramento, California, to give his uncle something to do. At the time, offices were seen as unnecessary and costly overhead for discount brokerage firms.

Subsequently, Schwab noticed that Sacramento was significantly outperforming other cities that had no offices. There was no obvious explanation. By exploring this anomaly carefully, Schwab discovered that retail sales offices had a number of important advantages even for a firm that typically dealt with customers by telephone. Local offices provided a rich source of customer leads through walk-in traffic and reassured those new customers who had concerns about trusting a broker they had heard of only from television. The offices provided a sense of solidity and a place customers could go to transact business. Schwab discovered that even in a high-tech age, customers like knowing that there is an office down the street or at least across town. Fully probing this anomaly led Schwab to build a large retail network.

LOOK FOR DISECONOMIES IN THE INDUSTRY'S VALUE CHAIN. Today, in industry after industry, companies are innovating the management of their value chain in ways that are more rewarding for consumers. When the Schwab firm entered the mutual fund business, its first thought was to create its own family of funds. Careful analysis of the industry value chain, however, revealed a bigger opportunity. Only a handful of the largest companies had sufficient economies of scale to distribute their funds cost-effectively—and those companies lost the ability to talk directly to their individual customers. Schwab's solution was to become an intermediary between its own customer base and a large number of subscale mutual-fund companies. Through OneSource, the firm served the needs of the fund companies and at the same time interposed itself between the funds and the customer. Schwab's ownership of the direct customer relationship can now provide a platform for growth in other financial services, such as insurance.

LOOK FOR ANALOGOUS SOLUTIONS TO THE INDUSTRY'S COMPROMISES. Some of the best compromise-breaking ideas are probably already out there—in someone else's industry. Circuit City's CarMax borrows many practices from other retail sectors. For example, its idea of offering extended warranties on used cars is borrowed from appliance and consumer-electronics retailing. To keep inventory moving and selection fresh, CarMax has copied a practice used commonly in soft-goods retailing—automatically discounting inventory as it ages. CarMax's practice of offering flat sales commissions and its low-pressure selling tactics can be observed in a number of sectors. Best Buy Company, one of Circuit City's competitors in electronics retailing, uses that approach to create the kind of low-key, self-serve environment CarMax was looking for.

An Organizing Principle for Growth

Many companies today are searching for growth. But how and where should they look? Managers will often turn first to line extensions, geographic expansion, or acquisitions. In the right circumstances, each of those makes sense. But we believe that innovations that break fundamental compromises in a business are far more powerful.

Breaking compromises can, in fact, provide an organizing principle for the pursuit of growth. The CEO of a large financial-services company asked his initially skeptical management team to specify and value all the compromises imposed on its customers. The exercise was eye opening.

To get its employees to focus their energies on compromise breaking, a company should start by asking them to immerse themselves in the customer's experience. It is critical to develop a strong, almost visceral feel for the compromises consumers experience. Whirlpool Corporation, the $8 billion appliance maker, identified a specific individual who personified the compromises all its customers bore.

Whirlpool's market research showed consumers to be generally satisfied with the home appliances they owned. But digging deeper, Whirlpool discovered a reservoir of latent dissatisfaction with all the activities for which the appliances were used—doing laundry, preparing food, cleaning up after meals. Although consumers didn't expect a lot more of their washing machines, ranges, and dishwashers, they were nevertheless very dissatisfied with household chores.

Those latent dissatisfactions became the basis for Whirlpool's brand strategy. In 1992, after decades of competing mostly on cost with companies such as General Electric, Whirlpool wanted to build a new and more profitable strategy around a more sharply differentiated brand. Management knew it needed to articulate the strategy and mobilize all employees behind a vision. Someone at Whirlpool saw an interview on a national television-news program with an overworked woman named Gail and taped it, recognizing Gail as the embodiment of Whirlpool's target customer. Gail was a 40-year-old woman taking care of several children at home while holding down a full-time job. Gail did all the cooking, the laundry, and the housework. Her husband's role was apparently restricted to playing sports with the children and helping them with their homework. The image was consistent with Whirlpool's research, which showed that women in the United States who work as many hours as their husbands in jobs outside the home continue to do most of the household chores as well. Gail personified the pressed-for-time working woman.

At the end of the video clip, the interviewer turns to her and says, "You're taking care of everyone in this family. Who takes care of you?" Before she can reply, her husband answers for her, "I take care of Gail." Gail shoots him a look that could kill.

The video, which became a rallying point for Whirlpool's new strategy, challenged all employees to think about how Whirlpool could be the company that takes care of Gail. Why, for example, was it taking Gail so long to clean up after meals? The traditional stove top was obviously designed by someone who was spared the daily responsibility of keeping it clean. The top of Whirlpool's CleanTop stove is completely flat, eliminating all the grease traps of the old design. Dishwashers used to be deafening, but now Gail can work on her kitchen computer while Whirlpool's Quiet Partner dishwasher is running.

More compromises wait to be broken. Why is doing the laundry such a chore? Gail's washing machine takes less time than her dryer to complete its cycle. Gail compensates by starting with lighter, faster-drying loads first. But eventually the process bogs down, and Gail is wasting time and energy running to the basement because no one makes a synchronized washer and dryer.

Breaking compromises can be a powerful organizing principle to enlist an entire organization in thinking about growth. The lesson from all the high-growth compromise breakers we've observed is this: the opportunity to identify and exploit compromises for faster growth and improved profitability is there for the taking. But managers must go to customers and look for themselves. This isn't a job that can be delegated to the market research department. Managers must ask themselves why customers behave the way they do. An auto dealer told us how proud he was of his expansive, well-lit lot with no fences. "My customers like to come after hours to look at cars and trucks," he proclaimed. He apparently never asked himself why they would do such a strange thing. And it never occurred to him that they might be looking at cars after hours precisely because they didn't want to have to deal with *him.*

To find the kinds of growth opportunities companies like CarMax, Schwab, and Contadina are pursuing, managers have to get inside the customer's skin and ask, What compromises am I putting up with? What's wrong with this picture? Where's the minivan in this company?

3

Competing on Resources: Strategy in the 1990s

David J. Collis and Cynthia A. Montgomery

As recently as ten years ago, we thought we knew most of what we needed to know about strategy. Portfolio planning, the experience curve, PIMS, Porter's five forces—tools like these brought rigor and legitimacy to strategy at both the business-unit and the corporate level. Leading companies, such as General Electric, built large staffs that reflected growing confidence in the value of strategic planning. Strategy consulting boutiques expanded rapidly and achieved widespread recognition. How different the landscape looks today. The armies of planners have all but disappeared, swept away by the turbulence of the past decade. On multiple fronts, strategy has come under fire.

At the business-unit level, the pace of global competition and technological change has left managers struggling to keep up. As markets move faster and faster, managers complain that strategic planning is too static and too slow. Strategy has also become deeply problematic at the corporate level. In the 1980s, it turned out that corporations were often destroying value by owning the very divisions that had seemed to fit so nicely in their growth/share matrices. Threatened by smaller, less hierarchical competitors, many corporate stalwarts either suffered devastating setbacks (IBM, Digital, General Motors, and Westinghouse) or underwent dramatic transformation programs and internal reorganizations (GE and ABB). By the late 1980s, large multibusiness corporations were struggling to justify their existence.

Not surprisingly, waves of new approaches to strategy were proposed to address these multiple assaults on the premises of strategic planning. Many focused inward. The lessons from Tom Peters and Bob

Waterman's "excellent" companies led the way, closely followed by total quality management as strategy, reengineering, core competence, competing on capabilities, and the learning organization. Each approach made its contribution in turn, yet how any of them built on or refuted the previously accepted wisdom was unclear. The result: Each compounded the confusion about strategy that now besets managers.

A framework that has the potential to cut through much of this confusion is now emerging from the strategy field. The approach is grounded in economics, and it explains how a company's resources drive its performance in a dynamic competitive environment. Hence the umbrella term academics use to describe this work: the *resource-based view of the firm* (RBV).[1] The RBV combines the *internal* analysis of phenomena within companies (a preoccupation of many management gurus since the mid-1980s) with the *external* analysis of the industry and the competitive environment (the central focus of earlier strategy approaches). Thus the resource-based view builds on, but does not replace, the two previous broad approaches to strategy by *combining* internal and external perspectives.[2] It derives its strength from its ability to explain in clear managerial terms why some competitors are more profitable than others, how to put the idea of core competence into practice, and how to develop diversification strategies that make sense. The resource-based view, therefore, will be as powerful and as important to strategy in the 1990s as industry analysis was in the 1980s. (See "A Brief History of Strategy.")

A Brief History of Strategy

The field of strategy has largely been shaped around a framework first conceived by Kenneth R. Andrews in his classic book *The Concept of Corporate Strategy* (Richard D. Irwin, 1971). Andrews defined strategy as the match between what a company *can* do (organizational strengths and weaknesses) within the universe of what it *might* do (environmental opportunities and threats).

Although the power of Andrews's framework was recognized from the start, managers were given few insights about how to assess either side of the equation systematically. The first important breakthrough came in Michael E. Porter's book *Competitive Strategy: Techniques for Analyzing Industries and Competitors* (Free Press, 1980). Porter's work built on the structure-conduct-performance paradigm of industrial-organization economics. The essence of the model is that the structure of an industry determines the state of competition within that industry and sets the context for companies' conduct—that is, their strategy. Most important, structural forces (which Porter called the five forces) determine the average profitability of the industry and have a correspondingly strong impact on the profitability of individual corporate strategies.

This analysis put the spotlight on choosing the "right industries" and, within them, the most attractive competitive positions. Although the model did not ignore the characteristics of individual companies, the emphasis was clearly on phenomena at the industry level.

With the appearance of the concepts of core competence and competing on capabilities, the pendulum swung dramatically in the other direction, moving from outside to inside the company. These approaches emphasized the importance both of the skills and collective learning embedded in an organization and of management's ability to marshal them. This view assumed that the roots of competitive advantage were inside the organization and that the adoption of new strategies was constrained by the current level of the company's resources. The external environment received little, if any, attention, and what we had learned about industries and competitive analysis seemed to disappear from our collective psyche.

The emerging resource-based view of the firm helps to bridge these seemingly disparate approaches and to fulfill the promise of Andrews's framework. Like the capabilities approaches, the resource-based view acknowledges the importance of company-specific resources and competencies, yet it does so in the context of the competitive environment. The resource-based view shares another important characteristic with industry analysis: it, too, relies on economic reasoning. It sees capabilities and resources as the heart of a company's competitive position, subject to the interplay of three fundamental market forces: demand (does it meet customers' needs, and is it competitively superior?), scarcity (is it imitable or substitutable, and is it durable?), and appropriability (who owns the profits?). The five tests described in the article translate these general economic requirements into specific, actionable terms.

The RBV sees companies as very different collections of physical and intangible assets and capabilities. No two companies are alike because no two companies have had the same set of experiences, acquired the same assets and skills, or built the same organizational cultures. These assets and capabilities determine how efficiently and effectively a company performs its functional activities. Following this logic, a company will be positioned to succeed if it has the best and most appropriate stocks of resources for its business and strategy.

Valuable resources can take a variety of forms, including some overlooked by the narrower conceptions of core competence and capabilities. They can be *physical,* like the wire into your house. Potentially, both the telephone and cable companies are in a very strong position to succeed in the brave new world of interactive multimedia because they own the on-ramp to the information superhighway. Or valuable resources may be *intangible,* such as brand names or technological know-how. The Walt Disney Company, for example, holds a unique consumer franchise that makes Disney a success in a slew of businesses, from soft toys to theme parks to videos. Similarly, Sharp Corporation's knowledge of flat-panel display technology has enabled it to dominate the $7 billion worldwide liquid-crystal-display (LCD) business. Or the valuable resource may be an organizational capability embedded in a company's routines, processes, and culture. Take, for example, the skills of the Japanese automobile companies—first in low-cost, lean manufacturing; next in high-quality production; and then in fast product development. These capabilities, built up over time, transform otherwise pedestrian or commodity inputs into superior products and make the companies that have developed them successful in the global market.

Competitive advantage, whatever its source, ultimately can be attributed to the ownership of a valuable resource that enables the company to perform activities better or more cheaply than competitors. Marks & Spencer, for example, possesses a range of resources that demonstrably yield it a competitive advantage in British retailing. (See Exhibit I.) This is true both at the single-business level and at the corporate level, where the valuable resources might reside in a particular function, such as corporate research and development, or in an asset, such as corporate brand identity. Superior performance will therefore be based on developing a *competitively distinct* set of resources and deploying them in a well-conceived strategy.

Competitively Valuable Resources

Resources cannot be evaluated in isolation, because their value is determined in the interplay with market forces. A resource that is valuable in a particular industry or at a particular time might fail to have the same value in a different industry or chronological context.

Exhibit I.

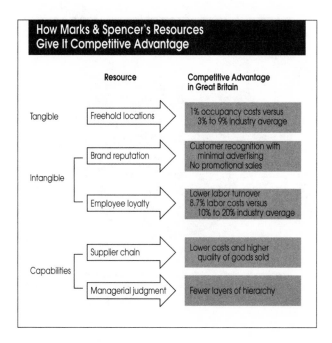

For example, despite several attempts to brand lobsters, so far no one has been successful in doing so. A brand name was once very important in the personal computer industry, but it no longer is, as IBM has discovered at great cost. Thus the RBV inextricably links a company's internal capabilities (what it does well) and its external industry environment (what the market demands and what competitors offer). Described that way, competing on resources sounds simple. In practice, however, managers often have a hard time identifying and evaluating their companies' resources objectively. The RBV can help by bringing discipline to the often fuzzy and subjective process of assessing valuable resources. (See Exhibit II.)

For a resource to qualify as the basis for an effective strategy, it must pass a number of external market tests of its value. Some are so straightforward that most managers grasp them intuitively or even unconsciously. For instance, a valuable resource must contribute to the production of something customers want at a price they are willing to pay. Other tests are more subtle and, as a result, are commonly misunderstood or misapplied. These often turn out to cause strategies to misfire.

Exhibit II.

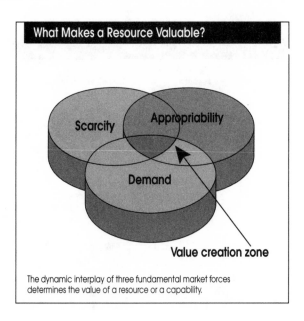

What Makes a Resource Valuable?

Scarcity   Appropriability

Demand

Value creation zone

The dynamic interplay of three fundamental market forces determines the value of a resource or a capability.

1. THE TEST OF INIMITABILITY: IS THE RESOURCE HARD TO COPY? Inimitability is at the heart of value creation because it limits competition. If a resource is inimitable, then any profit stream it generates is more likely to be sustainable. Possessing a resource that competitors easily can copy generates only temporary value. But because managers fail to apply this test rigorously, they try to base long-term strategies on resources that are imitable. IBP, the first meat-packing company in the United States to modernize, built a set of assets (automated plants located in cattle-rearing states) and capabilities (low-cost "disassembly" of beef) that enabled it to earn returns of 1.3% in the 1970s. By the late 1980s, however, ConAgra and Cargill had replicated these resources, and IBP's returns fell to 0.4%.

Inimitability doesn't last forever. Competitors eventually will find ways to copy most valuable resources. But managers can forestall them—and sustain profits for a while—by building their strategies around resources that have at least one of the following four characteristics:

The first is *physical uniqueness*, which almost by definition cannot be copied. A wonderful real estate location, mineral rights, or Merck

& Company's pharmaceutical patents simply cannot be imitated. Although managers may be tempted to think that many of their resources fall into this category, on close inspection, few do.

A greater number of resources cannot be imitated because of what economists call *path dependency*. Simply put, these resources are unique and, therefore, scarce because of all that has happened along the path taken in their accumulation. As a result, competitors cannot go out and buy these resources instantaneously. Instead, they must be built over time in ways that are difficult to accelerate.[3]

The Gerber Products Company brand name for baby food, for example, is potentially imitable. Re-creating Gerber's brand loyalty, however, would take a very long time. Even if a competitor spent hundreds of millions of dollars promoting its baby food, it could not buy the trust that consumers associate with Gerber. That sort of brand connotation can be built only by marketing the product steadily for years, as Gerber has done. Similarly, crash R&D programs usually cannot replicate a successful technology when research findings cumulate. Having many researchers working in parallel cannot speed the process, because bottlenecks have to be solved sequentially. All this builds protection for the original resource.

The third source of inimitability is *causal ambiguity*. Would-be competitors are thwarted because it is impossible to disentangle either what the valuable resource is or how to re-create it. What *really* is the cause of Rubbermaid's continued success in plastic products? We can draw up lists of possible reasons. We can try, as any number of competitors have, to identify its recipe for innovation. But, in the final analysis, we cannot duplicate Rubbermaid's success.

Causally ambiguous resources are often organizational capabilities. These exist in a complex web of social interactions and may even depend critically on particular individuals. As Continental and United try to mimic Southwest's successful low-cost strategy, what will be most difficult for them to copy is not the planes, the routes, or the fast gate turnaround. All of those are readily observable and, in principle, easily duplicated. However, it will be difficult to reproduce Southwest's culture of fun, family, frugality, and focus because no one can quite specify exactly what it is or how it arose.

The final source of inimitability, *economic deterrence*, occurs when a company preempts a competitor by making a sizable investment in an asset. The competitor could replicate the resource but, because of limited market potential, chooses not to. This is most likely when strategies are built around large capital investments that are both scale sensitive and specific to a given market. For example, the minimum efficient scale for float-glass plants is so large that many markets can support only one such facility. Because such assets cannot be redeployed, they represent a credible commitment to stay and fight it out with competitors who try to replicate the investment. Faced with such a threat, potential imitators may choose not to duplicate the resource when the market is too small to support two players the size of the incumbent profitably. That is exactly what is now occurring in Eastern Europe. As companies rush to modernize, the first to build a float-glass facility in a country is likely to go unchallenged by competitors.

2. THE TEST OF DURABILITY: HOW QUICKLY DOES THIS RESOURCE DEPRECIATE? The longer lasting a resource is, the more valuable it will be. Like inimitability, this test asks whether the resource can sustain competitive advantage over time. While some industries are stable for years, managers today recognize that most are so dynamic that the value of resources depreciates quickly. Disney's brand name survived almost two decades of benign neglect between Walt Disney's death and the installation of Michael D. Eisner and his management team. In contrast, technological know-how in a fast-moving industry is a rapidly wasting asset, as the list of different companies that have dominated successive generations of semiconductor memories illustrates. Economist Joseph A. Schumpeter first recognized this phenomenon in the 1930s. He described waves of innovation that allow early movers to dominate the market and earn substantial profits. However, their valuable resources are soon imitated or surpassed by the next great innovation, and their superior profits turn out to be transitory. Schumpeter's description of major companies and whole industries blown away in a gale of "creative destruction" captures the pressure many managers feel today. Banking on the durability of most core competencies is risky. Most resources have a limited life and will earn only temporary profits.

3. THE TEST OF APPROPRIABILITY: WHO CAPTURES THE VALUE THAT THE RESOURCE CREATES? Not all profits from a resource automatically flow to the company that "owns" the resource. In fact, the value is always subject to bargaining among a host of players, including customers, distributors, suppliers, and employees. What has happened to leveraged buyout firms is revealing. A critical resource of LBO firms was the network of contacts and relationships in the investment banking community. However, this resource often resided in the individuals doing the deals, not in the LBO firms as a whole. These individuals could—and often did—depart to set up their own LBO funds or move to another firm where they could reap a greater share of the profits that their resource generated. Basing a strategy on resources that are not inextricably bound to the company can make profits hard to capture.

4. THE TEST OF SUBSTITUTABILITY: CAN A UNIQUE RESOURCE BE TRUMPED BY A DIFFERENT RESOURCE? Since Michael E. Porter's introduction of the five-forces framework, every strategist has been on the lookout for the potential impact of substitute products. The steel industry, for example, has lost a major market in beer cans to aluminum makers in the past 20 years. The resource-based view pushes this critical question down a level to the resources that underpin a company's ability to deliver a good or service. Consider the following example. In the early 1980s, People Express Airlines challenged the major airlines with a low-price strategy. Founder Donald C. Burr pursued this strategy by developing a unique no-frills approach and an infrastructure to deliver low-cost flights. Although the major airlines were unable to replicate this approach, they nevertheless were able to retaliate using a *different* resource to offer consumers equivalent low-cost fares—their computer reservation systems and yield-management skills. This substitution eventually drove People Express into bankruptcy and out of the industry.

5. THE TEST OF COMPETITIVE SUPERIORITY: WHOSE RESOURCE IS REALLY BETTER? Perhaps the greatest mistake managers make when evaluating their companies' resources is that they do not assess them relative to competitors'. Core competence has too often become a "feel good" exercise that no one fails. Every company can identify one activity that it does relatively better than other activities and claim that as its core competence. Unfortunately, core competence should not be an internal assessment of which activity, of all its activities, the company performs best. It should be a harsh external assessment of what it does better than competitors, for which the term *distinctive competence* is more appropriate. How many consumer packaged-goods companies assert that their core competence is consumer marketing skills? They may indeed all be good at that activity, but a corporate strategy built on such a core competence will rapidly run into trouble because other competitors with better skills will be pursuing the same strategy.

The way to avoid the vacuousness of generic statements of core competence is to disaggregate the corporation's resources. The category *consumer marketing skills,* for example, is too broad. But it can be divided into subcategories such as effective brand management, which in turn can be divided into skills such as product-line extensions, cost-effective couponing, and so on. Only by looking at this level of specificity can we understand the sources of a company's uniqueness and measure by analyzing the data whether it is competitively superior on those dimensions. Can anyone evaluate whether Kraft General Foods' or Unilever's consumer marketing skills are better? No. But we can demonstrate quantitatively which is more successful at launching product-line extensions.

Disaggregation is important not only for identifying truly distinctive resources but also for deriving actionable implications. How many companies have developed a statement of their core competencies and then have struggled to know what to do with it? One manufacturer of medical-diagnostics test equipment, for example, defined one of its core competencies as instrumentation. But this intuitively obvious definition was too broad to be actionable. By pushing to deeper levels of disaggregation, the company came to a powerful insight. In fact, its strength in instrumentation was mainly attributable to its competitive superiority in designing the interface between its machines and the people who use them. As a result, the company decided to reinforce its valuable capability by hiring ergonomists, and it expanded into doctors' offices, a fast-growing segment of its market. There, the company's resources created a real competitive advantage, in part because its equipment can be operated by office personnel rather than only by technicians.

Although disaggregation is the key to identifying competitively superior resources, sometimes the valuable resource is a combination of skills, none of which is superior by itself but which, when combined, make a better package. Honeywell's industrial automation systems are successful in the marketplace—a measure that the company is good at something. Yet each individual component and software program might not be the best available. Competitive superiority lies either in the weighted average (the company does not rank first in any resource, but it is still better on average than any competitor) or in its system-integration capability.

The lesson for managers is that conclusions about critical resources should be based on objective data from the market. In our experience, managers often treat core competence as an exercise in intuition and skip the thorough research and detailed analysis needed to get the right answer.

Strategic Implications

Managers should build their strategies on resources that meet the five tests outlined above. The best of these resources are often intangible, not physical, hence the emphasis in recent approaches on the softer aspects of corporate assets—the culture, the technology, and the transformational leader. The tests capture how market forces determine the value of resources. They force managers to look inward and outward at the same time.

However, most companies are not ideally positioned with competitively valuable resources. More likely, they have a mixed bag of resources—some good, some mediocre, and some outright liabilities, such as IBM's monolithic mainframe culture. The harsh truth is that most companies' resources do not pass the objective application of the market tests. (See "What Ever Happened to the Dogs and the Cash Cows?")

What Ever Happened to the Dogs and Cash Cows?

In the late 1960s and early 1970s, the wisdom of the day was that companies could transfer the competitive advantage of professional management across a broad range of businesses. Many companies responded to the perceived opportunity: Armed with decentralized structures and limited, but tight, financial controls, they diversified into a number of related and unrelated businesses, mostly through acquisition. In time, such conglomerates came to resemble miniature economies in their own right. There appeared to be no compelling limits to the scope of corporations.

As the first oil crisis hit in 1973, corporate managers faced deteriorating performance and had little advice on how to act. Into this vacuum came the Boston Consulting Group and portfolio management. In BCG's now famous growth/share matrix, corporate management was finally given a tool with which to reassert control over its many divisions.

This simple matrix allowed managers to classify each division, since renamed a strategic business unit, into a quadrant based on the growth of its industry, and the relative strength of the unit's competitive position. There was a prescribed strategy for each position in the matrix: sustain the cash-generating cows, divest or harvest the dogs, take cash from the cows and invest in question marks in order to make them stars, and increase the market share of the stars until their industry growth slowed and they became the next generation of cash cows. Such simple prescriptions gave corporate management both a sense of what their strategy should accomplish—a balanced portfolio of businesses—and a way to control and allocate resources to their divisions.

The problem with the portfolio matrix was that it did not address how value was being created across the divisions, which could be as diverse as semiconductors and hammers. The only relationship between them was cash. As we have come to learn, the relatedness of businesses is at the heart of value creation in diversified companies. The portfolio matrix also suffered from its assumption that corporations had to be self-sufficient in capital. That implied that they should find a use for all internally generated cash and that they could not raise additional funds from the capital market. The capital markets of the 1980s demonstrated the fallacy of such assumptions.

In addition, the growth/share matrix failed to compare the competitive advantage a business received from being owned by a particular company with the costs of owning it. In the 1980s, many companies built enormous corporate infrastructures that created only small gains at the business-unit level. During the same period, the market for corporate control heated up, focusing attention on value for shareholders. Many companies with supposedly model portfolios were accordingly dissolved.

Even those companies that are fortunate enough to have unusual assets or capabilities are not home free. Valuable resources must still be joined with other resources and embedded in a set of functional policies and activities that distinguish the company's position in the market—after all, competitors can have core competencies, too.

Strategy requires managers to look forward as well. Companies fortunate enough to have a truly distinctive competence must also be wise enough to realize that its value is eroded by time and competition. Consider what happened to Xerox. During what has become known as its "lost decade," the 1970s, Xerox believed its reprographic capability to be inimitable. And while Xerox slept, Canon took over world leadership in photocopiers.

In a world of continuous change, companies need to maintain pressure constantly at the frontiers—building for the next round of competition. Managers must therefore continually invest in and upgrade their resources, however good those resources are today, and leverage them with effective strategies into attractive industries in which they can contribute to a competitive advantage.

INVESTING IN RESOURCES. Because all resources depreciate, an effective corporate strategy requires continual investment in order to maintain and build valuable resources. One of Eisner's first actions as CEO at Disney was to revive the company's commitment to animation. He invested $50 million in *Who Framed Roger Rabbit?* to create the company's first animated feature-film hit in many years and quadrupled its output of animated feature films—bringing out successive hits, such as *Beauty and the Beast, Aladdin,* and *The Lion King.*

Similarly, Marks & Spencer has periodically reexamined its position in its only business—retailing—and has made major investments to stay competitive. In the early 1980s, the British company spent billions on store renovation, opened new edge-of-town locations, and updated its procurement and distribution systems. In contrast, the U.S. retailer Sears, Roebuck and Company diversified into insurance, real estate, and stock brokerages, while failing to keep up with the shift in retailing to new mall locations and specialty stores.

The mandate to reinvest in strategic resources may seem obvious. The great contribution of the core competence notion is its recognition that, in corporations with a traditional divisional structure, investment in the corporation's resources often takes a backseat to optimizing current divisional profitability. Core competence, therefore, identifies the critical role that the corporate office has to play as the guardian of what are, in essence, the crown jewels of the corporation. In some instances, such guardianship might even require explicitly establishing a corporate officer in charge of nurturing the critical resources. Cooper Industries, a diversified manufacturer, established a manufacturing services group to disseminate the best manufacturing practices throughout the company. The group helped "Cooperize" acquired companies, rationalizing and improving their production facilities. The head of the services group, Joseph R. Coppola, was of a caliber to be hired away as CEO of Giddings & Lewis, the largest U.S. machine tool manufacturer. Similarly, many professional service firms, such as Coopers & Lybrand, have a senior partner in charge of their critical capabilities—client-relationship management, staff training, and intellectual development. Valuable corporate resources are often supradivisional, and, unless someone is managing them on that basis, divisions will underinvest in them or free ride on them.

At the same time, investing in core competencies without examining the competitive dynamics that determine industry attractiveness is dangerous. By ignoring the marketplace, managers risk investing heavily in resources that will yield low returns. Masco Corporation did exactly that. It built a competence in metalworking and diversified into tightly related industries. Unfortunately, the returns from this strategy were lower than the company had expected. Why? A straightforward five-forces analysis would have revealed that the structure of the industries Masco entered was poor—buyers were price sensitive with limited switching costs, entry barriers were low, and suppliers were powerful. Despite Masco's metalworking expertise, its industry context prevented it from achieving exceptional returns until it developed the skills that enabled it to enter more attractive industries.

Similarly, if competitors are ignored, the profits that could result from a successful resource-based strategy will dissipate in the struggle to acquire those resources. Consider the value of the cable wire into your house as a source of competitive advantage in the multimedia industry. Companies such as Time Warner have been forced by competitors, who can also see the value of that wire, to bid billions of dollars to acquire control of even modest cable systems. As a result, they may never realize substantial returns on their investment. This is true not only for resources acquired on the market but also for those core competencies that many competitors are simultaneously trying to develop internally.

UPGRADING RESOURCES.   What if a company has no unusually valuable resources? Unfortunately, that is a common experience when resources are evaluated against the standard of competitive superiority. Or what if a company's valuable resources have been imitated or substituted by competitors? Or perhaps its resources, like Masco's, are valuable only in industries so structurally unattractive that, regardless of how efficiently it operates, its financial returns will never be stellar. In these cases—indeed, in nearly all cases—companies must continually upgrade the number and quality of their resources and associated competitive positions in order to hold off the almost inevitable decay in their value.

Upgrading resources means moving beyond what the company is already good at, which can be accomplished in a number of ways. The first is by adding new resources, the way Intel Corporation added a brand name, Intel Inside, to its technological resource base. The second is by upgrading to alternative resources that are threatening the company's current capabilities. AT&T is trying to build capabilities in multimedia now that its physical infrastructure—the network—is no longer unique or as critical as it once was. Finally, a company can upgrade its resources in order to move into a structurally more attractive industry, the way Nucor Corporation, a U.S. steel company, has made the transition from competitive, low-margin, downstream businesses, such as steel joists, into more differentiated, upstream businesses, such as thin-slab cast-steel sheets.

Perhaps the most successful examples of upgrading resources are in companies that have added new competencies sequentially, often over extended periods of time. Sharp provides a wonderful illustration of how to exploit a virtuous circle of sequentially upgrading technologies and products, what the Japanese call "seeds and needs." In the late 1950s, Sharp was an assembler of televisions and radios, seemingly condemned to the second rank of Japanese consumer electronics companies. To break out of that position, founder Tokuji Hayakawa, who had always stressed the importance of innovation, created a corporate R&D facility. When the Japanese Ministry of International Trade and Industry blocked Sharp from designing computers, the company used its limited technology to produce the world's first digital calculator in 1964. To strengthen its position in this business, Sharp backward integrated into manufacturing its own specialized semiconductors and made a strong commitment to the new liquid-crystal-display technology. Sharp's bet on LCD technology paid off and enabled it to develop a number of new products, such as the Wizard electronic organizer. Over time, the superiority of its display technology gave Sharp a competitive advantage in businesses it had previously struggled in, such as camcorders. Its breakthrough product, Viewcam, captured 20% of the Japanese market within six months of release in 1992.

At each stage, Sharp took on a new challenge, whether to develop or improve a technology or to enter or attack a market. Success in each endeavor improved the company's resources in technology, distribution, and organizational capability. It also opened new avenues for expansion. Today, Sharp is the dominant player in the LCD market and a force in consumer electronics.

Cooper provides another example. Challenged to justify its plan to acquire Champion Spark Plug Company in 1989, when fuel injection was replacing spark plugs, Cooper reasoned that it had the resources to help Champion improve its position, as it had done many times before with products such as Crescent wrenches, Nicholson files, and Gardner-Denver mining equipment. But what really swung the decision, according to Cooper chairman and CEO Robert Cizik, was the recognition that Cooper lacked a critical skill it needed for the future—the ability to manage international manufacturing. With its numerous overseas plants, Champion offered Cooper the opportunity to acquire global management capabilities. The Champion acquisition, in Cizik's view, was a way to upgrade Cooper's resources. Indeed, a review of the company's history shows that Cooper has deliberately sought to improve its capabilities gradually by periodically taking on challenges it knows will have a high degree of difficulty for the organization.

LEVERAGING RESOURCES.   Corporate strategies must strive to leverage resources into all the markets in which those resources contribute to competitive advantage or to compete in new markets that improve the corporate resources. Or, preferably, both, as with Cooper's acquisition of Champion. Failure to do so, as occurred with Disney following the death of its founder, leads a company to be undervalued. Eisner's management team, which extended the scope of Disney's activities into hotels, retailing, and publishing, was installed in response to a hostile-takeover threat triggered by the underutilization of the company's valuable resources.

Good corporate strategy, then, requires continual reassessment of the company's scope. The question strategists must ask is, How far can the company's valuable resource be extended across markets? The answer will vary widely because resources differ greatly in their specificity, from highly fungible resources (such as cash, many kinds of machinery, and general management skills) to much more specialized resources (such as expertise in narrow scientific disciplines and secret product formulas). Specialized resources often play a critical role in securing competitive advantage, but, because they are so specific, they lose value quickly when they are moved away from their original settings. Shell Oil Company's brand name, for example, will not transfer well outside autos and energy, however valuable it is within those fields. Highly fungible resources, on the other hand, transfer well across a wide range of markets but rarely constitute the key source of competitive advantage.

The RBV helps us understand why the track record of corporate diversification has been so poor and identifies three common and costly strategic errors companies make when they try to grow by leveraging resources. First, managers tend to overestimate the transferability of specific assets and capabilities. The irony is that because valuable resources are hard to imitate, the company itself may find it difficult to replicate them in new markets. Despite its great success in Great Britain, Marks & Spencer has failed repeatedly in attempts to leverage its resources in the North American market—a classic example of misjudging the important role that context plays in competitive advantage. In this case, the concepts of path dependency and causal ambiguity are both at work. Marks & Spencer's success is rooted in its 100-year reputation for excellence in Great Britain and in the skills and relationships that enable it to manage its domestic supply chain effectively. Just as British competitors have been unable to duplicate this set of advantages, Marks & Spencer itself struggles to do so when it tries to enter a new market against established competitors.

Second, managers overestimate their ability to compete in highly profitable industries. Such industries are often attractive precisely because entry barriers limit the number of competitors. Entry barriers are really resource barriers: The reason competitors find it so hard to enter the business is that accumulating the necessary resources is difficult. If it could be done easily, competitors would flock to the opportunity, driving down average returns. Many managers fail to see the connection between company-level resources and industry-level profits and convince themselves that they can vault the entry barrier, without considering which factors will ultimately determine success in the industry. Philip Morris Companies' entry into soft drinks, for example, foundered on the difficulties it faced managing the franchise distribution network. After years of poor performance in that business, it gave up and divested 7-Up.

The third common diversification mistake is to assume that leveraging generic resources, such as lean manufacturing, will be a major source of competitive advantage in a new market—regardless of the specific competitive dynamics of that market. Chrysler Corporation seems to have learned this lesson. Expecting that its skills in design and manufacturing would ensure success in the aerospace industry, Chrysler acquired Gulfstream Aerospace Corporation—only to divest it five years later in order to concentrate on its core businesses.

Despite the common pitfalls, the rewards for companies that leverage their resources appropriately, as Disney has, are high. Newell Company is another stunning example of a company that has built a set of capabilities and used them to secure commanding positions for products in a wide range of industries. Newell was a modest manufacturer of drapery hardware in 1967, when a new CEO, Daniel C. Ferguson, articulated its strategy: The company would specialize in high-volume production of a variety of household and office staple goods that would be sold through mass merchandisers. The company made a series of acquisitions, each of which benefited from Newell's capabilities—its focused control systems; its computer links with mass discounters, which facilitate paperless invoicing and automatic inventory restocking; and its expertise in the "good-better-best" merchandising of basic products, in which retailers typically choose to carry only one brand, with several quality and price levels. In turn, each acquisition gave Newell yet another opportunity to strengthen its capabilities. Today, Newell holds leading market positions in drapery hardware, cookware, glassware, paintbrushes, and office products and maintains an impressive 15% earnings growth annually. What differentiates this diversified company from a host of others is how it has been able to use its corporate resources to establish and maintain competitive advantage at the business-unit level.

However, even Newell benefits from the attractiveness of the markets in which it competes. All its products are infrequently purchased, low-cost items. Most consumers will not spend time comparison shopping for six glasses, nor do they have a sense of the market price. Do you know if $3.99 is too much to pay for a brass curtain rod? Thus Newell's resources are all the more valuable for being deployed in an attractive industry context.

Whether a company is building a strategy based on core competencies, is developing a learning organization, or is in the middle of a transformation process, those concepts can all be interpreted as a mandate to build a unique set of resources and capabilities. However, this must be done with a sharp eye on the dynamic industry context and competitive situation, rigorously applying market tests to those resources. Strategy that blends two powerful sets of insights about capabilities and competition represents an enduring logic that transcends management fads.

That this approach pays off is demonstrated by the impressive performance of companies such as Newell, Cooper, Disney, and Sharp. Although these companies may not have set out explicitly to craft resource-based strategies, they nonetheless capture the power of this logic and the returns that come to those who do.

Notes

1. A number of insightful articles have been written on the resource-based view, including: Birger Wernerfelt, "A Resource-Based View of the Firm," *Strategic Management Journal,* September–October 1984, 171; J.B. Barney, "Strategic Factor Markets: Expectations, Luck and Business Strategy," *Management Science,* October 1986, 1,231; Richard P. Rumelt, "Theory, Strategy, and Entrepreneurship," in *The Competitive Challenge: Strategies for Industrial Innovation and Renewal,* ed. David J. Teece (Cambridge, Mass.: Ballinger, 1987), 137; Ingemar Dierickx and Karel Cool, "Asset Stock Accumulation and Sustainability of Competitive Advantage," *Management Science,* December 1989, 1,504; Kathleen R. Conner, "A Historical Comparison of Resource-Based Theory and Five Schools of Thought Within Industrial Organization Economics: Do We Have a New Theory of the Firm?" *Journal of Management,* March 1991, 121; Raphael Amit and Paul J.H. Schoemaker, "Strategic Assets and Organizational Rent," *Strategic Management Journal,* January 1993, 33; and Margaret A. Peteraf, "The Cornerstones of Competitive Advantage: A Resource-Based View," *Strategic Management Journal,* March 1993, 179.

2. To date, the most attention paid to the integration of the two perspectives has been by Michael E. Porter in *Competitive Advantage: Creating and Sustaining Superior Performance* (New York: Free Press, 1985) and, in the dynamic context, in his article "Towards a Dynamic Theory of Strategy," *Strategic Management Journal,* Winter 1991, 95.

3. These ideas were first discussed in two articles published in *Management Science:* Ingemar Dierickx and Karel Cool, "Asset Stock Accumulation and Sustainability of Competitive Advantage," December 1989, p. 1,504; and J.B. Barney, "Asset Stocks and Sustained Competitive Advantage," December 1989, 1,512.

PART

IV

Managing Innovation

1
Tough-Minded Ways to Get Innovative

Andrall E. Pearson

Most chief executives fervently want their companies to be more competitive, not just on one or two dimensions but across the board. Yet outstanding competitive performance remains an elusive goal. A few companies achieve it. Most do not.

What distinguishes outstanding competitors from the rest? Two basic principles. First, they understand that consistent innovation is the key to a company's survival. Being innovative some of the time, in one or two areas, just won't work. Second, they know that the most powerful changes they can make are those that create value for their customers and potential customers. The result? Competitive companies constantly look for ways to change every aspect of their businesses. Then, when they've found them, they make sure that they translate those changes into advantages customers will appreciate and act on.

Lincoln Electric has understood and applied these principles for years. That's why it has been able to offer its customers better products at lower cost year after year. Yet many people see only Lincoln's success in cutting costs. They miss the fact that the company is a great innovator too because they think about innovation too narrowly—in terms of home runs only and not all the hits players make, inning after inning, game after game.

Lincoln Electric and other outstanding performers look at innovation systematically. They know that their competitive success is built on a steady stream of improvements in production, finance, distribution, and every other function, not just a big hit in sales or marketing or R&D. So they make sure they've got players who can deliver consistently. And they create organizations that give those players all the backup they need. That means:

- Creating and sustaining a corporate environment that values better performance above everything else.
- Structuring the organization to permit innovative ideas to rise above the demands of running the business.
- Clearly defining a strategic focus that lets the company channel its innovative efforts realistically, in ways that will pay off in the market.
- Knowing where to look for good ideas and how to leverage them once they're found.
- Going after good ideas at full speed, with all the company's resources brought to bear.

Individually, none of these activities may be very complicated or hard to do. But keeping a company focused on all five, all the time, takes tremendous discipline and persistence. That systematic effort to institutionalize innovation is what gives market leaders their competitive edges. And it's what other companies can learn from them.

Begin with the Right Mind-set

To convert a solid performer into an aggressive competitor, you have to create an organization that not only values better performance but also sustains the commitment year after year. That means a major shift in values, not a slight step-up in the number of new ideas for next year.

Even a brief exposure to companies that are consistently successful innovators shows their constant dedication to changing things for the better. Everyone in the business thinks and acts that way, not just a few people at the top. Just picture what it was like to work at Apple Computer or Cray Research or Nike in their early years. Or the way things are today at innovative leaders like Wal-Mart Stores or Toys "R" Us or Progressive Mutual Insurance. Or ask anyone at Heinz about the pressure on innovation since Tony O'Reilly introduced risk taking into that once sleepy outfit. Change is a way of life in companies like these.

To sharpen an organization's receptivity to change, several ingredients are essential. First and foremost, top management must be deeply and personally involved in the process.

Innovative companies are led by innovative leaders. It's that simple.

Leaders who set demanding goals for themselves and for others, the kinds of goals that force organizations to innovate to meet them. Specific, measurable goals that constitute outstanding relative performance—like becoming number one in a particular market. Not vague, easily reached objectives.

Innovative leaders aren't necessarily creative, idea-driven people themselves (though obviously many are). But they welcome change because they're convinced that their competitive survival depends on innovation. That's a mind-set most executives can develop—if their conviction is based on a specific understanding of a particular competitive environment, not just a bromidic generality.

Look at what Cummins Engine has done to stay alive and gain market share in a truck engine market that's dramatically off. As any key Cummins executive will tell you, the company cut its costs and prices per engine by close to 40% and materially improved its products for one simple reason: to prevent the Japanese from repeating their auto triumph in the truck engine business. To accomplish all this Cummins had to overhaul nearly everything that, historically, had made it the industry leader: products, processes, prices, distribution methods—the works.

People throughout Cummins found the grit to make these changes by looking at their business through the eyes of a Japanese competitor. Other innovative companies do the same thing. They get their people to focus on beating a particular competitor, not just on doing better. One-on-one competition pushes the entire organization to be bolder, to take more risks, and to change faster than companies that have no particular target for their innovative efforts. It also makes a company a tighter, more effective competitor because its innovative efforts are designed to cut away at a particular opponent's current competitive advantages.

For instance, in the 1960s and early 1970s, Pepsi was a much more aggressive and innovative company than Coca-Cola. It had to outflank Coke just to survive. When Coke finally woke up—after losing its market leadership—it did a terrific job of innovating too. Why? Coke's new management began to focus on beating Pepsi, not just on doing better. And when Pepsi's managers responded by revving up their already aggressive culture, the result made history. There has been more innovation in soft drinks in the past 5 years than there had been in the previous 20. Industry growth has doubled, and both companies' market shares are the highest ever.

The same thing happened in the beer business when Miller began to take market share from Anheuser-Busch. Suddenly Busch became a much more aggressive, innovative competitor because it was focused on Miller. In contrast, I believe IBM paid a huge price in the 1970s and early 1980s because the company wasn't focused on a number of specialized competitors who were eroding its leadership, segment by segment.

If you don't have any major competitors you can't focus on them, of course. But targeting smaller local competitors is just as effective and invigorating. It's also a good way to ward off the complacency that undoes a lot of winners. At one time, for example, Frito-Lay thought that it didn't have to pay attention to its regional competitors since its market share was more than 50%. Then, collectively, the little guys cut the company's growth rate in half. Frito became very focused very fast.

Finally, innovative companies have lots of experiments going on all the time. This encourages more risk taking since people don't expect every experiment to succeed. It contains the cost since tests and trials don't get expanded until they show real promise. And it improves the odds of success because you're betting on a portfolio, not on one or two big, long-odds projects.

Sometimes, however, the work environment is so risk-averse that management has to bring in outsiders who haven't been intimidated by the sins of the past. That was what happened when PepsiCo acquired Taco Bell, which had been run by an ultraconservative management that regarded all new ideas with suspicion. It took an infusion of three or four outsiders to create a critical mass and get the company moving again.

Unfortunately, it's very easy for managers to convey the wrong messages about risk taking. Appearing to be short-term oriented, giving the impression that only winners get promoted, searching for people to blame, second-guessing managers who take risks (often before they even have time to work out the bugs)—actions like these send a much clearer signal than all the speeches about innovation a chief executive may make. We learned that at PepsiCo when we surveyed our middle managers and found out that many of them thought we were saying one thing and doing another. We had to correct signals and practices like these before they'd credit what we said.

All three of these ingredients—commitment, a specific villain, and risk taking—are soft requirements. Not tangible things like structure and process. But just because they're soft doesn't mean they're unimportant. In fact, unless all three are in place, I question whether you'll ever emerge as a leader.

Unsettle the Organization

Most big organizations are designed mainly to operate the business: to get the work done, control performance, spot problems, and bring in this year's results. And for the most part, that's as it should be.

But the structures, processes, and people that keep things ticking smoothly can also cut off the generation of good ideas and block their movement through the business system. Excessive layering, for example, kills ideas before they ever get considered by senior managers. Barriers fencing off R&D, marketing, production, and finance bottle up functional problems until it's too late for effective solutions. Elaborate approval systems grind promising innovations to a halt. Staff nitpick ideas or put financial yardsticks on them long before they are mature enough to stand rigorous scrutiny.

To get around organizational roadblocks like these you have to differentiate between what's needed to run the business and what's needed to foster creative activity. Most successful innovations require four key inputs:

1. A champion who believes that the new idea is really critical and who will keep pushing ahead, no matter what the roadblocks.
2. A sponsor who is high up enough in the organization to marshal its resources—people, money, and time.
3. A mix of bright, creative minds (to get ideas) and experienced operators (to keep things practical).
4. A process that moves ideas through the system quickly so that they get top-level endorsement, resources, and perspective early in the game—not at the bottom of the ninth inning.

There are, of course, lots of ways to organize your company to bring these four elements together. One is to use task forces on either a full- or part-time basis. Even Procter & Gamble (the ultimate product-manager company) has begun to superimpose multifunctional project teams, often headed by senior managers, onto its old structure. Other companies use full-time task forces to achieve similar goals. They've found their old structures didn't allow enough cross-functional interaction early on. Or enough top-level involvement and support.

Still other companies, like Hasbro, rely on frequent, consistent, and freewheeling meetings with top management to achieve their integration goals. They work within the existing structure but install a process to prevent rigidity and delay. Johnson & Johnson, on the other hand, has thrived largely by spinning off operations into small divisions to encourage its general managers to act more like freestanding entrepreneurs. In all these cases, the companies are striving to create the freedom needed to cross lines, get a variety of inputs, and take risks. They've tried to organize the creative parts of the company differently from the operational ones.

These efforts aren't cost free, of course. When you're trying to change and run the business at the same time, there's bound to be some competition and conflict. But bright people can live with that, and sooner or later the bumps get smoothed out. The risk I'd worry about is leaving one of the critical bases uncovered—by trying to make a champion out of someone who isn't committed to a project, say, or neglecting to temper your whiz kids with some seasoned people who'll be able to tell them whether the product they envision can actually be made. Because if you announce you're going to innovate more aggressively, yet consistently come up short, people will get discouraged and turn off.

Be Hardheaded about Your Strategy

Once the entire organization is committed to stepping up the pace of innovation, you have to decide where to direct your efforts. One way, of course, is to put smart and talented people to work and pray that they'll come up with something great. But more often than not, an unfocused approach like that produces lots of small ideas that don't lead anywhere, big costs and embarrassing write-offs, and a great deal of frustration and stop-and-go activity.

In contrast, successful innovators usually have a pretty clear idea of the kind of competitive edges they're seeking. They've thought long and hard about what's practical in their particular businesses. And just as hard about what's not.

Frequently, you'll hear CEOs say that their companies are committed to becoming the low-cost producer, or the industry leader in new products and production processes, or the best service provider. All are worthy visions or concepts—provided they apply to that particular business and company. But in many cases, the vision and the reality don't match up.

For much of smokestack America, for example, the concept of becoming the low-cost producer is simply a cruel fantasy. The Japanese already occupy that position, in many cases permanently. So the best that U.S. manufacturers can possibly hope for is to close the gap, which isn't likely to bring them back to being number one.

Likewise, leading the way in new products has turned out to be a fool's mission for most companies in mature industries like packaged goods. The reason? Fewer than ten new products a year are successful, despite expenditures of literally tens of millions of dollars by the major companies.

Finally, superior service can be an illusory and impractical goal for many large retailers. It simply takes more management and discipline than they can muster to bring so many outlets up to a higher-than-average level of service and keep them there.

The moral here is that your strategic vision has to be grounded in a deep understanding of the competitive dynamics of your business. You have to know the industry and your competitors cold. You have to know how you stack up on every performance dimension. (The way Ford did before it was able to close the gap on some 300 product features on which it lagged Japanese competitors.) And you have to be hardheaded about using this knowledge to position your company to gain a competitive edge. Are you big enough? Technically strong enough? Good enough at marketing? In short, you must be practical—not go after a pie in the sky.

Hasbro, a $1.5 billion (and growing) toy company, has a strategic vision that works. Unlike most of its competitors, Hasbro doesn't focus on inventing new blockbuster toys. Its management will take blockbusters if they come along, of course. But the company doesn't spend the bulk of its product development dollars on such long-odds bets. Instead, it centers its efforts on staples—toy lines like G.I. Joe, Transformers, games, and preschool basics that can be extended and renewed each year.

Another fine example is Crown Cork & Seal, one of America's best-performing companies for more than 30 years despite its five-star terrible business—tin cans. How did Crown do it, especially when it was number four in a mature business dominated by two giants (American Can and Continental Can), where size and scale appear to be essential? Simple. Crown focused its efforts on growth segments (beverages), on being the lowest-cost producer in each local area (instead of nationally), on growing in lesser developed countries (too small for the biggies to worry about), and on taking over the profitable, residual business left open as Continental and American diversified out of cans.

Both Hasbro and Crown Cork & Seal are tightly focused; they don't try to be all things to all customers. And because their directions are so clearly set, their creative people can channel their efforts toward things that will work against competitors in their particular businesses. Strategic focus works—in real life, not just in articles about strategy.

Look Hard at What's Already Going On

How do you find good, concrete ideas? Brainstorming is one approach, but I've never found that very helpful except when nobody in the group knows much and nobody cares whether the output is realistic. No, I firmly believe the best backdrop for spurring innovation is knowledge—knowing your business cold. Good ideas most often flow from the process of taking a hard look at your customers, your competitors, and your business all at once. So in looking for ways to innovate, I'd concentrate on:

- What's already working in the marketplace that you can improve on and expand.
- How you can segment your markets differently and gain a competitive advantage in the process.
- How your business system compares with your competitor's.

Looking hard at what's already working in the marketplace is the tactic that's likely to produce the quickest results. I call this robbing a few gas stations so that you don't starve to death while you're planning the perfect crime.

Lots of companies think that the only good innovations are the ones they develop themselves, not the ideas they get from smaller competitors—the familiar not-invented-here syndrome. In my experience, the opposite is usually true. Normally, outside ideas are useful simply because your competitors are already doing your market research for you. They're proving what customers want in the marketplace, where it counts.

I've found that good ideas come from all over—conventional competitors, regionals, small companies, even international competitors in Europe and Japan. So it may not surprise you to learn that most of PepsiCo's major strategic successes are ideas we borrowed from the marketplace—often from small regional or local competitors.

For example, Doritos, Tostitos, and Sabritos (whose combined sales total roughly $1 billion) were products developed by three small chippers on the West Coast. The idea for pan pizza (a $500 million business for Wichita-based Pizza Hut) originated with several local pizzerias in Chicago. And the pattern for Wilson 1200 golf clubs (the most successful new club line ever) came from a small golf clubber in Arizona.

In each case, PepsiCo spotted a promising new idea, improved on it, and then out-executed the competition. To some people this sounds like copycatting. To me it amounts to finding out what's already working with consumers, improving on the idea, and then getting more out of it. You can decide how much this idea appeals to you. But in PepsiCo it led to $2 billion to $3 billion worth of successful innovations without which the company's growth would have been a lot less dynamic.

Next, I'd look at how to create new segments or markets for the kinds of products you can produce. It sounds simple, but, believe me, it takes a lot of creativity and skill to: segment a market beyond simple demographics (which rarely ever produce meaningful edges); ferret out what each group of consumers really wants (as opposed to what it says it wants); and actually create distinctive product performance features (despite the technological and operational problems you usually encounter).

Several examples will illustrate what I have in mind. At Taco Bell, the biggest Mexican fast-food restaurant chain in the United States, top management found that working women were avoiding its outlets like the plague. Women felt Taco Bell's food was "too heavy," "too spicy." So the company developed a taco salad served in a light flour tortilla and seasoned very mildly. That salad increased per-store sales more than 20%, with 70% of the sales coming from women—mostly new customers. It also added about $100 million to Taco Bell's sales in its first full year.

It sounds simple, I'm sure: pick out a big segment you're not reaching, find out what consumers don't like about existing products, and develop a product to serve them better. But it took Taco Bell nearly two years to get the idea, develop it in R&D, test market several versions of the salad, and finally launch the winner nationally.

Another example, much more familiar, is what the Japanese have done in the camera business. They decided there was a segment of camera users who couldn't afford German top-of-the-line models but wanted vastly better pictures than those they could get from their existing Kodaks or Polaroids. Camera technology has been around for a long time, and the Japanese just hammered away at improving it until they succeeded in making superior 35mm cameras at a price people could afford. In the process, they created and now dominate a new (and huge) segment that no one else had seen.

Finally, there's Budget Gourmet, a four-year-old company you may never have heard of. Its management developed a very profitable $300 million business from scratch in a field—frozen foods—characterized by enormous price pressures, undistinguished products, little innovation, and low returns. Its founder's strategic vision was to offer working families high-quality-recipe products intended for microwave ovens and aimed at the low end of the market. So the company started out by developing a process to make and sell a line of entrees for $1.69, which gave it a good price advantage. But unlike other low-priced lines, Budget Gourmet's products were comparable to the over-$2 competition. And it backed up the product with first-class packaging, promotion, and advertising (the kind its low-end competitors didn't think of investing in). The result—a remarkable success in an extremely competitive field previously dominated by three of America's largest, most successful food companies. It's a terrific example of how segmentation and strategic focus interact. And like most good ideas it looks obvious—once you see how it works.

As these examples show, successful segmentors are very clear about what they're trying to do: offer their customers better value than their competitors do. This usually takes one of three forms: lower prices, better performing products, or better features for certain uses (a niche). Unless you can beat your competitors on one of these three dimensions, your innovation probably won't be a big success. The key idea, of course, is that you're trying to outperform the competition on a specific performance dimension and scale, not with vague platitudes. And successful innovators don't give up until customers reassure them that they've done just that.

The third place to look for good innovative ideas is in your business system. Beyond its products, every company has a business system by which it goes to market. That system is the whole flow of activities starting with product design and working its way through purchasing, production, MIS, distribution, customer sales, and product service. It will come as no surprise that these systems differ from one competitor to another, even in the same industry. And in almost every case, each competitor's system has particular strengths and vulnerabilities that can provide a fruitful focus for your innovative energies.

The underlying concept here is that a distinctive system can give you a big competitive edge for all your products because it will help you leverage their inherent consumer appeals in ways your competitors find hard to match. And once you understand how your business' system works at each step—both in terms of the marketplace and comparative system costs—it's surprising how often you'll uncover weak spots in a competitor's system or potential strengths in your own.

The number of Pizza Hut outlets (4,500), for example, dwarfs that of its nearest competitor (about 500). Scale like that is no guarantee of success. But it means that only the Pizza Hut system can market pizza products on a national basis virtually overnight—and thereby preempt local competition.

At one time, the biggest marketing problem Pizza Hut faced was lunch. Compared with McDonald's, its restaurants had virtually no lunchtime sales, and neither did any of its pizza competitors. The reason, of course, is that it takes 20 minutes to cook a pizza from scratch in a traditional pizza oven, and most people won't spend that long at lunchtime waiting to be served. By using a new, continuous-broiling technology adapted from the burger business, Pizza Hut developed a personal pan pizza that could be served in less than five minutes. It was quick, tasty, and moderately priced. And Pizza Hut rolled it out to all 4,500 stores and locked up the pizza-lunch business almost everywhere, almost overnight.

A good example of using a business system to maintain a competitive edge comes from the cookie business. P&G decided it could produce better cookies than Nabisco, the current leader. So the company came out with a great new cookie that tasted and looked better than Nabisco's Chips Ahoy!, the market leader. Duncan Hines cookies were the kind of superior product P&G has used to become the market leader in scores of products.

But its managers didn't count on the retaliatory strength of Nabisco's store-door distribution system and its intense desire to protect that big, profitable base system. Nabisco quickly matched P&G's cookie, in addition to expanding and improving its entire cookie line, and it used the leverage of its bigger system to get trade support and consumer impact. Despite the inherent superiority of P&G's single-product entry, it stood no chance against Nabisco's system strengths.

Virtually any part of your business system can be the basis for building competitive edges. Product technology has been a fruitful source of systemic advantages for Cray Research. Lincoln Electric's decades-long leadership is based largely on a systemic edge in production. Truly superior marketing and service have made Fidelity Investments' Fidelity Funds the dominant player in a business in which it was once an also-ran.

Naturally, in analyzing your business system and your competitors', you have to look at them dynamically since structural changes are usually at work altering what's required for success. When Philip Morris bought 7-Up, for example, its management knew they were entering an industry that historically had allowed smaller brands to prosper nicely. In fact, many Coke and Pepsi bottlers also handled 7-Up. But the battle between Coke and Pepsi was heating up, and as it became more intense, those cola competitors put tremendous pressure on their bottlers to launch new products, promote more often, and scramble for supermarket space. Both 7-Up and its new cola brand were left out in the cold. A one-time forgiving industry had become downright hostile.

Go for Broke

Even the best concepts or strategies tend to develop incrementally. They rarely ever work the first time out or unfold just as they were planned. In fact, the original concept or its execution usually gets changed considerably before it's ready to be implemented broadly. Pizza Hut's pan pizza, for instance, went through four or five different iterations. So even after you spot a promising segment and develop a product to serve it, you've usually still got at least one major hurdle to jump before you can capitalize on your new idea.

Tab initially flopped as a diet cola because consumers couldn't tell the difference between Tab with 1 calorie and Diet Pepsi, which then had 100. Then Coke figured out that it could dramatize the difference by surrounding a bathing beauty with 100 empty Tab bottles. Armed with that insight, it flooded the TV screen with ads and backed them up in stores with displays, signs, and samples. It was frightening to see how quickly that one idea, which sounds pretty small, changed the competitive dynamics.

To take another example, the Wilson Sting was developed to sell for half the price of the Prince graphite tennis racket. But very few high-end consumers believed they could get the same quality for $125 as Prince provided for $250, even though it was true. Fortunately, an alert marketing person at Wilson then uncovered a new segment for the Sting—people who were buying metal rackets because they couldn't afford graphite. Sting's pitch became "a graphite racket for the same price as steel," and that positioning made it a major success.

Once an idea or concept is properly developed, it seems logical to assume that any sensible company would throw the book at it to make it a success. Yet I've found that reality is often quite different. Looking back, most of the new-product mistakes I've seen grew from the company's failure to back up the innovation with enough resources— not from overspending.

Several factors explain this phenomenon. First and most important, many people fail to recognize that their competitors will retaliate—especially if their innovation takes customers away. People get so captivated by their own product that they plan new launches implicitly assuming there will be no significant competitive response. Almost inevitably, that turns out to be a poor assumption.

Second, people try to stretch their resources to finance too many projects at once because the prospect of four or five successes instead of one or two is so attractive. But new products generally involve considerable front-end investment and lots of management attention. So in a world in which money, people, and programs are necessarily limited, this usually means that none of the projects gets enough sustained support and effort to ensure its success. The only way around it is to be disciplined enough to say "next year" to most of the good ideas available.

Finally, people are often in such a hurry to get into the market with a new product that they neglect to think through all the things needed to launch it properly. These include programs to get adequate retailer support, advertising to generate high customer awareness, and above all, trial-inducing devices to entice consumers to pick the new product instead of the one they're already using. One or more of these essentials often goes by the boards.

In contrast, the big winners make careful plans to throw everything needed at new products to ensure their success—money, people, programs in every functional area. They don't just allocate resources, they marshal them, and then they execute like the Russian hockey team or the Boston Celtics. They've learned that doing it right the first time is lots more effective (and usually far less costly) than doing the job on a shoestring and then scrambling to fix things when what happens doesn't meet expectations. They also know they're never going to have the first-blood advantage again, and that the best way to preempt or block out competition is to do it right the first time.

I'm a firm believer in developing innovations as fast as you can do each one properly, which includes stopping to be sure you've got everything needed to generate a big success and then going to war to make the idea a winner. Sounds so obvious, you wonder why so many companies fail to do either of these pieces properly.

To sum up quickly, I believe there are five steps you can take to make your company more dynamic and innovative. Create a corporate environment that puts constant pressure on everyone to beat your specific competitors at innovation. Structure your organization so that you promote innovation instead of thwarting it. Develop a realistic strategic focus to channel your innovative efforts. Know where to look for good ideas and how to use your business system to leverage them once they're found. Throw the book at good ideas once you've developed them fully.

It all sounds simple because, of course, it is. Simple but not easy, since each innovation is a constant challenge from beginning to end. Yet innovation is a challenge you have to meet because that's what builds market leadership and competitive momentum. That's the bottom line. And that's why it's worth the extra effort to become an innovative company.

2
Managing Innovation in the Information Age

Rebecca Henderson

The continued vitality of the most successful U.S. and European pharmaceutical companies, in the face of accelerating scientific and technological change, holds valuable lessons for managers in all industries trying to respond to turbulent times. The pharmaceutical industry faces some serious challenges in the future, most notably the proposed reform of the U.S. health care system. Yet its success to date in the crucial area of research can serve as a benchmark for companies seeking to become more innovative in the overloaded environment of the information age.

New competitors skillfully exploiting a wave of technological change have displaced or seriously challenged the companies that once dominated such industries as machine tools, steel, xerography, automobiles, semiconductors, and computers. In contrast, companies founded in the 1940s and 1950s continue to dominate the pharmaceutical industry. These companies have demonstrated an ability to learn and grow that confounds conventional wisdom. Despite their age, size, and success, the best of these companies have found ways to retain the flexibility and responsiveness of companies one-tenth their size and age. And they have already solved some of the competitive challenges in the research arena that companies in other industries are just starting to grapple with.

New research that I conducted with Iain Cockburn, professor of strategic management at the University of British Columbia, suggests that the longevity of pharmaceutical companies attests to a unique managerial competency: the ability to foster a high level of specialized knowledge within an organization, while preventing that information from becoming embedded in such a way that it permanently fixes the organization in the past, unable to respond to an ever-changing competitive environment.

GM, IBM, and DEC are not in trouble today because they are run by incompetents. Rather, their difficulties are the natural result of their success. They have become prisoners of the deeply ingrained assumptions, information filters, and problem-solving strategies that make up their world views, turning the solutions that once made them great into new problems to be resolved. The best pharmaceutical companies have not fallen into this trap. Instead, they have managed to remake themselves even as the science on which they rely has changed dramatically. Studying these successful companies provides an opportunity to learn how to innovate continuously in the face of rapidly changing scientific and technological information.

Management Matters

To outside observers, the drug-discovery process can seem a random procedure in which inspired scientists, working around the clock, come upon major breakthroughs in the middle of the night. Drug discovery is risky, but the process is much less random than it appears. While 20 years ago, organic chemists might have had little more than hunches to guide them in the synthesis and elaboration of new compounds, today's chemists have much more information and far more sophisticated tools to guide them in their work. The random screening of compounds remains important, but leading-edge drug discovery is most often the result of a guided search. And effective management can greatly increase the efficiency of the discovery process.

In a three-year study of ten pharmaceutical companies, Professor Cockburn and I found that the research efforts of the most successful pharmaceutical companies can be as much as 40% more productive than their rivals. Interpreted with some care, this result is substantial enough to suggest that it takes more than hiring the best possible people and giving them funds to be successful. Indeed, management plays a crucial role in the innovation process. The best managers do not merely administer a static system. Instead, they constantly challenge the company's conventional wisdom and stimulate the dynamic exchange of ideas.

Modern-day drug discovery requires the integration of knowledge from a broad array of disciplines. A major drug house, for example,

Exhibit I.

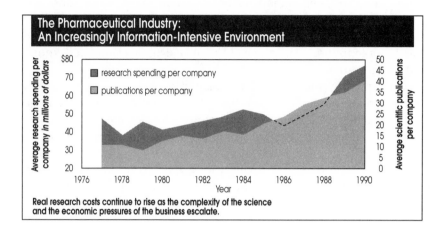

**The Pharmaceutical Industry:
An Increasingly Information-Intensive Environment**

■ research spending per company

□ publications per company

Average research spending per company in millions of dollars

Average scientific publications per company

Year

Real research costs continue to rise as the complexity of the science and the economic pressures of the business escalate.

today employs large numbers of molecular biologists, physiologists, and biochemists, as well as specialists in the traditional disciplines of synthetic chemistry and pharmacology, and more esoteric specialists like molecular kineticists. All of these disciplines are advancing at an extraordinarily rapid rate. For instance, there were over 80,000 articles published in the cardiovascular field alone in just the last half of 1992. Good drug discovery, therefore, requires tight ties to the larger intellectual community. But a unique competence in just one scientific specialty—say, in synthetic chemistry—is not enough to sustain a prolonged competitive advantage. Successful companies must keep abreast of the changes within particular scientific disciplines and successfully integrate this knowledge within and across company boundaries, often in new and unexpected ways. (See Exhibit I.)

As a result, successful pharmaceutical companies have been forced to acquire the key competitive advantage of the 1990s: the ability to innovate in an information-intensive environment. Over a period of 30 years, the most successful companies in our study obtained more than twice the number of patents per research dollar, advanced to clinical trials more often, and, most important, were more than twice as likely to bring new drugs to market than their less successful competitors. As a result, these companies had sales and profits far above the industry average.

In addition, the managers of these companies did all the things that business pundits recommend: they used sophisticated resource-allocation procedures, hired the best people, and encouraged cross-functional and cross-disciplinary communication. More important, they didn't view these innovations as quick fixes to a static system. Instead, they focused on continuously refurbishing the innovative capabilities of the organization. They actively managed their companies' knowledge and resources.

Our study revealed three characteristics shared by the most successful pharmaceutical companies: first, they kept abreast of the changes in their field by making and maintaining close connections with the scientific community at large; second, they allocated resources across a wide range of therapeutic areas, ending up with the most advantageous mix of projects; and, finally, they actively confronted the tension between organizing by function and organizing by product group.

Keeping Connected

The scientific and medical knowledge needed to make significant advances in drug discovery is changing too fast for any one company to hope to master it all. The most successful companies in our study therefore ensured that they were efficiently connected to the scientific community and to their peers.

All companies in our sample had scientific advisory boards, for example, but the boards had been in existence for many years in the most successful companies. All companies permitted their employees to publish in scientific journals and to attend conferences, but, in the most successful companies, eminence in the scientific community was an important criterion for promotion. At one of the less successful companies, for example, the director of research commented, "Of course people are free to publish if they want, but in general I haven't encouraged it. After all, the effort that goes into writing a paper could be employed to search for new drugs." In sharp contrast, the research director at one of the most successful companies was proud to have recently sponsored a major scientific conference in the field.

Of course, a company that focuses on scientific excellence alone runs the risk of creating an organization staffed by world-class scientists who produce excellent papers but no useful drugs. The successful companies balanced the ability to reach out beyond the company for new scientific knowledge with the ability to link that knowledge to therapeutically useful goals.

Allocating Scarce Resources

Budgeting is a contentious process. Yet in the pharmaceutical industry, it is made more difficult because large amounts of money must be invested years before any return can be expected. (See "Scientific Management at Merck: An Interview with CFO Judy Lewent," by Nancy A. Nichols, *Harvard Business Review,* January–February, 1994.)

Successful resource allocation is not simply a matter of picking winners or diversifying financial risk. Our study suggests that the most productive companies are those whose project portfolios are not only diverse enough to enable them to leverage their specialized scientific expertise but also related sufficiently to allow them to benefit from the cross-fertilization of ideas. (See Exhibit II.) Well managed resource-allocation processes also have important implications for the effective management of knowledge within a company. Effective resource-allocation processes encourage lively debate and in turn stimulate the rapid transfer of information across the company, while ensuring that the opportunities this information flow presents are reflected in the set of projects chosen.

In companies with relatively little communication across boundaries, resource allocation was more likely to be managed with a "last year plus 5%" or a "don't bother me, and I won't bother you" tactic. Strong individuals carved out personal fiefdoms, and resources rarely shifted dramatically from year to year across disciplines or therapeutic classes. Any individual area might conduct world-class science or make the occasional breakthrough. However, the static nature of the resource-allocation process encouraged a certain narrowness of vision.

In contrast, in the successful companies, resource allocation was a much more contentious process. Two models seemed to work particularly well. In the first model, a single, highly respected and knowledgeable individual took primary responsibility. He or she was widely read in the field and actively questioned the leading scientists on every project, pushing for more detail and suggesting new connections, questions, and perspectives. This method of decision making is risky because its effectiveness is solely dependent on the ability of the key decision maker. Some of the worst performing companies, for instance, were commanded by resource-allocation dictators who made the wrong calls or alienated key personnel with their arrogance. Still, when this method works well, it works very well, because the cross-boundary connections are made in the mind of a single individual who

Exhibit II.

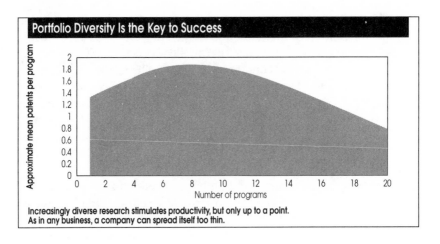

Portfolio Diversity Is the Key to Success

Increasingly diverse research stimulates productivity, but only up to a point.
As in any business, a company can spread itself too thin.

can encourage those around him or her to think in boundary-breaking terms.

The second successful resource-allocation model was the relatively high-conflict committee. Key decisions were made at annual or biannual meetings. There, each group presented its project and budget requirements, and decisions were arrived at through constructive confrontations across the group. While at its worst this type of decision making tends toward "last year plus 5%," at its best it encourages senior scientists to be aware of the nature and status of research being conducted in other areas of the company, encouraging the fluid flow of information and ideas throughout the organization.

Our results suggest that the companies that take advantage of knowledge generated from all areas of the organization are significantly more productive than their rivals. (See Exhibit III.) All other things being equal, for example, our results suggest that moving a program from one of the least diversified companies in the sample to one running twice the number of programs would increase its productivity by more than 20%. The best resource-allocation processes not only encourage the flow of information across the company, they also reflect an awareness that choosing the right set of projects is more than a financial decision. If projects are interrelated, failure in one program can be redeemed by the ability to use the knowledge it generated in other areas of the company. And if projects are diverse, then the company can remain open to unexpected possibilities and unanticipated connections.

Exhibit III.

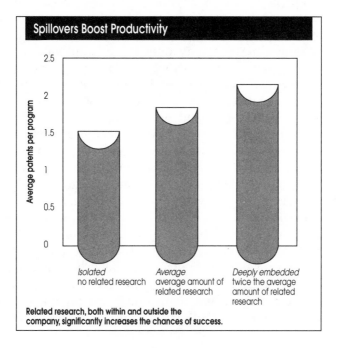

Spillovers Boost Productivity

Average patents per program

Isolated
no related research

Average
average amount of
related research

Deeply embedded
twice the average
amount of related
research

Related research, both within and outside the
company, significantly increases the chances of success.

Managing Tension in Organizational Design

Every organization must choose between organizing by function and organizing by product. Organization by function ensures that the in-depth, specialized knowledge fundamental to long-term innovation is preserved and enhanced. However, it opens the company to developing the "functional silos" that have bedeviled so much of U.S. industry. Organization by product, on the other hand, focuses the energies of the organization on the customer and encourages rich communication across functions. But it often does so at the cost of a steadily eroding base of functional knowledge. After a while, the functional specialists have spent so much time thinking about the whole product that they lose the functional expertise that was their core strength.

Our study suggests that either approach to organizational design can be, at best, only a temporary solution. A senior research manager at one of the most successful companies reflected, "We've tried organizing by therapeutic class. We've tried organizing by scientific discipline.

We've tried using project teams. Nothing works as well as being continually aware of the need to be both at the leading edge of the science and in total command of the important developments in other areas."

Success is not a function of a particular organizational choice or a particular form of boundary-spanning mechanism. Indeed, the most successful companies in our study were those that were never satisfied with any single answer. They continually expended organizational energy to ensure that neither the disciplinary nor the therapeutic perspective took the upper hand for too long. In some companies, this meant refocusing from disciplinary to therapeutic area and vice versa on a regular basis. In others, it meant continuous experimentation with boundary-spanning devices such as tiger teams or "heavyweight" team leaders. In still others, it meant the active cultivation of a culture in which every individual was continually reminded to wear "two hats": a functional, or disciplinary, hat and a product-oriented, or therapeutic, hat. A senior scientist at one of the most successful companies said of his company's tactic, "They have given me all the resources that I could have asked for, and we've been able to do some world-class science. But I'm very much aware that if we don't come up with some promising new compounds soon, my role here will be called into question. And that's OK. I want to see the science used to make some major therapeutic breakthroughs."

The problem of innovation is never solved. Cross-functional teams, organizing by product, or organizing by function may increase cross-disciplinary communication, but they may do so at the expense of disciplinary excellence. Companies succeed by attending to this tension, devoting organizational energy to ensuring that neither end of the continuum dominates the process. Their experience underlines the need to revisit and rebalance the organization's flow of knowledge continuously.

Success Is Dangerous

Health care reform presents the pharmaceutical industry with a new set of challenges. Can the industry respond with the flexibility that it has shown in adapting its research efforts to the biomedical revolution? For example, in their development functions (the processes of testing drugs on humans), some companies in our study displayed the kinds of deeply ingrained assumptions and rigid behavior patterns that have crippled established companies in other industries.

If it is to avoid the fate of so much of U.S. industry, the pharmaceutical industry will have to be just as sophisticated in developing and selling its products as it has been in generating them.

Author's note

This study was funded by the Sloan Foundation and four pharmaceutical companies, drawing on the internal records of ten major European and U.S. pharmaceutical companies and a variety of public data. The companies account for approximately 28% of U.S. research-and-development and sales. Professor Iain Cockburn and I believe that they are representative of the industry in terms of size and technical and commercial performance.

Our statistical results rely on a database that contains information about the inputs and outputs of more than 120 programs over a period of up to 30 years. Our primary input measure is research spending on discovery; our output measures include important patents, numbers of investigational new drug applications, new drug applications, new drug approvals, sales, and market share. These data were supplemented by interviews with 84 people at the sample companies, a number of industry experts, and a variety of measures of scientific opportunity and pharmaceutical demand derived from public sources.

3
Research That Reinvents the Corporation

John Seely Brown

The most important invention that will come out of the corporate research lab in the future will be the corporation itself. As companies try to keep pace with rapid changes in technology and cope with increasingly unstable business environments, the research department has to do more than simply innovate new products. It must design the new technological and organizational "architectures" that make possible a continuously innovating company. Put another way, corporate research must reinvent innovation.

At the Xerox Palo Alto Research Center (PARC), we've learned this lesson, at times, the hard way. Xerox created PARC in 1970 to pursue advanced research in computer science, electronics, and materials science. Over the next decade, PARC researchers were responsible for some of the basic innovations of the personal-computer revolution— only to see other companies commercialize these innovations more quickly than Xerox. (See "PARC: Seedbed of the Computer Revolution.") In the process, Xerox gained a reputation for "fumbling the future," and PARC for doing brilliant research but in isolation from the company's business.

PARC: Seedbed of the Computer Revolution

Former Xerox CEO C. Peter McColough created the Palo Alto Research CENTER (PARC) in 1970 to perform basic research in computing and electronics and to study what McColough called "the architecture of information"—how complex organizations use information. PARC hired some of the best computer scientists in the world and gave them virtually unlimited funding to pursue their ideas.

The scientific payoff from PARC was immediate. Throughout the 1970s, PARC researchers produced a series of fundamental innovation in computer technology that would prove to be the building blocks of the personal-computer revolution: "bit map" display computer screens that make easy-to-use graphic interfaces possible, local area networks for distributed computing, overlapping screen windows, point-and-click editing using a "mouse," and Smalltalk, the first object-oriented programming language.

Xerox never became a dominant player in the personal-computer industry. But PARC's research has nevertheless directly fed the company's strategic business. PARC developed the first prototype of laser printing in 1973. By 1990, laser printing was a several-billion-dollar business at Xerox. And PARC's innovations in local area networks and its distinctive computer interface designs have been successfully incorporated in Xerox copiers and printers, an innovation that was crucial to the company's successfully meeting the challenge from Japanese competition in the 1980s.

Where PARC scientists of the 1970s had a technical vision, today the center is increasingly focusing on the interrelationships between technology and work. In 1990, anthropologists, sociologists, linguists, and psychologists complement PARC's traditional staff of computer scientists, physicists, and engineers. And much of the center's computer-science research emphasizes how information technology can be used to support effective group collaboration—a field known as computer-supported cooperative work.—Robert Howard

That view is one-sided because it ignores the way that PARC innovations *have* paid off over the past 20 years. Still, it raises fundamental questions that many companies besides Xerox have been struggling with in recent years: What is the role of corporate research in a business environment characterized by tougher competition and nonstop technological change? And how can large companies better assimilate the latest innovations and quickly incorporate them in new products?

One popular answer to these questions is to shift the focus of the research department away from radical breakthroughs toward incremental innovation, away from basic research toward applied research. At PARC, we have chosen a different approach, one that cuts across both of these categories and combines the most useful features of each. We call it pioneering research.

Like the best applied research, pioneering research is closely connected to the company's most pressing business problems. But like the best basic research, it seeks to redefine these problems fundamentally in order to come up with fresh—and sometimes radical—solutions. Our emphasis on pioneering research has led us to redefine what we mean by technology, by innovation, and indeed by research itself. (See "Letter to a Young Researcher.") Here are some of the new principles that we have identified:

1. RESEARCH ON NEW WORK PRACTICES IS AS IMPORTANT AS RESEARCH ON NEW PRODUCTS. Corporate research is traditionally viewed as the source of new technologies and products. At PARC, we believe it is equally important for research to invent new prototypes of organizational practice. This means going beyond the typical view of technology as an artifact—hardware and software—to explore its potential for creating new and more effective ways of working, what we call studying "technology in use." Such activities are essential for companies to exploit successfully the next great breakthrough in information technology: "ubiquitous computing," or the incorporation of information technology in a broad range of everyday objects.

2. INNOVATION IS EVERYWHERE; THE PROBLEM IS LEARNING FROM IT. When corporate research begins to focus on a company's practice as well as its products, another principle quickly becomes clear: innovation isn't the privileged activity of the research department. It goes on at all levels of a company—wherever employees confront problems, deal with unforeseen contingencies, or work their way around breakdowns in normal procedures. The problem is, few companies know how to learn from this local innovation and how to use it to improve their overall effectiveness. At PARC, we are studying this process of local innovation with employees on the front lines of Xerox's business and developing technologies to harvest its lessons for the company as a whole. By doing so, we hope to turn company size, so often seen as an obstacle to innovation, into an advantage—a rich seedbed of fresh insights about technology and new work practices.

3. RESEARCH CAN'T JUST PRODUCE INNOVATION; IT MUST "COPRODUCE" IT. Before a company can learn from the innovation in its midst, it must rethink the process by which innovation is transmitted

Xerox Corporation
Palo Alto Research Center

3333 Coyote Hill Road
Palo Alto, California 94304
415 494-4000

Letter to a Young Researcher

When we hire someone at PARC, there is one qualification we consider more important than technology expertise or intellectual brilliance: intuition. A well-honed intuition and the ability to trust it are essential tools for doing the kind of research we do here.

Our approach to research is "radical" in the sense conveyed by the world's original Greek meaning: "to the root." At PARC, we attempt to pose and answer basic questions that can lead to fundamental breakthroughs. Our competitive edge depends on our ability to invent radically new approaches to computing and its uses and then bring these rapidly to market.

This is different from what goes on at most corporate research centers, where the focus is on improving current technology and advancing the status quo. If you take a job somewhere else, when you embark on the project you will probably have a pretty good idea of how and when your work will pay off. The problems you address will be well defined. You will help to improve computer technology state of the art by going one step farther along a well-plotted path.

If you come to work here, there will be no plotted path. The problems you work on will be ones you help to invent. When you embark on a project, you will have to be prepared to go in directions you couldn't have predicted at the outset. You will be challenged to take risks and to give up cherished methods or beliefs in order to find new approaches. You will encounter periods of deep uncertainty and frustration when it will seem that your efforts are leading nowhere.

That's why following your instinct is so important. Only by having deep intuitions, being able to trust them, and knowing how to run with them will you be able to keep your bearings and guide yourself through uncharted territory. The ability to do research that gets to the root is what separates merely good researchers from world-class ones. The former are reacting to a predictable future; the latter are enacting a qualitatively new one.

Another characteristic we look for in our research staff is a commitment to solving real problems in the real world. Our focus is on technology *in use,* and people here are passionate about seeing their ideas embedded in products that shape the way people work, interact, and create.

At Xerox, both corporate executives and research scientists are strongly committed to making research pay off. Over the last few years, new channels of dialogue have opened between research and other parts of the company. In particular, corporate strategy and research shape and inform each other. PARC's strategic role will undoubtedly be further strengthened by the emergence of digital copying and the company's new focus on documents of all kinds, whether in digital or paper form. The fusion of the two previously separate Xerox businesses—information systems and copying—means that the company will be able to capitalize on PARC's expertise in ways it has been unable to do in the past.

This is an exciting time to be embarking on a career in systems research. New tools and technologies make it possible to deliver large amounts of computing power to users, and this increase in power opens up possibilities for using computation in new ways.

If you come to work here, you will sacrifice the security of the safe approach in which you can count on arriving at a predictable goal. But you will have an opportunity to express your personal research "voice" and to help create a future that would not have existed without you.

Sincerely,

John Seely Brown   Frank Squires
Corporate Vice President   Vice President, Research Operations

throughout the organization. Research must "coproduce" new technologies and work practices by developing with partners throughout the organization a shared understanding of why these innovations are important. On the one hand, that means challenging the outmoded background assumptions that so often distort the way people see new technologies, new market opportunities, and the entire business. On the other, it requires creating new ways to communicate the significance of radical innovations. Essentially, corporate research must prototype new mental models of the organization and its business.

4. THE RESEARCH DEPARTMENT'S ULTIMATE INNOVATION PARTNER IS THE CUSTOMER. Prototyping technology in use, harvesting local innovation, coproducing new mental models of the organization—all these activities that we are pursuing inside Xerox are directly applicable to our customers as well. In fact, our future competitive advantage will depend not just on selling information-technology products *to* customers. It will depend on coproducing these products *with* customers—customizing technology and work practices to meet their current and future needs. One role of corporate research in this activity is to invent methods and tools to help customers identify their "latent" needs and improve their own capacity for continuous innovation.

At PARC, we've only begun to explore the implications of these new principles. Our activities in each of these areas are little more than interesting experiments. Still, we have defined a promising and exciting new direction. Without giving up our strong focus on state-of-the-art information technologies, we are also studying the human and organizational barriers to innovation. And using the entire Xerox organization as our laboratory, we are experimenting with new techniques for helping people grasp the revolutionary potential of new technologies and work practices.

The result: important contributions to Xerox's core products but also a distinctive approach to innovation with implications far beyond our company. Our business happens to be technology, but any company—no matter what the business—must eventually grapple with the issues we've been addressing. The successful company of the future must understand how people really work and how technology can help them work more effectively. It must know how to create an environment for continual innovation on the part of *all* employees. It must rethink traditional business assumptions and tap needs that customers don't even know they have yet. It must use research to reinvent the corporation.

Technology Gets Out of the Way

At the foundation of our new approach to research is a particular vision of technology. As the cost of computing power continues to plummet, two things become possible. First, more and more electronic technology will be incorporated in everyday office devices. Second, increased computing power will allow users to tailor the technology to meet their specific needs.

Both these trends lead to a paradoxical result. When information technology is everywhere and can be customized to match more closely the work to be done, the technology itself will become invisible. The next great breakthrough of the information age will be the disappearance of discrete information-technology products. Technology is finally becoming powerful enough to get out of the way.

Consider the photocopier. Ever since Chester Carlson first invented xerography some 50 years ago, the technology of photocopiers has been more or less the same. In a process somewhat similar to photography, a light-lens projects an image of the page onto a photoreceptor. The image is then developed with a dry toner to produce the copy. But information technology is transforming the copier with implications as radical as those accompanying the invention of xerography itself.

Today our copiers are complex computing and communications devices. Inside Xerox's high-end machines are some 30 microprocessors linked together by local area networks. They continually monitor the operations of the machine and make adjustments to compensate for wear and tear, thus increasing reliability and ensuring consistent, high copy quality. Information systems inside our copiers also make the machines easier to use by constantly providing users with information linked to the specific task they are performing. (See "How Xerox Redesigned Its Copiers.") These innovations were crucial to Xerox's success in meeting Japanese competition and regaining market share during the past decade.

How Xerox Redesigned Its Copiers

In the early 1980s, Xerox's copier business faced a big problem. Service calls were increasing, and more and more customers were reporting that our newest copiers were "unreliable." The complaints couldn't have come at a worse time. We had been late to recognize market opportunities for low- and mid-range copiers, and Japanese competitors like Canon were cutting into our market share. Now Xerox's reputation for quality was at stake.

After interviewing some customers, we discovered that unreliability was not the real problem. Our copiers weren't breaking down more frequently than before; in fact, many of the service calls were unnecessary. But customers were finding the copiers increasingly difficult to use. Because they couldn't get their work done, they perceived the machines were unreliable.

The source of the problem was our copier design. Traditionally, Xerox technology designers—like most engineers—have strived to make machines "idiot proof." The idea was to foresee in advance all the possible things that could go wrong, then either design them out of the system or provide detailed instructions of what to do should they occur.

But as we kept adding new functions, we had to add more and more information, usually stored on flip cards attached to the machine. The copiers became so complex that it was harder for the new user to figure out how to do any particular task. To learn a new operation meant a time-consuming search through the flip cards. And whenever something went wrong—a paper jam, say, or a problem with the toner—the machines would flash a cryptic code number, which would require more flipping through the cards to find the corresponding explanation.

In many instances, users would encounter some obstacle, not be able to find out how to resolve it, and simply abandon the machine in mid-procedure. The next user to come along, unaware of the previous problem, would assume the machine was broken and call a repair person.

We had to make radical changes in copier design, but it was difficult to sell that message within the company. The idea that there might be serious usability problems with our machines met with resistance in the Xerox development organization that designs our copier. After all, they had tested their designs against all the traditional "human factors" criteria. There was a tendency to assume that any problems with the machines must be the users' fault.

When researchers from PARC began to study the problem, we discovered that the human-factors tests used by the development group didn't accurately reflect how people actually used the machines. So, a PARC anthropologist set up a video camera overlooking one of our new copiers in use at PARC, then had pairs of researchers (including some leading computer scientists) use the machine to do their own copying. The result was dramatic footage of some very smart people, anything but idiots, becoming increasingly frustrated and angry as they tried and failed to figure out how to get the machine to do what they wanted it to do.

The videos proved crucial in convincing the doubters that the company had a serious problem. Even more important, they helped us define what the real problem was. The videos demonstrate that when people use technology like a copier they construct interpretations of it. In effect, they have a conversation with the machine much as two people have a conversation with each other. But our traditional idiot-proof design provided few cues to help the user interpret what was going on.

We proposed an alternative approach to design. Instead of trying to eliminate "trouble," we acknowledged that it was inevitable. So the copier's design should help users "manage" trouble—just as people manage and recover from misunderstandings during a conversation. This meant keeping the machine as transparent as possible by making it easy for the user to find out what is going on and to discover immediately what to do when something goes wrong.

Xerox's most recent copier families—the 10 and 50 series—reflect this new design principle. Gone are the flip cards of earlier machines. Instead, we include enough computing power in the machines to provide customized instructions on the display panel linked to particular procedures or functions. The information the user receives is immediately put in the context of the task he or she is trying to perform. The new design also incorporates ideas from PARC's research on graphical user interfaces for computers. When something goes wrong, the display panel immediately shows a picture of the machine that visually indicates where the problem is and how to resolve it.

The results of these changes have been dramatic. Where it once took 28 minutes on average to clear a paper jam, it takes 20 seconds with the new design. And because such breakdowns are easier to fix, customers are more tolerant of them when they occur.

But these changes are only the beginning. Once copiers become computing devices, they also become sensors that collect information about their own performance that can be used to improve service and product design. For example, Xerox recently introduced a new standard feature on our high-end copiers known as "remote interactive communication" or RIC. RIC is an expert system inside the copier that monitors the information technology controlling the machine and, using some artificial-intelligence techniques, predicts when the machine will next break down. Once RIC predicts a breakdown will occur, it automatically places a call to a branch office and downloads its prediction, along with its reasoning. A computer at the branch office does some further analysis and schedules a repair person to visit the site *before* the expected time of failure.

For the customer, RIC means never having to see the machine fail. For Xerox, it means not only providing better service but also having a new way to "listen" to our customer. As RIC collects information on the performance of our copiers—in real-world business environments, year in and year out—we will eventually be able to use that information to guide how we design future generations of copiers.

RIC is one example of how information technology invisible to the user is transforming the copier. But the ultimate conclusion of this technological transformation is the disappearance of the copier as a stand-alone device. Recently, Xerox introduced its most versatile office machine ever—a product that replaces traditional light-lens copying techniques with "digital copying," where documents are electronically scanned to create an image stored in a computer, then printed out whenever needed. In the future, digital copiers will allow the user to scan a document at one site and print it out somewhere else—much like a fax. And once it scans a document, a copier will be able to store, edit, or enhance the document—like a computer file—before printing it. When this happens, the traditional distinction between the copier and other office devices like computers, printers, and fax machines will disappear—leaving a flexible, multifunctional device able to serve a variety of user needs.

What is happening to the copier will eventually happen to all office devices. As computing power becomes ubiquitous—incorporated not only in copiers but also in filing cabinets, desktops, white boards, even electronic "post-it" notes—it will become more and more invisible, a taken-for-granted part of any work environment, much as books, reports, or other documents are today. What's more, increased computing power will make possible new uses of information technology that are far more flexible than current systems. In effect, technology will become so flexible that users will be able to customize it ever-more precisely to meet their particular needs—a process that might be termed "mass customization."

We are already beginning to see this development in software design. Increased computing power is making possible new approaches to writing software such as "object-oriented programming" (developed at PARC in the 1970s). This technique makes it easier for users to perform customizing tasks that previously required a trained programmer and allows them to adapt and redesign information systems as their needs change. From a purely technical perspective, object-oriented programming may be less efficient than traditional programming techniques. But the flexibility it makes possible is far more suited to the needs of constantly evolving organizations.

Indeed, at some point in the not-too-distant future—certainly within the next decade—information technology will become a kind of generic entity, almost like clay. And the "product" will not exist until it enters a specific situation, where vendor and customer will mold it to the work practices of the customer organization. When that happens, information technology as a distinct category of products will become invisible. It will dissolve into the work itself. And companies like ours might sell not products but rather the expertise to help users define their needs and create the products best suited to them. Our product will be our customers' learning.

Harvesting Local Innovation

The trend toward ubiquitous computing and mass customization is made possible by technology. The emphasis, however, is not on the technology itself but on the work practices it supports. In the future, organizations won't have to shape how they work to fit the narrow confines of an inflexible technology. Rather, they can begin to design information systems to support the way people really work.

That's why some of the most important research at PARC in the past decade has been done by anthropologists. PARC anthropologists have studied occupations and work practices throughout the company— clerks in an accounts-payable office who issue checks to suppliers, technical representatives who repair copying machines, designers who develop new products, even novice users of Xerox's copiers. This research has produced fundamental insights into the nature of innovation, organizational learning, and good product design.

We got involved in the anthropology of work for a good business reason. We figured that before we went ahead and applied technology to work, we had better have a clear understanding of exactly how people do their jobs. Most people assume—we did too, at first—that the formal procedures defining a job or the explicit structure of an organizational chart accurately describe what employees do, especially in highly routinized occupations. But when PARC anthropologist Lucy

Suchman began studying Xerox accounting clerks in 1979, she uncovered an unexpected and intriguing contradiction.

When Suchman asked the clerks how they did their jobs, their descriptions corresponded more or less to the formal procedures of the job manual. But when she observed them at work, she discovered that the clerks weren't really following those procedures at all. Instead, they relied on a rich variety of informal practices that weren't in any manual but turned out to be crucial to getting the work done. In fact, the clerks were constantly improvising, inventing new methods to deal with unexpected difficulties and to solve immediate problems. Without being aware of it, they were far more innovative and creative than anybody who heard them describe their "routine" jobs ever would have thought.

Suchman concluded that formal office procedures have almost nothing to do with how people do their jobs. People use procedures to understand the goals of a particular job—for example, what kind of information a particular file has to contain in order for a bill to be paid—not to identify the steps to take in order to get from here to there. But in order to reach that goal—actually collecting and verifying the information and making sure the bill is paid—people constantly invent new work practices to cope with the unforeseen contingencies of the moment. These informal activities remain mostly invisible since they do not fall within the normal, specified procedures that employees are expected to follow or managers expect to see. But these "workarounds" enable an all-important flexibility that allows organizations to cope with the unexpected, as well as to profit from experience and to change.

If local innovation is as important and pervasive as we suspect, then big companies have the potential to be remarkably innovative—*if* they can somehow capture this innovation and learn from it. Unfortunately, it's the rare company that understands the importance of informal improvisation—let alone respects it as a legitimate business activity. In most cases, ideas generated by employees in the course of their work are lost to the organization as a whole. An individual might use them to make his or her job easier and perhaps even share them informally with a small group of colleagues. But such informal insights about work rarely spread beyond the local work group. And because most information systems are based on the formal procedures of work, not the informal practices crucial to getting it done, they often tend to make things worse rather than better. As a result, this important source of organizational learning is either ignored or suppressed.

At PARC, we are trying to design new uses of technology that leverage the incremental innovation coming from within the entire company. We want to create work environments where people can legitimately improvise, and where those improvisations can be captured and made part of the organization's collective knowledge base.

One way is to provide people with easy-to-use programming tools so they can customize the information systems and computer applications that they work with. To take a small example, my assistant is continually discovering new ways to improve the work systems in our office. She has more ideas for perfecting, say, our electronic calendar system than any researcher does. After all, she uses it every day and frequently bumps up against its limitations. So instead of designing a new and better calendar system, we created a programming language known as CUSP (for "customized user-system program") that allows users to modify the system themselves.

We've taken another small step in this direction at EuroPARC, our European research lab in Cambridge, England. Researchers there have invented an even more advanced software system known as "Buttons"—bits of computer code structured and packaged so that even people without a lot of training in computers can modify them. With Buttons, secretaries, clerks, technicians, and others can create their own software applications, send them to colleagues throughout the corporation over our electronic mail network, and adapt any Buttons they receive from others to their own needs. Through the use of such tools, we are translating local innovation into software that can be easily disseminated and used by all.

New technologies can also serve as powerful aids for organizational learning. For example, in 1984 Xerox's service organization asked us to research ways to improve the effectiveness of their training programs. Training the company's 14,500 service technicians who repair copying machines is extremely costly and time-consuming. What's more, the time it takes to train the service work force on a new technology is key to how fast the company can launch new products.

The service organization was hoping we could make traditional classroom training happen faster, perhaps by creating some kind of expert system. But based on our evolving theory of work and innovation, we decided to take another approach. We sent out a former service technician, who had since gone on to do graduate work in anthropology, to find out how reps actually do their jobs—not what they or their managers *say* they do but what they really do and how they learn the skills that they actually use. He took the company training program, actually worked on repair jobs in the field, and interviewed tech-reps about their jobs. He concluded that the reps learn the most not from formal training courses but out in the field—by working on real problems and discussing them informally with colleagues. Indeed, the stories tech-reps tell each other—around the coffee pot, in the lunchroom, or while working together on a particularly difficult problem—are crucial to continuous learning.

In a sense, these stories are the real "expert systems" used by tech-reps on the job. They are a storehouse of past problems and diagnoses, a template for constructing a theory about the current problem, and the basis for making an educated stab at a solution. By creating such stories and constantly refining them through conversation with each other, tech-reps are creating a powerful "organizational memory" that is a valuable resource for the company.

As a result of this research, we are rethinking the design of tech-rep training—and the tech-rep job itself—in terms of lifelong learning. How might a company support and leverage the storytelling that is crucial to building the expertise not only of individual tech-reps but also of the entire tech-rep community? And is there any way to link that expertise to other groups in the company who would benefit from it—for example, the designers who are creating the future generations of our systems?

One possibility is to create advanced multimedia information systems that would make it easier for reps and other employees to plug in to this collective social mind. Such a system might allow the reps to pass around annotated videoclips of useful stories, much like scientists distribute their scientific papers, to sites all over the world. By commenting on each other's experiences, reps could refine and disseminate new knowledge. This distributed collective memory, containing all the informal expertise and lore of the occupation, could help tech-reps—and the company—improve their capacity to learn from successes and failures.

Coproducing Innovation

Our approach to the issue of tech-rep training is a good example of what we mean by "pioneering" research. We started with a real business problem, recognized by everyone, then reframed the problem to come up with solutions that no one had considered before. But this raises another challenge of pioneering research: How to communicate fresh insights about familiar problems so that others can grasp their significance?

The traditional approach to communicating new innovations—a process that usually goes by the name of "technology transfer"—is to treat it as a simple problem of transferring information. Research has to pour new knowledge into people's heads like water from a pitcher into a glass. That kind of communication might work for incremental innovations. But when it comes to pioneering research that fundamentally redefines a technology, product, work process, or business problem, this approach doesn't work.

It's never enough to just *tell* people about some new insight. Rather, you have to get them to experience it in a way that evokes its power and possibility. Instead of pouring knowledge into people's heads, you need to help them grind a new set of eyeglasses so they can see the world in a new way. That involves challenging the implicit assumptions that have shaped the way people in an organization have historically looked at things. It also requires creating new communication techniques that actually get people to experience the implications of a new innovation.

To get an idea of this process, consider the strategic implications of an innovation such as digital copying for a company like Xerox. Xerox owes its existence to a particular technology—light-lens xerography. That tradition has shaped how the company conceives of products, markets, and customer needs, often in ways that are not so easy to identify. But digital copying renders many of those assumptions obsolete. Therefore, making these assumptions explicit and analyzing their limitations is an essential strategic task.

Until recently, most people at Xerox thought of information technology mainly as a way to make traditional copiers cheaper and better. They didn't realize that digital copying would transform the business with broad implications not just for copiers but also for office information systems in general. Working with the Xerox corporate strategy office, we've tried to find a way to open up the corporate imagination—to get people to move beyond the standard ways they thought about copiers.

One approach we took a couple of years ago was to create a video for top management that we called the "unfinished document." In the video, researchers at PARC who knew the technology extremely well discussed the potential of digital copying to transform people's work. But they didn't just talk about it; they actually acted it out in skits. They created mock-ups of the technology and then simulated how it might affect different work activities. They attempted to portray not just the technology but also the technology "in use."

We thought of the unfinished document as a "conceptual envisioning experiment"—an attempt to imagine how a technology might be used before we started building it. We showed the video to some top corporate officers to get their intuitional juices flowing. The document was "unfinished" in the sense that the whole point of the exercise was to get the viewers to complete the video by suggesting their own ideas for how they might use the new technology and what these new uses might mean for the business. In the process, they weren't just learning about a new technology; they were creating a new mental model of the business.

Senior management is an important partner for research, but our experiments at coproduction aren't limited to the top. We are also involved in initiatives to get managers far down in the organization to reflect on the obstacles blocking innovation in the Xerox culture. For example, one project takes as its starting point the familiar fact that the best innovations are often the product of "renegades" on the periphery of the company. PARC researchers are part of a company group that is trying to understand why this is so often the case. We are studying some of the company's most adventuresome product-development programs to learn how the larger Xerox organization can sometimes obstruct a new product or work process. By learning how the corporation rejects certain ideas, we hope to uncover those features of the corporate culture that need to change.

Such efforts are the beginning of what we hope will become an ongoing dialogue in the company about Xerox's organizational practice. By challenging the background assumptions that traditionally stifle innovation, we hope to create an environment where the creativity of talented people can flourish and "pull" new ideas into the business.

Innovating with the Customer

Finally, research's ultimate partner in coproduction is the customer. The logical end point of all the activities I have described is for corporate research to move outside the company and work with customers to coproduce the technology and work systems they will need in the future.

It is important to distinguish this activity from conventional market research. Most market research assumes either that a particular product already exists or that customers already know what they need. At PARC, we are focusing on systems that do not yet exist and on needs that are not yet clearly defined. We want to help customers become aware of their latent needs, then customize systems to meet them. Put another way, we are trying to prototype a need or use before we prototype a system.

One step in this direction is an initiative of Xerox's Corporate Research Group (of which PARC is a part) known as the Express project. Express is an experiment in product-delivery management designed to commercialize PARC technologies more rapidly by directly involving customers in the innovation process. The project brings together in a single organization based at PARC a small team of Xerox researchers, engineers, and marketers with employees from one of our customers—Syntex, a Palo Alto-based pharmaceutical company.

Syntex's more than 1,000 researchers do R&D on new drugs up for approval by the Food and Drug Administration. The Express team is exploring ways to use core technologies developed at PARC to help the pharmaceutical company manage the more than 300,000 "case report" forms it collects each year. (The forms report on tests of new drugs on human volunteers.) Syntex employees have spent time at PARC learning our technologies-in-progress. Similarly, the Xerox members of the team have intensively studied Syntex's work processes—much as PARC anthropologists have studied work inside our own company.

Once the project team defined the pharmaceutical company's key business needs and the PARC technologies that could be used to meet them, programmers from both companies worked together to create some prototypes. One new system, for example, is known as the Forms Receptionist. It combines technologies for document interchange and translation, document recognition, and intelligent scanning to scan, sort, file, and distribute Syntex's case reports. For Syntex, the new system solves an important business problem. For Xerox, it is the prototype of a product that we eventually hope to offer to the entire pharmaceutical industry.

We are also treating Express as a case study in coproduction, worth studying in its own right. The Express team has videotaped all the interactions between Xerox and Syntex employees and developed a computerized index to guide it through this visual database. And a second research team is doing an in-depth study of the entire Xerox-

Syntex collaboration. By studying the project, we hope to learn valuable lessons about coproduction.

For example, one of the most interesting lessons we've learned from the Express project so far is just how long it takes to create a shared understanding among the members of such product teams—a common language, sense of purpose, and definition of goals. This is similar to the experience of many interfunctional teams that end up reproducing inside the team the same conflicting perspectives the teams were designed to overcome in the first place. We believe the persistence of such misunderstandings may be a serious drag on product development.

Thus a critical task for the future is to explore how information technology might be used to accelerate the creation of mutual understandings within work groups. The end point of this process would be to build what might be called an "envisioning laboratory"—a powerful computer environment where Xerox customers would have access to advanced programming tools for quickly modeling and envisioning the consequences of new systems. Working with Xerox's development and marketing organizations, customers could try out new system configurations, reflect on the appropriateness of the systems for their business, and progressively refine and tailor them to match their business needs. Such an environment would be a new kind of technological medium. Its purpose would be to create evocative simulations of new systems and new products before actually building them.

The envisioning laboratory does not yet exist. Still, it is not so farfetched to imagine a point in the near future where major corporations will have research centers with the technological capability of, say, a multimedia computer-animation studio like Lucasfilm. Using state-of-the-art animation techniques, such a laboratory could create elaborate simulations of new products and use them to explore the implications of those products on a customer's work organization. Prototypes that today take years to create could be roughed out in a matter of weeks or days.

When this happens, phrases like "continuous innovation" and the "customer-driven" company will take on new meaning. And the transformation of corporate research—and the corporation as a whole—will be complete.

Executive Summaries

Increasing Returns and the New World of Business

W. Brian Arthur

Our understanding of how markets and businesses operate was passed down to us more than a century ago by English economist Alfred Marshall. It is based on the assumption of diminishing returns: products or companies that get ahead in a market eventually run into limitations so that a predictable equilibrium of prices and market shares is reached. The theory was valid for the bulk-processing, smokestack economy of Marshall's day. But in this century, Western economies have gone from processing resources to processing information, from the application of raw energy to the application of ideas. The mechanisms that determine economic behavior have also shifted—from diminishing returns to increasing returns.

Increasing returns are the tendency for that which is ahead to get further ahead and for that which is losing advantage to lose further advantage. If a product gets ahead, increasing returns can magnify the advantage, and the product can go on to lock in the market.

Mechanisms of increasing returns exist alongside those of diminishing returns in all industries. But, in general, diminishing returns hold sway in the traditional, resource-processing industries. Increasing returns reign in the newer, knowledge-based industries. Modern economies have split into two interrelated worlds of business corresponding to the two types of returns. The two worlds have different economics. They differ in behavior, style, and culture. They call for different management techniques, strategies, and codes of government regulation.

The author illuminates those differences by explaining how increasing returns operate in high tech and in service industries. He also offers advice to managers in knowledge-based markets.

Strategy As Revolution

Gary Hamel

How often does the strategic-planning process start with senior executives asking what the rest of the organization can teach them about the future? Not often enough, argues Gary Hamel.

In many companies, strategy making is an elitist procedure and "strategy" consists of nothing more than following the industry's rules. But more and more companies, intent on overturning the industrial order, are rewriting those rules. What can industry incumbents do? Either surrender the future to revolutionary challengers or revolutionize the way their companies create strategy. What is needed is not a tweak to the traditional strategic-planning process, Hamel says, but a new philosophical foundation: strategy is revolution.

Hamel offers ten principles to help a company think about the challenge of creating truly revolutionary strategies. Perhaps the most fundamental principle is that so-called strategic planning doesn't produce true strategic innovation. The traditional planning process is little more than a rote procedure in which deeply held assumptions and industry conventions are reinforced rather than challenged. Such a process harnesses only a tiny proportion of an organization's creative potential.

If there is to be any hope of industry revolution, senior managers must give up their monopoly on the creation of strategy. They must embrace a truly democratic process that can give voice to the revolutionaries that exist in every company. If senior managers are unwilling to do this, employees must become strategy activists.

The opportunities for industry revolution are mostly unexplored. One thing is certain: if you don't let the revolutionaries challenge you from within, they will eventually challenge you from without—in the marketplace.

How Architecture Wins Technology Wars

Charles R. Morris and Charles H. Ferguson

Signs of revolutionary transformation in the global computer industry are everywhere. A roll call of the major industry players reads like a waiting list in the emergency room.

The usual explanations for the industry's turmoil are at best inadequate. Scale, friendly government policies, manufacturing capabilities, a strong position in desktop markets, excellent software, top design skills—none of these is sufficient, either by itself or in combination, to ensure competitive success information technology.

A new paradigm is required to explain patterns of success and failure. Simply stated, success flows to the company that manages to establish proprietary architectural control over a broad, fast-moving, competitive space.

Architectural strategies have become crucial to information technology because of the astonishing rate of improvement in microprocessors and other semiconductor components. Since no single vendor can keep pace with the outpouring of cheap, powerful, mass-produced components, customers insist on stitching together their own local systems solutions. Architectures impose order on the system and make the interconnections possible. The architectural controller is the company that controls the standard by which the entire information package is assembled. Microsoft's Window is an excellent example of this. Because of the popularity of Windows, companies like Lotus must conform their software to its parameters in order to compete for market share.

In the 1990s, proprietary architectural control is not only possible but indispensable to competitive success. What's more, it has broader implications for organizational structure: architectural is giving rise to a new form of business organization.

The Right Game: Use Game Theory to Shape Strategy

Adam M. Brandenburger and Barry J. Nalebuff

Business is a high-stakes game. The way we approach this game is reflected in the language we use to describe it. Business language is full of expressions borrowed from the military and from sports. Unlike war and sports, however, business is not about winning and losing. Companies can succeed without requiring others to fail. And they can fail no matter how well they play if they play the wrong game.

The essence of business success lies in making sure you're playing the right game. How do you know if it's the right game? What can you do if it's the wrong game? To help managers answer those questions, the authors have developed a framework that draws on the insights of game theory.

The primary insight of game theory is the importance of focusing on others—of putting yourself in the shoes of other players and trying to play out all the reactions to their actions as far ahead as possible. By adopting this perspective, a company may, for example, discover that its chances for success are greater if it creates a win-win, rather than a win-lose, situation with other players. In other words, companies should consider both cooperative and competitive ways to change the game.

Who are the participants in the game of business? The authors introduce a schematic map that represents all the players and all the interdependencies among them. Drawing this map for your business is the first step toward changing the game. The second step is identifying all five elements of the game—players, added values, rules, tactics, and scope— and changing one or more of them. By using these tools, the authors say, companies can design a game that's right for them.

The Options Approach to Capital Investment

Avinash K. Dixit and Robert S. Pindyck

Companies make capital investments to create and exploit profit opportunities. Opportunities are options rights but not obligations to take some future action. The old net present value presumption that investment decisions are either reversible or now-or-never propositions turns out to be flawed. Irreversibility, uncertainty, and the choice of timing alter the investment decision in critical ways.

Investment expenditures are irreversible when they are specific to a company or to an industry. When a company exercises its option by making an irreversible investment, it effectively kills its option: The company has given up the possibility of waiting for new information that might affect the desirability or timing of the investment. Thus the simple NPV rule should be modified: Instead of being merely positive, the present value of the expected stream of cash from a project must exceed the cost of the project by an amount equal to the value of keeping the investment option alive.

As with a financial call option, the greater the uncertainty over the profitability of a capital investment, the greater the value of the opportunity and the greater the incentive to wait and keep the opportunity alive. If a company can identify some situations that would cause it to rethink a go-ahead decision (such as a drop in demand for its product), then the ability to wait and avoid those eventualities is valuable.

Because they create and preserve options, decisions such as those to test a market or conduct R&D enhance a company's flexibility and should be made more readily than a naive NPV would suggest; but decisions that reduce flexibility should be made more hesitantly and be subjected to stiffer hurdle rates than the cost of capital.

When Is Virtual Virtuous? Organizing for Innovation

Henry W. Chesbrough and David J. Teece

Champions of virtual corporations are urging managers to subcontract anything and everything. Because a number of high-profile corporate giants have been outperformed by more nimble, "networked" competitors, the idea of the virtual organization is tantalizing. But is virtual really the best way to organize for innovation?

Henry W. Chesbrough and David J. Teece argue that the virtual corporation has been oversold. Innovation is not monolithic, and it is critically important to understand the type of innovation in question. For some innovations, joint ventures, alliances, and outsourcing can play a useful role. But for others, they are inappropriate—and strategically dangerous. The initial success—and subsequent failure—of the IBM PC illustrate the strategic mistake of using a virtual approach for the kind of complex technology that should have been controlled in-house.

The authors present a framework to help managers determine when to innovate by going virtual, when to form alliances, and when to rely on internal development. They provide a range of cases to illustrate how to match organizational strategy to the type of innovation being pursued. General Motors, for example, used the wrong approach to develop disk brake technology and paid the price: getting to market later than its competitors. To realize its vision of "tetherless communication," Motorola must choose an organizational strategy allowing it more control over the direction and timing of technological change than a virtual approach could provide. In contrast, the virtues of the virtual organization are illustrated by Ameritech's use of alliances to influence the innovation path in multimedia.

Disruptive Technologies: Catching the Wave

Joseph L. Bower and Clayton M. Christensen

One of the most consistent patterns in business is the failure of leading companies to stay at the top of their industries when technologies or markets change. Why is it that established companies invest aggressively—and successfully—in the technologies necessary to retain their current customers but then fail to make the technological investments that customers of the future will demand? The fundamental reason is that leading companies succumb to one of the most popular, and valuable, management dogmas: they stay close to their customers.

Customers wield extraordinary power in directing a company's investments. But what happens when a new technology emerges that customers reject because it doesn't address their needs as effectively as a company's current approach? In an ongoing study of technological change, the authors found that most established companies are consistently ahead of their industries in developing and commercializing new technologies as long as those technologies address the next-generation-performance needs of their customers. However, an industry's leaders are rarely in the forefront of commercializing new technologies that don't initially meet the functional demands of mainstream customers and appeal only to small or emerging markets.

To remain at the top of their industries, managers must first be able to spot the technologies that fall into this category. To pursue these technologies, managers must protect them from the processes and incentives that are geared to serving mainstream customers. And the only way to do that is to create organizations that are completely independent of the mainstream business.

Breaking Compromises, Breakaway Growth

George Stalk, Jr., David K. Pecaut, and Benjamin Burnett

Many companies today are searching for growth. But how and where should they look? Breaking compromises can be a powerful organizing principle. Even in the most mature businesses, compromise breakers have emerged from the pack to achieve breakaway growth—far outpacing the rest of their industry. Examples include Chrysler Corporation, Contadina, CarMax, and the Charles Schwab Corporation.

Compromises are concessions customers are forced to make. Unlike trade-offs, which are the legitimate choices customers make between different product or service offerings, compromises are imposed. For instance, in choosing a hotel, a customer can *trade off* luxury for economy. But the entire hotel industry makes customers *compromise* by not permitting early check-in. Trade-offs are very visible, but most compromises are hidden.

Compromises mean it's the industry's way or no way. Often, customers assume the industry must be right; they accept compromises as the way the business works. That is why traditional market research rarely uncovers compromise-breaking opportunities.

The authors propose a number of alternative approaches to finding the compromises hidden in any business. One approach is to look for the compensatory behaviors customers engage in because using the product or service as intended would not fully meet their needs. Other approaches include paying attention to performance anomalies and looking for diseconomies in the industry's value chain. If managers think like customers, the authors say, they will be able to find and exploit compromises for faster growth and improved profitability.

Competing on Resources: Strategy in the 1990s

David J. Collis and Cynthia A. Montgomery

How do you create and sustain a profitable strategy? Many of the approaches to strategy that have been championed in the past decade have focused the attention of managers inward, urging them to build a unique set of resources and capabilities. In practice, however, notions like core competence have too often become a "feel good" exercise that no one fails. The authors explain how a company's resources drive its performance in a dynamic competitive environment, and they propose a new framework that moves strategic thinking forward in two ways: (1) by laying out a pragmatic and rigorous set of market tests to determine whether a company's resources are truly valuable enough to serve as the basis for strategy; and (2) by integrating this market view of capabilities with earlier insights about competition and industry structure. Where a company chooses to play will determine its profitability as much as its resources.

The authors explain in clear managerial terms why some competitors are more profitable than others, how to put the idea of core competence into practice, and how to develop diversification strategies that make sense. Case examples such as Disney, Cooper, Sharp, and Newell illustrate the power of resource-based strategies. The authors show how these organizations have been able to use corporate resources to establish and maintain competitive advantage at the business-unit level, and also how they have benefited from the attractiveness of the markets in which they have chosen to compete.

Tough-Minded Ways to Get Innovative

Andrall E. Pearson

Consistent innovation is the key to market leadership. Outstanding competitors know that and build their success on it. Other companies can do the same by making a systematic effort to concentrate on five key activities.

Innovation begins at the top—with a CEO or general manager who believes change is the way to survive. Spread that mind-set through the organization by: setting challenging, measurable goals; getting everyone focused on beating a specific competitor; and supporting people who take risks.

The systems and people that run your business can choke off innovation. New ideas need: a champion, a sponsor, a mix of creative types (for ideas), and operators (to keep thinks practical), and a separate system to get ideas to top management early and fast.

Know the competitive dynamics of your business cold. A realistic strategic vision will channel innovative efforts to ideas that will pay off in the market place.

Look hard at your customers to find new segments, your competition to see what's already working, and your business to see where you can leverage existing strengths.

Once an idea is well developed, go for broke. Expect heavy retaliation from competitors. Set priorities. Think through every step of the launch.

Managing Innovation in the Information Age

Rebecca Henderson

The continued vitality of the most successful U.S. and European pharmaceutical companies in the face of accelerating scientific and technological change holds valuable lessons for managers in all industries trying to respond to turbulent times. The pharmaceutical industry faces some serious challenges in the future, most notably, the proposed reform of the U.S. health care system. Yet its success in the crucial area of research can serve as a benchmark for companies seeking to become more innovative in the overloaded environment of the information age.

New competitors skillfully exploiting a wave of technological change have displaced or seriously challenged the companies that once dominated industries such as machine tools, steel, xerography, automobiles, semiconductors, and computers. In contrast, companies founded in the 1940s and 1950s continue to dominate the pharmaceutical industry. These companies have demonstrated an ability to learn and grow that confounds conventional wisdom. Despite their age, size, and success, they have found ways to retain the flexibility and responsiveness of companies one-tenth their size and age. And they have already solved some of the competitive challenges in the research arena that companies in other industries are just starting to grapple with.

New research conducted by Rebecca Henderson of MIT and Iain Cockburn of the University of British Columbia suggests that the longevity of pharmaceutical companies attests to a unique managerial competency: an ability to foster a high level of specialized knowledge within an organization, while preventing that information from fixing the company in the past, unable to respond to an ever-changing environment.

Research That Reinvents the Corporation

John Seely Brown

The most important invention that will come out of the corporate research lab in the future will be the corporation itself. As companies try to keep pace with rapid changes in technology and cope with unstable business environments, the research department has to do more than simply innovate new products. It must design the new technological and organizational "architectures" that make a continuously innovating company possible.

In this article, John Seely Brown, director of the Xerox Palo Alto Research Center (PARC), describes the business logic behind this distinctive vision of research's role and the ways PARC has tried to realize that vision. PARC researchers are prototyping new work practices as well as new technologies and products. They are designing new uses of technology to support the naturally occurring "local innovation" that takes place at all levels of any big company. And they are experimenting with new techniques for "coproducing" technological and organizational innovations—not only with other departments at Xerox but with the company's customers as well.

Xerox's business is technology, but Brown argues that any company, no matter what the business, must eventually grapple with the issues he raises. The successful company of the future must understand how people really work and how technology can help them work more effectively. It must know how to create an environment for continual innovation on the part of all employees. It must rethink traditional business assumptions and tap needs that customers don't even know they have yet. It must use research to reinvent the corporation.

About the Contributors

W. Brian Arthur is the Citibank Professor at the Santa Fe Institute in Santa Fe, New Mexico, and the Dean and Virginia Morrison Professor of Economics and Population Studies and a professor of human biology at Stanford University. He is the author of *Increasing Returns and Path Dependence in the Economy* and various articles published in *Scientific American*, the *Harvard Business Review*, and *American Economics Review*. Professor Arthur's Web site is www.santafe.edu/arthur.

Joseph L. Bower is the Donald K. David Professor of Business Administration at the Harvard Business School and a leading expert in the fields of corporate strategy and public policy. He has devoted his research to the problems that top management faces in dealing with the rapidly changing political economy and competitive circumstances of the contemporary world economy. Professor Bower's books include *When Markets Quake: The Management Challenge of Restructuring Industry* (HBS Press, 1986) and *The Two Faces of Management: An American Approach to Leadership in Business and Government*.

A professor in the Competition and Strategy area at the Harvard Business School, **Adam M. Brandenburger** is both a scholar and a consultant. He is the co-author, with Barry Nalebuff, of the best-selling book *Co-opetition* as well as the author or co-author of numerous articles on game theory and business strategy. Professor Brandenburger's pioneering work in applying the science of game theory to the art of management has been featured in the *Wall Street Journal, Financial Times, The Economist,* and *Business Week,* and on CNN, CNBC, and National Public Radio.

Benjamin Burnett is a vice president in the consumer and retail practice of The Boston Consulting Group. During his 14 years with the company, he has worked extensively with clients in the packaged goods and retail sectors. His areas of expertise include corporate strategy, revitalizing mature brands, cost reduction, trade marketing organization, market segmentation, and promotional effectiveness.

Henry W. Chesbrough is a Ph.D. candidate in business strategy and innovation management at the Haas School of Business at the University of California-Berkeley. His research focuses on the organizational impact of innovation, organizational issues in managing strategic alliances, how organizations develop and manage capabilities, and the ways that innovation affects organizations in the United States differently from those in Japan. He previously worked in the computer industry for over 10 years, in positions in product management and strategic marketing.

Clayton M. Christensen is an associate professor of business administration at the Harvard Business School, where he holds a joint appointment with the Technology and Operations Management and General Management faculty groups. His research and writing focus on the management of technological innovation, problems of finding new markets for new technologies, and the identification and development of organizational capabilities. Prior to joining the Harvard Business School faculty, Professor Christensen served as chairman and president of Ceramics Process Systems Corporation, a firm he co-founded in 1984 with several MIT professors.

David J. Collis is an associate professor in the Business, Government, and Competition area at the Harvard Business School and a consultant to several large U.S. and European corporations. He is currently conducting an international comparison of the role of the corporate office in large multibusiness corporations. He is the author of many articles in periodicals, such as the *Harvard Business Review, Strategic Management Journal,* and *European Management Journal,* and in books, including *International Competitiveness, Managing the Multibusiness Company,* and *Beyond Free Trade* (HBS Press 1993).

Avinash K. Dixit has been a professor of economics at Princeton University since 1981, and was named the John J. F. Sherrerd '51 University Professor of Economics in 1989. He has contributed to theories of industrial organization, international trade, public finance, and economic growth and development. His current areas of research include the study of the political process by which economic policy is made, and the theory of irreversible capital investment under uncertainty and its applications. Professor Dixit has published seven books and nearly 150 articles and reviews in professional journals and collected volumes.

Formerly a researcher at MIT and consultant to high-technology firms, **Charles H. Ferguson** founded Vermeer Technologies in March 1994. Since the company was sold in 1996, Ferguson has been pursuing both consulting and academic interests. He has served as a visiting scholar at MIT and the University of California-Berkeley and is the co-author, with Charles Morris, of *Computer Wars: How the West Can Win in a Post-IBM World.*

Gary Hamel is a founder and chairman of Strategos, a company dedicated to helping its clients get to the future first. He is also Visiting Professor of Strategic and International Management at London Business School. Called "the world's reigning strategy guru" by *The Economist,* Hamel has originated such concepts as strategic intent, core competence, corporate imagination, strategic architecture, and industry foresight. With C.K. Prahalad, he has published *Competing for the Future* (HBS Press, 1994), hailed by numerous business journals as one of the decade's most influential business books, and several articles in the *Harvard Business Review.*

Rebecca Henderson is a tenured associate professor of strategic management at the Sloan School of Management at MIT and a research fellow at the National Bureau of Economic Research. She specializes in technology strategy and product and process management and has written various articles on these subjects in the *Rand Journal of Economics, Strategic Management Journal, Journal of Economics and Business Strategy,* and *Design Management Journal.*

The John G. McLean Professor of Business Administration at the Harvard Business School, **Cynthia A. Montgomery** focuses her research on corporate strategy and the competitiveness of diversified firms, particularly on issues relating to the markets in which multibusiness firms compete, the resource bases of the firms, and the creation of value across multiple lines of business. Professor Montgomery is the editor or co-editor of two books; the author of numerous articles in management journals; and a member of the board of directors of UNUM Corporation, Newell Company, and several Merrill Lynch mutual funds.

Charles R. Morris is a former partner at Devonshire Partners, a Cambridge, Massachusetts, technology consulting and financial advisory firm. He is the co-author, with Charles H. Ferguson, of *Computer Wars: How the West Can Win in a Post-IBM World*.

Barry J. Nalebuff is the Milton Steinbach Professor of Economics and Management at Yale University. An expert on game theory, he has written extensively on its applications for managers. He is the co-author of *Thinking Strategically: The Competitive Edge in Business, Politics, and Everyday Life*. His second book, *Co-opetition*, written with Adam Brandenburger, is an extension of the article included in this collection. Professor Nalebuff applies game theory in his teaching, research, consulting work with businesses on strategy, and antitrust litigation.

Formerly the 1958 Professor of Business Administration at Harvard Business School, **Andrall E. Pearson** is a principal of Clayton, Dubilier & Rice, Inc., a New York management buy-out firm that specializes in leveraged acquisitions, involving management participation, of large U.S. corporations. He serves on the boards of Alliant Food Services (formerly Kraft), PepsiCo, May Department Stores, Lexmark International, Homeland Stores, and Travelers Group, and is a trustee of the New York University Medical Center and the Good Samaritan Medical Center in Palm Beach, Florida.

A vice president of The Boston Consulting Group, **David K. Pecaut** focuses mainly on issues of competitive strategy and managing the organizational changes necessary to implement new strategies. He has managed projects worldwide on relative cost competitiveness, market segmentation, new product development, and mergers and acquisitions in sectors as diverse as forest products and aerospace. In addition, Mr. Pecaut has built an international practice as an adviser to various governments on economic and industrial policy.

Robert S. Pindyck is the Mitsubishi Bank Professor of Applied Economics at the Sloan School of Management at MIT. He is also a research associate of the National Bureau of Economic Research and a fellow of the Econometric Society. His research has covered industrial organization and econometric modeling and forecasting. Professor Pindyck's recent work examines the role of uncertainty in firm behavior and market structure, criteria for investing in risky projects, the role of R&D and the value of patents, and the value of flexibility. He has written many journal articles in these areas and seven books, including three textbooks.

John Seely Brown is the Chief Scientist of Xerox Corporation and the Director of its Palo Alto Research Center (PARC). At Xerox, he has been involved in expanding the role of corporate research to include such topics as organizational learning, ethnographies of the workplace, complex adaptive systems, and techniques for unfreezing the corporate mind. His research over the years has focused primarily on human learning and the management of radical innovation. Dr. Brown has published more than 60 papers in scientific journals and was given the *Harvard Business Review*'s 1991 McKinsey Award for "Research that Reinvents the Corporation," an article included in this volume.

A senior vice president of The Boston Consulting Group, **George Stalk, Jr.**, focuses his professional practice on international and time-based competition, and he speaks regularly to business and industry associations on time-based competition and other topics. Based in Toronto, he has served as a consultant to a variety of leading manufacturing, retailing, and technology- and consumer-oriented companies. Stalk is the co-author of the critically acclaimed *Competing Across Time* and of *Kaisha: The Japanese Corporation;* his articles have appeared in numerous business publications.

David J. Teece is the Mitsubishi Bank Professor at the Haas School of Business and director of the Institute of Management, Innovation, and Organization at the University of California-Berkeley. He is also the director of the Consortium on Competitiveness. His interests lie in industrial organization and the economics of technological change. Professor Teece is the co-author of more than 100 articles and publications, including *The Competitive Challenge*, and, with Richard P. Rumelt and Dan E. Schendel, the co-editor of *Fundamental Issues in Strategy* (HBS Press, 1994).

Index